JOURNAL FOR THE STUDY OF THE NEW TESTAMENT
SUPPLEMENT SERIES
107

Executive Editor
Stanley E. Porter

Editorial Board
Richard Bauckham, David Catchpole, R. Alan Culpepper,
Joanna Dewey, James D.G. Dunn, Craig A. Evans, Robert Fowler,
Robert Jewett, Elizabeth Struthers Malbon, Dan O. Via

Sheffield Academic Press

Prologue and Gospel

The Theology
of the Fourth Evangelist

Elizabeth Harris

Journal for the Study of the New Testament
Supplement Series 107

To Alexander
...ἐκεῖνος ἐξηγήσατο

Copyright © 1994 Sheffield Academic Press

Published by Sheffield Academic Press Ltd
Mansion House
19 Kingfield Road
Sheffield, S11 9AS
England

Typeset by Sheffield Academic Press
and
Printed on acid-free paper in Great Britain
by Bookcraft
Midsomer Norton, Somerset

British Library Cataloguing in Publication Data

A catalogue record for this book is available
from the British Library

ISBN 1-85075-504-3

CONTENTS

Preface   7

Abbreviations   8

Chapter 1
THE RELATION OF THE PROLOGUE TO THE REST OF THE GOSPEL   9

Chapter 2
JOHN AND HIS WITNESS   26

Chapter 3
MOSES   63

Chapter 4
THE DIFFICULTIES FOR THE TRANSLATOR OF JOHN 1.18   91

Chapter 5
CHRISTOLOGICAL EXPRESSIONS IN THE FOURTH GOSPEL:
THE SON OF MAN   116

Chapter 6
CHRISTOLOGICAL EXPRESSIONS IN THE FOURTH GOSPEL:
ἐγώ εἰμι   130

Chapter 7
CHRISTOLOGICAL EXPRESSIONS IN THE FOURTH GOSPEL:
THE SON (OF GOD)   155

Chapter 8
THE FINAL DAYS IN JERUSALEM OF THE LOGOS, JESUS CHRIST   173

Conclusion   189

Appendix:
THE LOGOS   196

Bibliography   202
Index of References   207
Index of Authors   214

PREFACE

This book had its origin as a thesis submitted for the degree of PhD in the University of London. It was supervised by Professor Christopher F. Evans, first when he was Professor of New Testament Studies at King's College, London, and then in his retirement. I am immensely grateful to him for the constant stimulus of his teaching of the New Testament in general and of St John's Gospel in particular, and for his patient direction in matters of method and presentation in New Testament study.

I am also much indebted to Professor Graham N. Stanton, Professor of New Testament Studies at King's College, London, for his kindly assistance and advice; to the examiners of the thesis, Professor J. Leslie Houlden and Dr John Ziesler, for their suggestion that the thesis should be extended with a view to publication; and to other scholars for their encouragement, among whom I would like to mention Dr Francis J. Moloney, SDB, Dr Philip Sherrard and the late Dr A. Marcus Ward.

ABBREVIATIONS

AB	Anchor Bible
ANCL	Ante-Nicene Christian Library
BAG	W. Bauer, W.F. Arndt and F.W. Gingrich, *Greek–English Lexicon of the New Testament*
BJRL	*Bulletin of the John Rylands University Library of Manchester*
BTB	*Biblical Theology Bulletin*
CChr	Corpus Christianorum
ETR	*Etudes théologiques et religieuses*
ExpTim	*Expository Times*
HNT	Handbuch zum Neuen Testament
HTR	*Harvard Theological Review*
IDBSup	*IDB*, Supplementary Volume
JBL	*Journal of Biblical Literature*
JETS	*Journal of the Evangelical Theological Society*
JSOTSup	*Journal for the Study of the Old Testament*, Supplement Series
JTS	*Journal of Theological Studies*
LD	Lectio divina
Neot	*Neotestamentica*
NovT	*Novum Testamentum*
NovTSup	*Novum Testamentum* Supplements
NTS	*New Testament Studies*
PW	Pauly–Wissowa, *Reäl-Encyclopadie der classischen Altertumswissenschaft*
SBLMS	SBL Monograph Series
SBT	Studies in Biblical Theology
SE	*Studia Evangelica I, II, III* (= TU 73 [1959], 87 [1964], 88 [1964], etc.)
SNTSMS	Society of New Testament Studies Monograph Series
TDNT	G. Kittel and G. Friedrich (eds.), *Theological Dictionary of the New Testament*
TS	*Theological Studies*
ZTK	*Zeitschrift für Theologie und Kirche*

Chapter 1

THE RELATION OF THE PROLOGUE TO THE REST OF THE GOSPEL

Although this question was broached as long ago as 1892 by A. von Harnack[1] it cannot be said to have received an agreed answer. This is partly because both the terms used, 'prologue' and 'gospel', have been so much matters of discussion. Thus, when the preoccupation of scholarship was with source-analysis of this gospel, and attention was focused on detecting antecedent written documents which the evangelist was supposed to have used in the construction of his work, the result inevitably was that the Gospel was seen as something of a patchwork, and therefore less as a conscious literary work to which a prologue would be appropriate. This is all the more so if the hand of a redactor or redactors is postulated to account for the Gospel in its present form; for then it becomes uncertain to which stage of production the prologue is intended to correspond. The problem is worse still if, in order to account for inconsistencies in the text of the Gospel in its present form, any large-scale disruption of the original text is assumed, and a consequent rearrangement attempted (as notably by R. Bultmann); for it then becomes even more uncertain what the shape and construction of the original document were to which the prologue was to serve as an introduction. Thus, before the prologue can be examined either in itself or in its relation to the rest of the Gospel, some consideration has to be given to the character of the Gospel as a whole. Is it a deliberately and carefully constructed work according to some ascertainable genre of literature?

The question of the genre of this gospel, as of the other gospels, has recently come up for renewed discussion. M.J. Suggs observes that to describe a writing as *sui generis* is to say that it was not congruent with its milieu, and so cannot be explained by reference to antecedent literary

1. In 'Über das Verhältnis des Prologs des vierten Evangeliums zum ganzen Werke', *ZTK* 2 (1892), pp. 189-231.

forms.[1] Justin's use of 'memoirs', it is claimed, shows that his readers would not readily have understood the term 'gospel'; but 'memoirs' suits only biography and historical narrative as literary forms, and 'memoirs of the apostles' might be held to imply the direct reports of eye-witnesses as lying immediately behind the Gospels. At the other end of the scale 'Sayings of the Sages' is unsatisfactory as an antecedent literary type since it implies a lack of any narrative material. Some have suggested aretalogies as closest to the genre of gospel, but H.C. Kee doubts whether there was a fixed aretalogy form.[2]

C.H. Talbert has devoted a whole book to this question.[3] His general conclusion is that gospels belong within the category of ancient biography, which was narrated within the context of myth. He defines ancient biography as 'prose narration about a person's life, presenting supposedly historical facts which are selected to reveal the character or essence of the individual, often with the purpose of affecting the behaviour of the reader'.[4] In this he is concerned to refute Bultmann's assertion that, in contrast to ancient biography, the Gospels are mythical, cultic and world-negating.[5] His analysis, however, would seem to be unsatisfactory on a number of counts, at least so far as the Fourth Gospel is concerned. For that gospel hardly seems to fit the definition. It is very little directed towards affecting the behaviour of individuals. Such an aim would hardly correspond with this gospel's emphasis on the divine gifts and presence as themselves bringing about qualitative difference in the lives of human beings, who become children of God through a divine quality transforming human life, and by a present, albeit partial, participation in and intimacy with the heavenly. Undoubtedly such an immediacy of God's gifts through belief in the Son and in the One who has sent him does affect human behaviour, but this is only by way of a proper response to the God of the Jews and his unique Son, which is a prerequisite.

Secondly, the mythical elements which Talbert discerns as the background of ancient biography are there limited, and are confined to certain compartments; whereas in this gospel the 'mythical elements' govern the whole composition. There is set out in the prologue the

1.   M.J. Suggs, 'Gospel, Genre', in *IDBSup*, pp. 370-72.
2.   H.C. Kee, 'Aretalogy', in *IDBSup*, pp. 52-53.
3.   *What is a Gospel?* (Philadelphia: Fortress Press, 1977).
4.   Talbert, *Gospel*, p.17.
5.   See *Gospel*, pp. 133-35 for a summary of his views.

relation of the Logos to God from the beginning, and the Logos is further explicated as the light, and as the only-begotten Son of a Father, and is named Jesus Christ, before any prose narrative of that person's life begins. On Talbert's hypothesis it is odd that this introduction is not followed by narratives of birth, records of childhood, parentage and so forth (Mark does not have these either, but he is not concerned with any 'life' of Jesus before his ministry). Moreover, the prose narrative that follows is permeated throughout with the 'mythical', that is, with the divine origin and the divine goal of the Jesus who acts and speaks. Further, it may be contested whether in John the supposed historical facts are chosen and presented in order to show 'the character and essence of Jesus'. The emphasis in the Gospel is consistently theocentric. The only Son points constantly beyond himself to God, the one who has sent him. He affirms his heavenly origin as the presupposition of all that he does or says ('I came forth from God and am come', 8.42), and his prayer for his followers is that they may have eternal life, which consists in knowing God as the one true God, and Jesus Christ as the sent one (17.3). The Johannine Jesus speaks and acts in a way that necessitates throughout the divine origin which is declared in the prologue at the outset. It is difficult to find here those categories which Talbert required for biography. For one who claims to be returning to where he was before 'character and essence' are hardly suitable terms. The Gospel is hardly a biography of Jesus in any sense of that term; nor is it an aretalogy, in which attention is concentrated on the personal achievements of a central figure. It is a work with a theological core, in which John (the Baptist) as the divinely ordained witness points people to the Logos, the light, Jesus, who in turn points them to God. And people are invited to respond, not in terms of changed behaviour, but in the areas of the cognizance of Jesus and of God through belief, and a right understanding of the things of God.

So long as the Synoptic Gospels were approached as biographical material and the Fourth Gospel considered in relation to them, usually with the aim of deciding which had the better chronological structure overall and the greater historical accuracy in respect of individual data, the skilfully constructed narratives of ancient writers (for example Plutarch) could be cited as providing in some measure antecedent literary models. It gradually came to be realized, however, that the questions posed by a quest for a 'life' of Jesus, or of subsidiary figures such as the Baptist, could not be answered precisely because the material was not

intended to answer that kind of question. It was intended for theological
edification in respect of the beliefs of Christians about Jesus, about the
Baptist and about human beings in their relations to the God of the
Jews. History is subsumed in the service of theology. The Gospels, therefore, and especially the Fourth Gospel, may have to be treated once
again as to a large extent *sui generis*, and to be understood from within
themselves as particular creations. This is not to say, however, that they
would have been for that reason unintelligible to ancient readers. A
study, for example, of a word such as δοξάζειν and its cognates and
equivalents in Greek, Roman and Jewish literature from the sixth
century BCE to the third century CE shows a wide variety of usage and
meaning, and would suggest that ancient readers were nurtured in traditions which allowed writers considerable freedom to express religious
beliefs in very differently constructed accounts of any figure, heavenly
or human, to whom honour, glory or worship were to be accorded.

These considerations of the literary genre of the Fourth Gospel as a
whole could have a bearing on the understanding of the first eighteen
verses of the Gospel and vice versa. These verses appear to constitute a
self-contained whole. As such they pose the questions of whether they
also rest on the background of any antecedent literary type, and whether
they give any hints of the character of the Gospel as a whole by the fact
that, and the way in which, they stand at the beginning of it. It has been
the custom of modern scholars to refer to these verses as 'the prologue'
(in some cases the word 'proem' has been used), and in this they may
have been consciously or unconsciously repeating ancient usage.[1] Is the
term a proper one to use of these verses? And is it being used in the
very general sense only of some kind of introduction, or in a more
specific sense which denotes something of its character and function?

The noun πρόλογος, derived from the verb προλέγειν in the sense
of 'to announce beforehand', means 'the statement announced in
advance'. It became a technical term of literary criticism and of rhetoric,
and would seem to have had a long period of development. It can be
seen emerging in the sixth century BCE, when Thespis created it in
carrying out certain simple but far-reaching innovations in one branch of
the complex literary group the dithyrambs. He was concerned with the
drama regularly presented in lyrical odes sung by a chorus of fifty
dancing round the Dionysian altar, and he broke with tradition in

---

1.   As that of Jerome, who refers to these verses as *proemium* in the Preface to
his Commentary on Matthew, CChr (Series Latina), LXXVII, p. 3.

introducing one more member into the drama, who opened the presentation with a spoken prologue. The function of this prologue was to announce beforehand the plot to the audience, even though the sacred tradition of the Epic dramas was already thoroughly familiar to them. The newly introduced actor delivered not only the prologue but also the subsequent speeches that were interspersed between the odes. In this emerging poetic and dramatic art form, which in Greek poetry was based not on rhythm but on length of metres, attention was focused entirely on the words spoken. With the absence of stage props, and with the actors wearing masks, there was no acting in the modern sense of the word. The drama was a linguistic creation which needed to be heard rather than seen. The words of the text rather than the performance of the actor as such provided the fullest understanding of the situation, the debate and the outcome.

These small innovations of Thespis in the old dramas began a process of profound change, and although they were not immediately taken up they eventually provided the basis of the development of tragedy, and then of comedy, in which the prologue becomes a stable, though also fluid, constituent. This can be seen in the variety of techniques employed in the surviving plays of the great tragedians, Aeschylus, Sophocles and Euripides.[1] Although the prologue was not confined to drama—it was, for example, used as the opening of a formal speech—it is in the sphere of dramatic literature that we are most able to trace its use, since that was a living tradition until the third century CE, although most of the wide range of material it covered is now lost. Thus A.E. Haigh provides details of productions of satyric dramas in Greece until the first century CE, and he refers to Hadrian's patronage of a poet, Gaius Julius, who was voted a statue in CE 127, and observes that the contests of Greek tragedy in Rome, established in 186 BCE, were a regular part of Roman life until CE 195.[2] Moreover, by way of the New Comedy Rome came to have its own plays in Plautus and Terence, who produced his last comedy there in BCE 160. Of the latter it has been observed that he reduced the prologue to a pure preface. He dispensed with the type of prologue which informed about the action to follow, inserting such material into the action of his plays. 'His introductory speech is the

---

1.   See A.E. Haigh, *Tragic Drama of the Greeks* (Oxford: Oxford University Press, 1925) for various uses in the classical tragedians.

2.   *Tragic Drama*, pp. 444-56.

14   *Prologue and Gospel*

vehicle for literary criticism or polemical discussion.'[1]

As well as the prologues themselves there have come down to us statements of how the prologues were viewed in the ancient world. There are two in particular, the famous contest between Aeschylus and Euripides in Aristophanes' *Frogs*, and Aristotle's observations on the matter in his *Rhetoric* and *Poetics*. Though of very different origin and character they approximate to each other. For, as F. Stoessl observes, when Aeschylus and Euripides criticize each other's prologues they are using familiar arguments, and are restating the literary criticism of the fifth century, which is to be taken back as far as the Sophists.[2] And this criticism appears to have arisen in a mode of thinking which was strongly influenced by rhetoric. What is said in the *Frogs*, being comic knockabout, hardly yields anything about the nature of prologues as such; they are simply referred to as 'the beginnings' of the plays.[3] Although Aristophanes nowhere mentions πρόλογος of the beginning of a comedy, it would seem that rhetoric treated prologues to comedy and tragedy alike on the analogy of the beginnings of speeches. It follows that of the four references to prologues in Aristotle later, the two most significant occur in the *Rhetoric,* and have the art of speech in view more than the art of tragedy. In the *Poetics* the πρόλογος occurs simply as an item in the enumeration of the parts of a tragedy, and is defined as 'the whole part of a tragedy before the parodos of the chorus'.[4] Thus Aristotle sees the prologue as a part of the whole and not as a preface separate from the action, and there is here a shift of meaning when the word leaves its original sense of 'prior announcement' and takes on more the idea of 'beginning'.

That the word was felt in certain quarters to be inadequate for what it was designating is shown, according to Stoessl, by the fact that scholia on the tragedies can introduce synonyms for it such as εἰσόδος, 'entrance',[5] ἀρχή, 'beginning'[6] and προοίμιον, 'proem',[7] while with

1. Haigh, *Tragic Drama*, p. 352.
2. See F. Stoessl, 'Prologos', in PW XXIII.I, cols. 631-41.
3. Stoessl, 'Prologos', col. 635.
4. The passages referred to are *Rhetoric* 3.1414b, 19-20 and 1415a, 9, *Poetics* 1425b, 19-20.
5. 'Prologos', col. 634 citing a scholion on Soph. Aj. 134.
6. 'Prologos', col. 634, scholion on Soph. Aj. (Einl. Schol. Soph. El. 1).
7. 'Prologos', col. 634, scholion on Soph. Aj. (Einl. Schol. Soph. Oid. Tyr. 14); cf. Aristotle, *Rhetoric* 1414b, 19.

reference to comedy εἰσβολή, 'way of entering', is found. Later still, when the word was transliterated into the Latin *prologus*, the *pro-* prefix would have reintroduced something of the original sense of 'beforehandedness'. Nevertheless, the word πρόλογος maintained itself, no doubt because of its origin in literary criticism and rhetoric. But Aristotle's definition quoted above could be said to be defective, and not borne out by the evidence. E.A. Havelock remarks of it that 'the anonymous author (Aristotle could scarcely have been so dogmatic or so wrong) reflects those standards of mechanical formalism current in the period of the drama's decline'; and of Aristotle's statement that the prologue as defined by him occurs in all the tragedies, he says that it is simply erroneous.[1] Hence there are to be found in the literary tradition other, non-Aristotelian definitions of πρόλογος without express limitation to tragedy and comedy. Thus, 'Prologue is a pre-statement of the things which are to be introduced in the drama: *rhēsis* is the subsequent speech spoken to the audience: *amoibē* is the dialogue of the actors introduced'.[2] Or, on a different analysis of the structure of drama, there is the Latin definition of Euanthius, 'The prologue is, as it were, a pre-face to the story, in which alone is anything allowed to be said to the audience outside the argument, for the convenience of the poet, the story or the actor'.[3] Very similar, but in relation now to a prologue which stands on its own separate from the action (as in several of the plays of Plautus and Terence, and probably in those of the New Comedy) is the definition of Donatius, 'The prologue is the opening speech, called by the Greeks πρῶτος λόγος, preceding the real composition of the story'.[4]

This variety of definition and terminology would seem to point to a certain fluidity and development over a considerable period, and it cannot be ruled out in advance that it could have provided something of a background for the author of the Fourth Gospel and his readers. The Greek literary sphere is the only one that furnished instances of a self-contained, concentrated poetic unit acting as an introduction to, and pre-statement of, what was to follow; there are no instances of this to be

---

1. In his Introduction to H. Lloyd-Jones, *The Eumenides of Aeschylus* (Prentice Hall Drama Series; Englewood Cliffs, NJ: Prentice Hall, 1970), p. xi.
2. In the *Scholia Londinensia* to Dionysius Thrax, cited by Stoessl, 'Prologos', col. 636.
3. Cited by Stoessl, 'Prologos', col. 636.
4. Cited by Stoessl, 'Prologos', col. 636.

found in Jewish literature.[1] If the author of the Fourth Gospel and his
readers had any acquaintance with the variety of forms and functions of
a 'prologue', they would accept that the writer was free to re-present
any known account of a personage or god in terms which suited the
author's choice and emphasis. They would be aware that the manifold
re-presentations of the old, well-known stories in the Greek and Greco-
Roman literary and religious traditions were saturated with rhetoric and
philosophy, even though the plays 'are all taken from the old
mythology, in accordance with the sacred traditions of the drama, which
it was impossible to disobey'.[2] From this standpoint it would not have
been difficult for early Christians to accept that the very different gospel
that John's Gospel is should be introduced in this way, and to recognize
the prologue for what it was. In that case it could be that, as in Greek
drama, which had no playbill but sometimes had a prologue as a kind of
substitute, so in the Fourth Gospel the prologue is verbal scenery, giving
information about the coming action, introducing the main characters,
stating the subject of the whole and so preparing the recipients for a true
understanding of the state of affairs, which is ordained from heaven,
concerning the relationship of humankind to heaven. The characters
introduced in the Johannine prologue—the Logos who is the only Son,
who is Jesus Christ, and the divine witness John—are those who effect
the divinely conceived plans, while the mention of Moses is able to act as
a shorthand reference for the ancient and prestigious traditions claimed
by the Jews as their prerogatives. The background indicated is one of
cosmic conflict which embraces all humankind. The results of
appropriating the heavenly gifts are universal, but since they originate
from God who is the God of the Jews, the conflict has to be set out in
terms which allow for the development of the theme, not only of the
ignorance and culpability of humankind in general, but also of the Jews
who worship him.

The structure and contents of the prologue will be dealt with in more
detail in the following chapters. Here a brief survey may be made of
previous treatments of the matter in so far as they have a bearing on the
relation of the prologue to the Gospel as a whole. In Harnack's original
magisterial treatment there is much that is of permanent value, both in

1.   Thus the so-called hymns to Wisdom in Prov. 8, Ecclus. 24 and Wis. 7,
which are often appealed to as parallels, at least to the thought of the prologue, do not
stand at the beginning as an introduction.

2.   Haigh, *Tragic Drama*, p. 237.

his analysis of the thought of the Gospel in terms of a heavenly pre-existent Son of God present on earth as the human Jesus, and in his analysis of the emphases and sequence of thought in the prologue. He was, however, writing in conscious opposition to certain positions of his own day (those of Weizsäcker, Holtzmann and so on) in which 'the narrative itself, as also the words of Jesus in the Fourth Gospel, cannot deny their origin in the Logos doctrine', which doctrine 'is not a mantle hung over the story and the faith; rather it governs the concept throughout'. Harnack set out to refute this in so far as it implied that the evangelist saw Jesus, the Son, as a divine figure in the sense of eternally-begotten (as in later Christian doctrine), or that the Logos was more for him than a current conception by which to introduce one whose nature and function are most adequately defined as those of the unique Son. Harnack sees messiahship as the key concept in the Gospel, though messiahship of a heavenly and pre-existent kind (the 'Son of Man' he defines as 'the heavenly messiah'), and this is the link with the prologue when it comes to rest with the only Son and with Jesus Christ. He thus reaches the conclusion that

> The Prologue is not the key to the understanding of the Gospel, but pre-pares the Greek reader for that understanding. It attaches itself to a known entity, the Logos, adapts and transforms it—by implication opposing false Christologies—in order to substitute for it Jesus Christ, the μονογενὴς θεός, and consequently to reveal it as this Jesus Christ. From the moment this happened the Logos concept was discarded. The author then speaks only of Jesus in order to establish the faith that he is the Messiah, the Son of God.[1]

Apart from the contemporary assumptions and character of the debate, which strike one now as too rigid and confined, it is questionable whether Harnack is right in seeing 'messiahship' either as a main thread of the Gospel, or as a major link between the Gospel and the prologue. He is undoubtedly correct when he says that the evangelist admittedly understood by 'messiah' both extensively and intensively something wholly different from what the Jews understood by this concept, but unfortunately he does not expound this wholly different understanding. Had he done so it might have become apparent that 'messiah' is hardly the title the evangelist wished to present for acceptance and belief, especially when in the prologue Christ appears only as a proper name.

---

1. Harnack, 'Das Verhältnis des Prologs zum ganzen Werke', pp. 191, 230.

Again, Harnack does not explore the Philonic conception of the Logos for any points of contact between it and the functions of the Logos-Son-Jesus Christ in the prologue. What is said in terms of the Logos is, it is true, said after the prologue in terms of Jesus Christ; but this does not exclude the possibility that the rest of the Gospel expands and explicates that upon which the Christian understanding of the Logos—the Johannine Logos who is also μονογενής God and Son—rests. It would seem that Harnack does not arrive at any full coinherence of gospel and prologue.

The approaches of scholars who have treated the matter more recently vary considerably, and are not amenable to any simple grouping. First may be considered the position that the prologue as it stands is the result of the redaction of an already existent unit. The criteria for this type of literary analysis were laid down by J.H. Bernard. They were: (1) in accordance with the character of Semitic poetry the verse lines must be short, roughly the same in length, and fall into parallel clauses; (2) as the unit is a hymn it must consist of statements; hence the argumentative verses (vv. 13, 17 and perhaps 18) are to be excluded; and (3) as it is an abstract statement proper names (John, Moses, Jesus Christ) are to be excluded (i.e. vv. 6-8, 15, 17).[1] The best known exponent of this approach is Bultmann.[2] According to Bultmann's analysis, the prologue has a literary character, which is that of a hymn, and is the hymn of a community. It is made up of couplets in poetic rhythm, and its entire form is governed by strict rules. However, this does not hold for vv. 6-8, 13 and 15, and these stand out as interruptions in being partly prose narrative either with a polemical purpose (vv. 6-8, 15) or as dogmatic definition (v. 13). Considerations of rhythm also require the excision of v. 2 as repetition of v. 1, of ἄνθρωπον in v. 9, of ἐν τῷ κόσμῳ ἦν καί in v. 10 and of ἐξουσίαν in v. 12. The analysis is not however purely literary, since Bultmann asks where the prologue first speaks of the incarnate Logos. His answer is that in the source this was at v. 14, and that the 'we' of vv. 14 and 16 are the same, the witness of John in v. 15 being an insertion into the original hymnic form. Similarly, while in the original hymn vv. 1-5 and vv. 9-12 spoke of the pre-existent Logos and

---

    1.   J.H. Bernard, *A Critical and Exegetical Commentary on the Gospel according to John* (2 vols.; Edinburgh: T. & T. Clark, 1928), I, p. cxlv; referred to by B. Lindars, *The Gospel of John* (London: Oliphants, 1972), pp. 80-81.
    2.   R. Bultmann, *The Gospel of John: A Commentary* (Oxford: Basil Blackwell, 1971), pp. 13-18.

his 'almost fruitless effect as Revealer in this form',[1] the evangelist takes v. 5—'the light shines in the darkness, and the darkness has not overcome it'—as a reference to the historical Jesus, and has therefore inserted vv. 6-8. These insertions 'are not to be eliminated as interpolations; they are the evangelist's own comments'.[2] Again, v. 12c and v. 13 are exegetical comments interpreting the idea of 'the children of God' in v. 12b, and v. 17 is an exegetical gloss on v. 16, while v. 18 is to be regarded on stylistic grounds as an addition by the evangelist. Bultmann concludes that the cultic hymn of the community which the evangelist has used as the basis of the prologue consisted of vv. 1-5, 9-12, which spoke of the pre-existent Logos, whose negative effect is offset by the statement of v. 14, which speaks of the incarnation of the Logos, which the evangelist already found in v. 5. 'It is only because he [the evangelist] found in the words τὸ φῶς ἐν τῇ σκοτίᾳ φαίνει κτλ., an expression of the revelation given by the historical Jesus that he is able to introduce the Baptist at this point as the witness to the light.'[3] Added to this theological consideration, Bultmann insists, is the polemical character of vv. 6-8, 15, which deny John the authority of Revealer. Further, by an appeal to the Mandaean literature he holds that the Baptist sect would have hymned John as a gnostic revealer. So the evangelist utilized a gnostic Baptist hymn, in which the cosmology of gnosticism had already given way to an expression of belief in the Creator-God of the Old Testament.

There are certain merits in Bultmann's analysis which account for its acceptance in general by a number of scholars, even when they modify it in detail. The chief of these is the isolation within the present prologue of an original whose rhythmic structure and form correspond to its subject matter, and on the basis of which the attitude of the evangelist may be detected in the additions and comments he has made which disturb this form. Its weaknesses may be said to be twofold. First, on this view the hymn to the Logos was not the evangelist's own deliberate construction, which he felt impelled to compose as a prolegomenon to his gospel, but something ready to hand which he felt he could use for the purpose. Secondly, the reasons that Bultmann gives for the evangelist's insertions and adaptations, and for his addition of vv. 17-18, by which he edits such a tightly-knit structure, are not particularly compelling. The

1. Bultmann, *John*, p. 17.
2. Bultmann, *John*, p. 16.
3. *John*, p. 17.

influence of Bultmann's type of analysis upon a whole range of scholars may be seen in the table printed by R.E. Brown in his commentary, where he gives the reconstructions of an original hymn made by J.H. Bernard, S. de Ausejo, P. Gaechter, H.C. Green, E. Haenchen, E. Käsemann and R. Schnackenburg. These reconstructions have a good deal in common, but they also vary considerably, particularly after v. 5. Brown himself offers tentatively his own reconstruction of the original hymn as consisting of four strophes—vv. 1-2, 3-5, 10-12b and 14-16. To this were added as explanatory expansions the statements in vv. 12c-13, and at a later stage a set of additions about the Baptist, vv. 6-8, 15, which may originally have constituted the opening of the Gospel, but which were displaced by a final redactor when he prefaced the Gospel with a prologue. At this point this type of analysis, in postulating such a complicated series of redactions, tends to run out into the sand.[1]

On the other hand there are scholars who forswear this type of analysis, and who see the prologue as it stands as a literary and theological unity from the evangelist's own hand. There is, however, no uniformity among these. They include, for example, J.A.T. Robinson, who believes that the prologue was written at a later stage than the composition of the Gospel, and therefore could not be held to have shaped and controlled what follows it.[2] At the opposite pole is C.K. Barrett, who rejects on literary grounds the view that a poetic structure underlies the prologue. There is no evidence here of Greek poetry, which was written in recognizable metres. Barrett argues that the Greek here is in prose rhythm, the content determining the length of the lines, and vv. 6-8 are not to be distinguished as prose from the rest which is in verse. His conclusion is that the prologue 'is one piece of solid theological writing', and that it is 'necessary to the Gospel, as the Gospel is necessary to the Prologue. The history explicates the theology, and the theology interprets the history.'[3] Unfortunately these conclusions cannot be systematically tested within the limits of the single lecture in which they are reached, though they are presupposed in Barrett's commentary on John.

1.   See R.E. Brown, *The Gospel according to John* (AB, 29, 29a; 2 vols.; Garden City, NY: Doubleday, 1966), pp.18-23.

2.   See his article 'The Relation of the Prologue to the Gospel of St John', *NTS* 9 (1963), pp. 120-29.

3.   See his Ethel M. Wood Lecture, 'The Prologue of St John's Gospel' (London: Athlone Press, 1971), pp. 27-28, reprinted in his *New Testament Essays* (SPCK, 1972). The quotation is from p. 48 (all references are to the SPCK edition).

In this group should be counted C.H. Dodd, who here, as elsewhere in his study of this gospel, takes the possibility of a Greek background into account. He uses both the word 'proem' and the word 'prologue'. Thus, 'Chapter 1 forms a proem to the whole gospel. It falls into two parts: 1-18, commonly designated the Prologue, and 19-51, which we may, from the nature of its contents, conveniently call the Testimony.'[1] After recalling Mk 1.1-15 as similarly constituting an introduction or proem to the Gospel, and discussing Logos and other problems, he concludes: 'The Prologue thus represents a thoroughgoing re-interpretation of the idea which in the later part of the chapter is expressed in terms of the "realised eschatology" of the primitive Church'. He suggests that the evangelist wishes 'to offer the Logos-idea as the appropriate approach—for those nurtured in the higher religion of hellenism—to the central purport of the Gospel, through which he may lead them to the historical actuality of its story, rooted as it is in Jewish tradition'.[2] Finally he observes that the two statements in 1.14 and 1.51 'contain in brief the substance of what the evangelist is now about to relate'.[3] Dodd's use of both 'proem' and 'prologue' recalls the dissatisfaction felt by ancient writers with the term 'prologue'. As there, so here, both terms suggest 'beginning', but clearly Dodd sees in the prologue in some sense an 'announcing beforehand', a new interpretation of an old set of ideas around a central figure now called 'Logos'. This is, as has been previously shown, in accordance with ancient usage, and could correspond with a state of literary creative freedom in the evangelist's own time and milieu. It may be noticed that nowhere is it suggested by Dodd that philosophical speculation or metaphysics are to be thought to provide the interpretive key.[4]

R.H. Lightfoot did not make a special study of the problem, though in a discussion of the opening of Mark's Gospel he made certain observations which bear on it, and which have been taken up by others. He notes certain general parallels between Mk 1.1-13 and Jn 1.1-18, and designates both 'prologue'. By his 'prologue' Mark wished to provide

---

1. C.H. Dodd, *The Interpretation of the Fourth Gospel* (Cambridge University Press, 1953), p. 292.
2. Dodd, *Interpretation*, p. 296.
3. Dodd, *Interpretation*, p. 296.
4. Hence Dodd hardly deserves the strictures directed against him on this score by H. Ridderbos in 'The Structure and Scope of the Prologue to the Gospel of John', *NovT* 8 (1966), p.181.

his readers from the outset with the key he intended them to have to
make it possible for them to understand the person and office of Jesus.[1]
There are however differences of a textual and theological kind. The
Markan prologue is prose, and is in the same style as the remainder of
the Gospel, so that there can be no question of the incorporation or later
addition of an originally independent source. In his commentary on
John's Gospel Lightfoot himself refers to 'a very small difference in
their opening narratives [the Markan and Johannine Prologues] to illustrate an important truth'. The Markan approach to the doctrine of the
Lord's person is said to be 'chiefly by way of the Jewish messianic
hope, and hope implies an attitude towards the future', whereas the
Johannine approach is said to be 'chiefly from the divine side', with the
prologue emphasizing 'the eternity of the Logos, and His equality with
God'.[2] The former, with its expectation of something yet to come, and
the latter, with its consciousness of a reality or truth already present, are
theological distinctions throughout the respective gospels and their
prologues.

   This point is touched on by M.D. Hooker in her paper on 'The
Johannine Prologue and the Messianic Secret'.[3] She notes that the
Markan prologue is, like the rest of the Gospel, in narrative form with
echoes of its vocabulary. The fourth evangelist is said 'to offer us
something...much closer to becoming a theological discourse', and the
discourse is said to be typical of this gospel until the passion narrative
begins.[4] There is some truth in this, though it is to be observed that
'discourse' is only one constituent part of the first seventeen chapters of
the Gospel. The so-called 'farewell discourses' of chs. 13–17 are rightly
called discourses, but a great deal of chs. 1–12 (for example 1.19-51;
2.1-25; 4.1-31, 39-54; 5.1-18; 6.1-25, 60-71) is hardly discourse, but
rather a peculiar blend of events theologically presented and isolated
sayings or Johannine themes. 'Discourse' as a description of the literary
form of the prologue may be questioned. It gains support from
Bultmann's hypothesis of a miracle source and a discourse source
having been available to the evangelist, but this is a hypothesis that has

   1.   R.H. Lightfoot, *The Gospel Message of St Mark* (Oxford: Clarendon Press,
1950), pp. 15-19.
   2.   R.H. Lightfoot, *St John's Gospel: A Commentary* (ed. C.F. Evans; Oxford:
Clarendon Press, 1956), p. 57.
   3.   *NTS* 21 (1974), pp. 40-58.
   4.   Hooker, 'Johannine Prologue', p. 41.

not been universally accepted, and which should probably be rejected. Recalling Lightfoot's assessment of Mk 1.1-13 Hooker explores the possibility that the Markan literary method might help in understanding the Johannine. She maintains that Jn 1.41, 49 indicates that the disciples acknowledged Jesus as the messiah from the beginning. What is hidden and occasions obtuseness in the disciples cannot be, as in Mark, his messiahship. It is rather his status as the Logos. The reference in 1.14 to the glory seen when the Logos tabernacled among us is regarded by her as a link with Moses, and the Logos is here already being contrasted with Moses. On this reading 'his own' is a designation of the Jews, and those who saw the glory are Christian believers thought of as the new people of God. This also may be questioned. For in view of the state of universal non-comprehension depicted in 1.1-5 'his own' could well be humankind, who are part of the created order referred to in 1.1-4. In that case the believers are Christians, but without any suggestion that they are a 'new Israel' or people of God in direct succession to the Jews. In any case 1.14 and 2.11 indicate that this glory, carefully introduced in respect of the divine Logos-Son in relation to a Father who is the God of the Jews, is clearly visible to all from the beginning, and there is here nothing corresponding to the messianic secret in Mark. Having placed the hidden Logos, the glory and Jesus Christ in a relation to Moses, Hooker proceeds to interpret 1.14-18 in the light of Exodus 33–34, where Moses is not allowed to see the face of God.

This raises the general question of the intended readers of this gospel, since it leans heavily on the view that they would be steeped in biblical knowledge and exegesis. But when the evangelist finds it necessary to transliterate *messias* in 1.41, or to explain the rite of purification as Jewish in 2.6, it suggests a wider, multi-racial audience of a more universal character. It may be that the statement in 1.18 that no human being has seen God at any time could include a reference to the Old Testament in its scope and involve a denial of Old Testament statements; but if so the reference is likely to have been wider than Exodus 33–34. For readers acquainted with the Old Testament could well have recalled Exod. 24.9-11, where not only Moses but his three companions and all the elders of Israel are said to have seen the Lord without paying any penalty, and there were prophets and seers for whom the same could be claimed. Indeed, it is not strictly true that in 1.14-18 Christ and Moses are contrasted. As a man effecting certain things for God Moses was temporarily commissioned for specific duties; and when they were performed they were not regarded as the very acts of God himself, the prerogatives of God alone, but as acts of a man doing certain things as God's agent. This cannot be the same with Jesus, who from the outset as Logos 'created all things', and thereafter performs the divine functions in total unity with God as Father. There is a partial contrast in terms of perfect and imperfect origins, which qualitatively affect the work which is effected. In that case 1.18 restates the authenticity of the claim and works of the Logos-Jesus in contrast to all other human claims, since this Son is both Logos and μονογενὴς θεός. The climax of the prologue is 1.18b, for with the credentials set out in 1.18a none can be placed in a position of superiority to him or of better authority than him. Nevertheless, it is significant that a certain unity of prologue and gospel can be found by way of the exploration of statements about Moses, and to this we shall return later.

Finally, in a very different vein is E. Käsemann's study 'The Structure and Purpose of the Prologue to John's Gospel'.[1] He believes that those scholars who hold that the prologue is in some way an overture to, or a summary of, the Gospel which follows have obscured rather than elucidated the problem. He devotes considerable attention to an analysis of the structure and genesis of the prologue. Underlying 1.1-13 is a Christian hymn, with v. 12 as its climax and v. 13 as a note added by the author (surely a weak point). Verses 14-18 are an epilogue to the whole. He rejects the view that vv. 5-13 are a proleptic picture of the appearance of the Revealer in history, seeing the language of these verses as characteristic rather of the portrayal of an epiphany. Since the prologue does not expressly say who it is with whom we have to deal in the historical Jesus, Käsemann opposes the view that Christology and ontology are at the centre of the prologue, though he roundly asserts that the parallelism between v. 5 and vv. 9-11 shows that 'his own' ought not to be understood of Israel, and that a cosmological slant characterizes the whole prologue, not just its opening verses. Nevertheless, for him the primary concern of the evangelist appears, with v. 12 as the climax underlined by his own note in v. 13, as 'the eschatological presence of salvation', with Jesus as 'the Creator of the eschatological sonship to God, and of the new world'.[2] Käsemann makes some important points, particularly that the universal understanding of eternal

1. In *New Testament Questions of Today* (London: SCM Press, 1969), pp. 138-67.
2. Käsemann, 'Structure and Purpose', p. 165.

life governs the eschatological perspective and the work of Jesus in this gospel. It may be questioned, however, whether the experiential awareness of the creator of eschatological sonship and of the new world constituted the real drive of the evangelist's work. At best they are one small part of a greater whole. The motif of 'new world' is hardly to the fore in Johannine theology, and in the body of the Gospel eschatological sonship is remarkable by its absence. If such had been a primary concern of the evangelist it is surprising that so little is said in the Gospel about the proper way of living as sons, or about any hope for an extended future with its inevitable temporal end. And if Christology and ontology are rejected in favour of Christ as the creator of eschatological sonship, it is curious that there is no reference to the problem of relating a 'Christian' claim to worship the Logos-Creator, Jesus Christ, as God alongside the worship of the Jewish God. In short, the theocentricity of the evangelist, and its dominance in his presentation of the gospel truths, are not here sufficently taken into account.

The foregoing brief account of the approaches to the question of the relation of the prologue to the rest of the Gospel shows some agreement, but also a wide range of disagreement. The matter remains open for further examination, particularly along the lines of the prologue as functioning like the prologue to a religious drama, with the fore-announcing of the past events, the present situation and the final outcome as being within the preordained will of God, and with the introduction in advance of principal figures as chief characters.

Chapter 2

JOHN AND HIS WITNESS

As indicated at the end of the previous chapter, no general consensus of opinion has emerged among scholars as to whether the prologue as it now stands had once existed independently, and had been incorporated by the evangelist *en bloc*, or had existed in a different form and had been redacted by the evangelist, and what that original form might have been. It is, therefore, still open to maintain that it was from the first the construction of the evangelist himself. This will be maintained here as a hypothesis, and I shall proceed to examine afresh the contents of the prologue and its purpose in relation to the remainder of the Gospel which the evangelist was to write. To do this I propose to start from precisely those elements which in most analyses have been taken as secondary and as redactional additions to an original hymn, and to examine in particular the roles of the three personal figures whom the evangelist has chosen to select for introduction into what is otherwise a somewhat impersonal and semi-metaphysical prologue, viz. John, Moses and Jesus Christ, and to enquire in what manner and for what purposes they are so introduced.

We begin, then, with John; since, significantly, the term 'the Baptist' is nowhere used in the Fourth Gospel he will be referred to by his proper name 'John'. The relation between theories of an original form of the prologue which has been incorporated and redacted by the evangelist and assessment of the theology of the Gospel as a whole is immediately raised by the figure of John. Thus, if Bultmann's theory is accepted that originally the prologue was a hymn to the Baptist as the Logos arising in a Baptist sect, then the statements about John in 1.6-8, regarded on grounds of rhythm as a prose interpolation into a hymn, are seen as deliberately introduced by the evangelist to demote him from any such position. Even apart from Bultmann's very precise hypothesis the majority of scholars would seem to have regarded these verses as a prose addition with this primarily negative purpose. If, on the other hand, Barrett is correct in his judgment that these verses are not a prose interpolation, but are sufficiently elevated in style to be continuous with the rest, then it is possible to ask again for what positive purpose the evangelist introduces John this early in the composition of the prologue, and what he intended to say through these verses, both of a positive and a negative kind, that was vital to his gospel.

Hooker also considers that vv. 6-8 (and v. 15) are not intrusions into the prologue, but 'have been used to link firmly the introductory philosophical passages to the rest of the Gospel'.[1] She detects two main sections, vv. 1-5 and vv. 9-13, which are themselves characterized by what she calls 'a certain chiastic structure', the second part of each section developing more fully what has been stated in the first part. The statements about John at vv. 6-8 and v. 15 stand, according to this analysis, at turning points from the first to the second part of each of these two sections of the prologue, so that John is made to be the witness who 'confesses the truth of what has just been said'. There is thus compressed into the brief statements of the prologue the witnessing function of John as it appears later in the Gospel in 1.19-34. While the chiastic structure is somewhat doubtful, Hooker has perhaps drawn attention to a positive link between the prologue and the rest of ch. 1 of the Gospel, though when she goes on to say that John is made 'to deny any position to himself',[2] she ignores the way in which the evangelist has made John apply to himself the scriptural words of Isa. 40.3 as divinely attesting that he is the voice, and so to make a self-acclamation of a highly authoritative kind.

C.H. Dodd, in his book *Historical Tradition in the Fourth Gospel*, was engaged in a particular and limited form of historical enquiry, in the course of which, however, he maintains that the evangelist's presentation of 'the mission' of the Baptist is governed by a threefold schematization. This first appears in the prologue in the statements 'was not the Light', 'came to bear witness to the Light' and 'in order that through his agency all might become believers'; and it can then be traced in the later passages in the Gospel concerned with John.[3] Dodd admits that this schematization cannot be applied too rigidly—the theme that all might

---

1. In 'John the Baptist and the Johannine Prologue', *NTS* 16 (1970), p. 358.
2. 'John the Baptist', p. 357.
3. C.H. Dodd, *Historical Tradition in the Fourth Gospel* (Cambridge: Cambridge University Press, 1963), pp. 248-49.

believe through his agency is not represented in 3.22-30. Nevertheless it
draws attention to one element of literary unity within the material in the
Gospel concerned with John. Outside this schema lies 1.15, about which
Dodd rightly observes that it is repeated at 1.30, and that both these are
to be linked with 3.28. These verses furnish three examples, one in the
prologue and two outside it, of a style of self-quotation which is ascribed
by the evangelist to John.[1]

E. Käsemann also insists that the prologue is to be understood as a
literary and theological whole, though his analysis of its literary structure
and growth is highly complicated, and indeed idiosyncratic. On this
analysis he locates the theological emphasis as being on Christ as the
creator of eschatological sonship to God and of the new world. The
objections to this understanding have been stated earlier. In this analysis,
however, both on its literary and theological sides, John is seen to play
an important role. For Käsemann insists that v. 5 and vv. 9-11 are to be
taken as parallel statements of the appearance of the Logos-Revealer in a
hostile world, and John is introduced between them as God's ordained
witness to the light for the benefit of all humankind in a scene of universal alienation. And since, in Käsemann's view, the climax of the prologue lies in the confession of the witnessing community in v. 12 of the
presence of Christ as the creator of eschatological sonship within this
alienated world, John in v. 15 'is in no way designed to have an exclusively polemic or apologetic character. The Gospel does not exist without the confessing community, whose first representative John the
Baptist was.'[2]

C.K. Barrett, from a different standpoint and with a different literary
analysis, can also say that '"the Baptist" verses are not an afterthought,
thrown in to injure the rival Baptist group, but part of a serious, connected, thought-out, theological purpose'. They contain a 'theological
evaluation' of the historical figure.[3] They are part of the setting in which
the narrative that is to follow is to be understood. As he points out,
Mark and Luke had made the Baptist the indispensable figure in the
beginning of their gospels, but in this the tradition had exaggerated, and
the fourth evangelist puts the true beginning of the Gospel before
creation, before time itself.[4] Of this John himself is the witness as witness

1. *Historical Tradition*, p. 271.
2. 'Structure and Purpose', p. 165.
3. 'Prologue', p. 44.
4. 'Prologue', p. 45.

to the light (vv. 6-8), as he is also the witness to the subsequent glorification of Jesus in his statement in v. 15.[1]

This brief survey is intended to show that a number of scholars with different approaches have given grounds for a further consideration of the figure of John in this gospel. In his monograph *John the Baptist in the Gospel Tradition*, which is the most detailed recent treatment of the subject,[2] W. Wink observes that the study of the Baptist had previously taken place entirely within the setting of the quest for reconstructing the historical Jesus, and was thought to have provided a particularly secure section in that reconstruction. And he further notes that even when the quest for the historical Jesus became less and less confident of success, this did not apply to what was said about John, which achieved a certain 'fixation on the level of historicity', so that 'every monograph on John which has thus far appeared has dealt with him from the point of view of historical biography'.[3]

One of the reasons for this, as Wink observes, is that in John's case, in contrast to that of Jesus, there is mention of him in the writings of Josephus, which were widely regarded as giving a valuable historical judgment from a non-Christian source. The question, however, whether the passage about the Baptist in *Ant.* 18.116-19 was simply a historical reference, or was itself shaped by theological motives, does not appear to have been considered. In the *Antiquities*, which may have been written partly at least to explain Judaism to outsiders, Josephus introduced the Baptist to show that Jews worshipped a just God who effectively punished those who harmed pious Jews, thus leading people to correct worship. With this aim he records the death of Herod, who had put the Baptist to death, as being understood by some Jews in terms of Jewish theodicy, and the details he gives regarding John are embellishments of the statement that 'John was a pious man'. When Josephus depicts him as summoning to baptism the Jews who practised virtue and exercised righteousness towards one another and piety towards God, he is selecting in his description what his intended readers are likely to appreciate, in itself and as the grounds for the high estimate of John in Jewish religious circles and for his popular following. His description of John's baptism as accepted by God for the purification of the body, the soul having been previously cleansed by righteousness, is highly

1. 'Prologue', p. 47.
2. SNTSMS, 7; Cambridge: Cambridge University Press, 1968.
3. Wink, *John the Baptist*, p. x.

distinctive. Possibly, it reflects an adjustment of Jewish theology to prevalent religious attitudes in the Greco-Roman world. It is also possible that in the words 'it seemed to him [God?] that baptismal ablution was acceptable if it were not used to seek remission of sins', Josephus is dissociating the rite from the kind of claim for it in the Christian tradition—represented by the Synoptic Gospels but not at all in the Fourth Gospel—of conferring the forgiveness of sins. It would seem, therefore, that Josephus's presentation of the Baptist was in its own way a theological rather than a purely historical one. If this is the case, it is highly probable that all other presentations of the Baptist are structured to perform a theological function within a given religious circle.

Wink's own approach to the Gospel traditions about the Baptist is to be welcomed in its attempt to rectify the previous situation, for it does not insist that irreconcilable data—for instance chronological contradictions, or the graphic inconsistencies in the figures depicted—be accounted for on historical grounds and with an eye to detailed historical accuracy. His treatment of John in the Fourth Gospel is, however, open to criticism since he brings it under an overall method of redaction criticism which is stated at the outset of his book, and while this is applicable to the procedures of the synoptic evangelists with respect to their use of already existing traditions, it is not necessarily applicable to the Fourth Gospel. The considerable extent of agreement between the variant traditions in the Synoptic Gospels makes observation of redactional activity of those evangelists possible, but this is hardly so with the Fourth Gospel. C.H. Dodd's study of historical tradition in this gospel reaches the conclusion that 'an ancient tradition independent of the other gospels' lay behind the Fourth Gospel, that this was an oral tradition, and that with respect to the Baptist it was more detailed and provided evidence of his work as a Jewish reformer. Further, Dodd accepts as a historical probability that the ministries of John and Jesus ran parallel, that both practised a rite of ablution. He accepts also that followers of the Baptist may have followed Jesus at some stage, though the text as it stands does not show the circumstances in which the two figures parted company.[1] It cannot be said, however, that in all this there can be observed any clear signs of the redaction of a previously existing tradition which can now be isolated from the forms and contexts in which the evangelist makes it appear.

1. *Tradition*, p. 429.

John is thus deliberately, and somewhat surprisingly, introduced as the first human figure in a prologue which is dealing with cosmic and ultimate issues; and is introduced as the object of a divine mission which is expressly defined as witness to the divine light, and as the necessary agency of believing response to the light on its appearance. As Wink observes, the overall conception which dominates the presentation of John in the Fourth Gospel is that of witness, and any investigation of John in the Gospel must be concerned with how and why this is so.[1] This concept is introduced as a general term (εἰς μαρτυρίαν) to describe the object of John's 'coming', which is his 'being sent from God' (1.7), and here the witness is twice specified as witness 'concerning the light' (1.7, 8). Before the prologue closes, however, John's witness is referred to again, not now in general terms, but by having him actually bear his witness (1.15). This witness is introduced by the solemn word κέκραγεν.

Before the content of this witness is examined, however, there is a preliminary textual question to be decided of how far the witness thus introduced is to be supposed to extend. There is evidence of some confusion in the matter. John Chrysostom opens his comment on 1.16 in *Homily* XIV on the Gospel of John with the words,

> I said the other day [the reference is to *Homily* XIII on 1.15], that John, to resolve the doubts of those who should question with themselves how the Lord, though he came after to the preaching, became before and more glorious than he, added, 'for He was before me'. And that is indeed one reason. But not content with this, he adds again a second, which he now declares. What is it? 'And of His fulness' says he, 'have we all received, and grace for grace'. With these again he mentions another. What is this? That 'the Law was given by Moses, but grace and truth came by Jesus Christ'.

The most natural interpretation of this is that by 'John' is meant 'the Baptist', and that his testimony is regarded as extending from v. 15 to v. 17. However, later in the *Homily* Chrysostom states, 'And therefore John said, "Of His fulness have we all received", and joins his own testimony to that of the Baptist; for the expression "of His fulness have we all received" belongs not to the forerunner but to the disciple'. It is evident, then, that Chrysostom regards 1.16-17 as the words of the evangelist and not of John (the Baptist), as he does also 1.18, when in *Homily* XV he introduces his comment on 'No man has seen God at any time' with the words, 'By what connection of thought does the

1. *John the Baptist*, p. 89.

Apostle come to say this?'[1] This has been almost the universal view of
commentators since. Before Chrysostom, however, there is evidence for
a different view. Origen, in his *Commentary on John,* when introducing
his theory that the Baptist has six testimonies in this Gospel, wrote:

> Accordingly John came to bear witness of the light, and in his witness-
> bearing he cried, saying, 'He that cometh after me exists before me; for He
> was before me; for of His fulness we have all received and grace for grace;
> for the law was given by Moses but grace and truth came through Jesus
> Christ. No one hath seen God at any time; the only begotten God, who is
> in the bosom of the Father, He hath declared him'. This whole speech is
> from the mouth of the Baptist bearing witness to the Christ. Some take it
> otherwise, and consider that the words from 'for of His fulness' to 'He
> hath declared Him' are from the writer John the Apostle. The true state of
> the case is that John's first testimony begins, as we said before, 'He that
> cometh after me', and ends, 'He hath declared Him'.[2]

Among the 'some who take it otherwise', to whom Origen refers here,
was Heracleon, though he held a peculiar position. When developing the
theory of the six testimonies of the Baptist in Book VI of his
Commentary Origen comments on Jn 1.19 as follows,

> 'And this is the witness of John.' This is the second recorded testimony
> of John the Baptist to Christ. The first begins with 'This was He of whom
> I said, He that cometh after me', and goes down to 'The only begotten Son
> of God, who is in the bosom of the Father, He hath declared Him'.
> Heracleon supposes the words, 'No one has seen God at any time', etc to
> have been spoken, not by the Baptist, but by the disciple. But in this he is
> not sound. He himself allows the words, 'Of his fulness we all received,
> and grace for grace; for the law was given by Moses, but grace and truth
> came by Jesus Christ' to have been spoken by the Baptist.[3]

1.   *Homilies of S. John Chrysostom on the Gospel according to St John*
(tr. Library of the Fathers; John Henry Parker, 1848), *Homily* XIV, pp. 111-12.
2.   Origen, *Commentary on S. John's Gospel* (ANCL Additional Volume;
Edinburgh: T. & T. Clark, 1896), p. 343. The Greek text is in *The Commentary of
Origen on S. John's Gospel: The Text Revised with a Critical Introduction and
indices* (ed. A.E. Brooke; 2 vols.; Cambridge: Cambridge University Press, 1896), I,
p. 103. As well as the Commentary from the MSS Brooke prints 110 fragments of the
Commentary which have survived elsewhere. Among these, Fragments 44–49
(*Commentary*, II, pp. 258-64) are concerned with the witness of the Baptist, and
suggest that for Origen it did not come to a close until 3.36.
3.   *Commentary*, VI, ANCL Additional Vol., p. 350; Greek text in Brooke (ed.),
Commentary, I, pp. 110-11.

Irenaeus also regarded at least 1.16 as spoken by the Baptist when, as an instance of the recognition of salvation, he writes,

> For this is the knowledge of salvation...which John made, saying; 'Behold the Lamb of God who takes away the sin of the world. This is he of whom I said, "After me comes a man who was made before me, because he was before me: and of his fulness have all we received"' (*Adv. Haer.* 3.10.2).

The same may be said of Clement of Alexandria, who in a discussion of whether the Greek philosophers were robbers of the Old Testament or not, observed 'For of the prophets it is said, "we have all received of his fulness"', indicating that for him the speaker of 1.16 is the Baptist as a prophet (*Strom.* 1.17).

While this understanding was replaced, at least from the time of Chrysostom, by that which sees 1.16-18 as statements of the evangelist, it did not entirely die out. For Aquinas in his *Catena Aurea* from the Fathers, by way of comment on Jn 1.16-17, places ahead of Chrysostom's judgment that the evangelist here adds his own testimony to that of the Baptist a summary of what he understands the evidence of Origen to be in the following words:

> This is to be considered a continuation of the Baptist's testimony to Christ, a point which has escaped the attention of many, who think that from this to 'He hath declared him' St John the Apostle is speaking. But the idea that on a sudden, and, as it would seem unseasonably, the discourse of the Baptist should be interrupted, by a speech of the disciple is inadmissable. And anyone able to follow the passage will discern a very obvious connection here. For having said, 'He is preferred before me, because he was before me', he proceeds, 'From this I know that he was before me because I and the Prophets who preceded me have received of His fulness and grace for grace' (the second grace for the first). For they too by the Spirit penetrated beyond the figure to the contemplation of the truth. And hence receiving, as we have done, of His fulness, we judge that the law was given by Moses, but that grace and truth were made by Jesus Christ—made, not given.[1]

Calvin also explicitly refers 1.16 to the Baptist when he begins his comment on it with

---

1. *Catena Aurea: Commentary on the Four Gospels collected out of the Works of the Fathers by S. Thomas Aquinas*. VI. *St John* (Oxford and London: James Parker, 1870), pp. 38-39.

Prologue and Gospel

> He [i.e. the Baptist, the subject of the comment on 1.15] begins now to
> preach about the office of Christ, that it contains within itself an abundance
> of all blessings, so that no part of salvation must be sought anywhere
> else... and John classes himself with the rest, not for the sake of modesty,
> but to make it more evident that no man whatever is excepted.

And when Calvin continues with 'All the godly, no doubt, who lived
under the law, drew out of the same fulness; but as John immediately
afterwards distinguishes between different periods', he implies that 1.17
is also to be attributed to the Baptist. In expounding 1.18 Calvin refers
continually to the evangelist, though even this is not clear, since he
introduces his comment on 1.19 with 'Hitherto the evangelist has related
the preaching of John about Christ'.[1]

These references would seem to indicate that in the second and third
centuries there was a significant weight of scholarly opinion—gnostic,
semi-gnostic and anti-gnostic—which saw one, two or three of the
statements after 1.15 in the prologue as having been intended by the
evangelist to belong to the testimony of John (the Baptist); and that long
after the contrary view—that they were the words of the evangelist—
had come to hold the field after Chrysostom in the fourth century it was
at least entertained as a possibility by Aquinas, and returned to by
Calvin. The question was unikely to have been raised by the liturgical
tradition, since for liturgical use as the Gospel reading for Christmas Day
the prologue was, no doubt, in the service of a doctrine of incarnation,
truncated at v. 14 (as also in its use as the last gospel at the Mass), and it
was taken over in that form in for example the English *Book of
Common Prayer*. In this way vv. 15-18 were inevitably considered as of
less importance, and there was less need to consider what their function
was in the prologue as a whole. It might have been expected that with
source criticism and form criticism, and their attempts to isolate
antecedent literary sources or oral units, the question would have been
raised again in connection with defining the limits and shape of the prologue, and hence of determining its theological function. On the whole
this has not been so, since in the analyses of the prologue mentioned in
the previous chapter the tendency has been to isolate an original hymn
on structural and rhythmic grounds, in relation to which vv. 15-18,
along with vv. 6-8, have been seen as insertions or additions from the
hand of either the evangelist or a previous redactor. Thus in his analysis

1. J. Calvin, *Commentary on the Gospel according to John* (Calvin Translation
Society, 1847), I, pp. 50, 55.

Bultmann sees vv. 6-8 and v. 15 as polemical insertions against a Baptist sect, and offers no particular comment on vv. 16-18 except to suggest that v. 16a might originally have belonged with v. 14. In their own way his analysis and interpretation of the prologue are governed by his belief that it expresses the paradox of the hiddenness of the divine glory in the flesh (vv. 14 and 16?), which leaves no room for a serious consideration of vv. 17-18 as part of the structure of the prologue.[1]

There are two points of detail which could be said to be illuminated if the content of John's witness is taken to include the whole of vv. 15-18. The first is the verb κέκραγεν by which it is introduced. Dodd's view is that this unusual verb is to be taken as the Johannine equivalent of κηρύσσειν.[2] This is hardly acceptable, as the concept of κήρυγμα is absent from this gospel, and in this context John, as the one who is later to designate himself the appointed voice of God himself, gives utterance to the very words of God about Jesus, the Logos and the light. Utterances of God through prophets or sages is what is suggested. Elsewhere the evangelist uses the verb to introduce solemn, oracular utterances of Jesus of some length (7.28, 37; 12.44), and inspired speech is one of its meanings. It comes as something of a disappointment if what is introduced by this emphatic verb is limited to the contents of v. 15b, John's statement of Jesus' priority to himself and his pre-eminence, especially since what is then said has been said more effectively in 1.1-4, 9-14, including Jesus' pre-eminence over John in respect of all things. The following verses, vv. 16-18, are then tacked on without introduction. If, on the other hand, John's first actual testimony, which has been prepared for by the general statement in 1.7-8 that witness was his vocation so that people might come to belief, includes vv. 16-18, itself introduced by his confession in v. 15 of his own inferior status, it would be more fittingly introduced by the solemn κέκραγεν as including an exalted theological witness to the status of Jesus, and as bringing the prologue to a conclusion which matches the beginning.

Secondly, if vv. 15-18 were all intended to be the witness of John it becomes possible to take the ὅτι which introduces both v. 16 and v. 17 as instances of ὅτι recitative, continuing the speech of the one who utters v. 15, and, so it may be claimed, to give them a more reasonable explanation. Reference to the commentaries will show the difficulties

1. For a table showing how various scholars accommodate the separate verses 1.15-18 in their analyses of the prologue, see Brown, *John*, I, p. 22.
2. *Interpretation*, p. 382 n. 1.

involved in taking the ὅτι in both cases as causal, and in establishing a causal relation between 'we all of his fulness have received' (v. 16), and John's statement about himself and Jesus' priority in v. 15; as also the difficulty (though it is less here) of a causal relation between the contrast of Moses and Jesus in v. 17 and 'of his fulness have we all received and grace for grace' in v. 16. Barrett indeed allows the possibility that ὅτι in v. 16 'may continue the words of the Baptist', though he adds that they 'more probably resume the thread of the argument', without however indicating how they do so if ὅτι is to be rendered 'because'; nor does he comment on the ὅτι at the beginning of v. 17.[1] Bultmann finds it impossible to decide here between the reading καί, which has considerable support in the MSS, versions and Fathers, and which he considers to have been characteristic of the style of the prologue's source, the evangelist having himself altered it to ὅτι; and the reading ὅτι, which is given by the weightiest MSS, but may have been introduced in accordance with the Alexandrian view, expressed by Origen, that John is here speaking as a representative of the Old Testament prophets.[2]

These and similar difficulties would be removed if the statements in v. 16 and v. 17 were regarded as made by John, and as introduced by ὅτι recitative. This, of course, still leaves v. 18 as loosely attached, but that is a problem on almost any view. Origen refers to Heracleon as having excluded this verse from John's testimony, but does not give the reason why he had done so. If the exclusion had been made on the stylistic grounds that the verse was unattached by any connecting particle, Origen is likely to have discussed the issue in grammatical terms. The fact that his argument for the inclusion of v. 18 in the testimony is conducted on deductive theological lines might indicate that Heracleon had also excluded the verse on theological grounds. He could, however, have regarded the strong parallelism in the structure of vv. 16 and 17 as evidence for extending the testimony of John to include them, and have excluded v. 18, with its very different structure, on stylistic grounds.

A further textual point in relation to the structure of the prologue as a whole and to its concluding verses may be raised here. What is the status and meaning of v. 19a? This is universally taken to introduce the following section 1.19-28, but Bultmann at least sees a problem here in

---

1. C.K. Barrett, *The Gospel according to St John: An Introduction with Commentary and Notes on the Greek Text* (London: SPCK, 2nd rev. edn, 1978), p. 168.

2. *John*, p. 76 n. 3.

translating the initial αὕτη. He regards v. 19 as a heading announcing a theme. It is a sentence of comment by the evangelist in which he picks up an important concept, witness, from the previous section, and does so by the demonstrative αὕτη. His comment is, 'Thus the καί does not simply lead on to what follows, as in 2.13 etc,...but points to v. 15, and means "and indeed"'.[1] He maintains that it is not possible to take καὶ αὕτη... Ἰωάννου as a complete sentence in itself; it is a heading which has run over into the narrative.[2] In translating καὶ αὕτη as 'And this is...', he takes αὕτη as referring backwards, which is what this demonstrative conveys in classical Greek and generally in Hellenistic Greek ('this' referring forwards would be ἥδε). It is also the case in this gospel, where it is used to refer backwards, often in an emphatic manner.[3] The only exceptions are those in which the demonstrative is used in clauses of definition, and the definition is introduced by ἵνα or ὅτι.[4] For Bultmann, however, this backward reference jumps over vv. 16-18 to v. 15, and does so of necessity since he has already committed himself to the opinion that 1.19-34 is not an original unit and 1.6-8, 13 and 15 'stand out as interruptions' which the evangelist has introduced into an original prologue. If, however, this analysis is rejected, and the prologue as it stands is seen as a deliberate theological construction of the evangelist throughout, then the backward reference of αὕτη could be to the whole of vv. 15-18, and v. 19a could be seen as rounding off the prologue. This admittedly leaves the rest of v. 19 with an abrupt beginning with ὅτε. Other occurrences of ὅτε in subordinate clauses in this gospel have οὖν to follow (except at 17.2, which, though a close, is not an exact parallel); but there are elsewhere in the Gospel, and in this opening chapter, instances of very abrupt beginnings without connecting particles (for example 1.29, 43; 4.31; 5.1; 6.1), and this could be accounted a feature of the author's style. There remains the problem of the καί at the beginning of v. 20, but this is awkward on any punctuation of vv. 19-20, though καί...καί is a strengthening device, and could be so used here.

It may then be suggested that the prologue is brought to an end by v. 19a with a backward reference to, and summary of, the contents of

1. *John*, p. 85 n. 2.
2. *John*, p. 86 n. 1.
3. As at 1.2, 7, 15, 30, 33, 42; 2.20; 3.2, 26; 4.29, 42, 47; 6.14, 42, and so on.
4. As at 1.34; 3.19; 7.26; 9.20, 24; 11.47; 15.12; 17.3. Both usages are less clear in 1 John.

the previous verses as being John's testimony. The evangelist intended
vv. 16-18 to be from the mouth of John and not his own reflections
upon themes already hinted at, and to be further developed later. They
are uttered by the one who speaks v. 15, which is not to be regarded as
a somewhat artificially preserved statement inserted for polemical
reasons (as it is in most analyses), but as a preface to the assertions in vv.
16-18, investing them with the authority of the very speech of God
through the mouth of the divinely ordained witness, and introduced by
the solemn κέκραγεν. Internal grammatical evidence may be held to
support these recommended changes in punctuation, and to prepare for
a fresh assessment of the intentions of the evangelist in writing a prologue *qua* prologue, in which, as it were, a second part, extending from
v. 15 to v. 18, is in the form of the first testimony of John. And this first
testimony is both a summary of earlier statements in the prologue and
also an extension of them, in which the reader is prepared through
certain highly compressed theological assertions for their gradual expan-
sion and explication in the body of the Gospel.

It may be observed that the prologue form in Greek literature is not
without parallel here. Frequently in Greek tragedy the prologue is
followed by the parodos. Peculiar in this respect is the *Electra* of
Sophocles, where the first 85 lines constitute the prologue and lines 100-
120 the parodos, between which Sophocles has placed a long monody
by Electra herself. It is possible to say that this belongs properly with
what follows, but it is taken by one commentator on internal grounds
with what precedes as a secondary prologue.[1] This shows a certain
literary agility on the part of Sophocles in comparison with, for example,
the somewhat stiff prologues of Euripides. Haigh, in one of several
appreciative passages on Sophoclean writings, remarks that 'The
prologues of Euripides...suffer by comparison with the opening scenes
of Sophocles—those skilful little dialogues in which the necessary facts
are disclosed, the characters are introduced, and the leading motive
suggested, with consummate ease and gracefulness'.[2]

It is not suggested that there are exact parallels here between the
Johannine prologue and those of Greek drama, but only that the
evangelist could be writing with a convention of this kind somewhere in
the background. Hooker has claimed, though on very different grounds,

1. See the commentary of J.C. Kamerbeek, *The Plays of Sophocles*. V. *The
Electra* (Leiden: Brill, 1974), p. 31.
2. *Tragic Drama*, pp. 248-49.

that the Johannine prologue does fall into two parts.[1] This second part, 1.15-18, would not be a monody, but the first and very important testimony of the one who has already been introduced in the first part as the divinely authorized witness to the light and to the benefits brought to humankind through belief. Its contents would be vital for the understanding of the author's theological presentation in literary form of a gospel. As in Greek drama, they would tell of the true state of affairs and of the divine will in relation to the situation. They introduce the Logos-Son who is in the closest intimacy with God. They also point forward in providing seminal statements about the figures who will recur in the unfolding of the story on the stage of history, and cryptic theological assertions which will be explicated thereafter. It is with the foreknowledge imparted by both sections of the prologue that the evangelist can develop his irony throughout the Gospel, since the attentive reader will be cognizant of the dilemma facing human beings as this Jesus, with his unquestionably authentic heavenly origins, effects a variety of human responses.

'Witness': Its Various Meanings

The word 'witness' is particularly connected with John in this Gospel. Both the verb μαρτυρεῖν and the noun μαρτυρία occur more frequently in the Fourth Gospel than in any other New Testament writing, and, if the Johannine Epistles be included, more frequently than in all the other New Testament writings put together. Indeed, the figures for its occurrence are so striking as to suggest that it is a word of primary importance in the evangelist's vocabulary, and carries a good deal of what he intends to say.[2] Moreover, it occurs in a wide range of contexts, and is attached to some of the principal themes. The following, each in their own way, are said to 'witness': John (1.7-8, 15, 19, 32-34; 3.26, 32-33; 5.32, 36); the Samaritan woman (4.39); the scriptures (5.29); the works of Jesus (10.25); the crowd (12.17); Jesus himself (3.11; 4.44; 7.7; 8.14, 18; 13.21; 18.37); God himself concerning Jesus (5.36-37; 8.18); the Paraclete concerning Jesus (15.26); disciples (15.27); and the beloved disciple (19.35; 21.24). It is therefore of supreme importance for the understanding of this gospel to decide what meaning the word carries;

---

1. 'John the Baptist', pp. 354-58.
2. The verb occurs in the Gospel 33 times, in the Johannine Epistles 10 times; the noun in the Gospel 14 times, in the Epistles 7 times.

but it is by no means easy to do this, or to find an English equivalent
that adequately covers what it intends to say.

On this scholars would seem to be divided roughly into two classes,
those who translate with 'confess', primarily in the sense of belief and
allegiance, and those who translate with 'testify' in a juridical (forensic)
sense of giving evidence. To the former belongs Wink, who is concerned
with the word only in its relation to John, and who understands John's
witness solely in terms of confessing Christ in the sense of a
'christological confession'. To the latter belong A.E. Harvey[1] and
A.A. Trites,[2] both of whom are concerned with the word throughout the
Gospel.

Wink nowhere considers the possibility of a juridical meaning, and
seeks to establish christological confession as the sole substance of
John's 'witness'. Thus he argues that since the verb and noun occur in
the description of John's vocation in 1.6-8, and since εἶπον in 1.15 does
not in fact refer back to anything previously said, 'what is important is
not what John says, but the fact that he is witness to Jesus' messiahship'.[3] But is this not immediately to reduce the word, since the witness
of John in 1.7-8 is said to be concerning the light, which has its origin in
the life of the Creator-Logos, and which has been in irreconcilable
opposition to the darkness? And Wink's view here hardly seems to be
supported by κέκραγεν in 1.15, which would at least suggest some
emphasis on what John actually says. Indeed, when Wink comes to his
theological assessment of 1.19-28 he does stress the content of John's
witness, though only in the sense that John's negative witness constitutes
a kind of confession of Jesus' messiahship. While it is likely, as Wink
observes, that in 1.19-28 the evangelist means to distinguish John from
'the Jews', the latter being unbelievers, this is not to say that John is for
that reason thought of as a confessing Christian—'he is a confessing
Christian, they are symbols of unbelief'[4]—since in 1.7-8 John is said to
occupy a unique position as the one through whom other people are to
come to belief.

Again, with reference to 1.20-23, Wink understands the triple denial of
John that he is the Christ, Elijah or the prophet as 'a negative confession

1. *Jesus on Trial: A Study in the Fourth Gospel* (London: SPCK, 1976).
2. *The New Testament Concept of Witness* (SNTSMS, 31; Cambridge
University Press, 1977).
3. *John the Baptist*, p. 88.
4. Wink, *John the Baptist*, p. 90.

that Jesus is the Christ'; but if that is its purpose why is it arrived at by mention of Elijah or the prophet at all? For these are not synonyms for the messiah, nor did the church envisage Jesus as all three. Wink supports his interpretation by taking the words 'he confessed, he did not deny, he confessed' as introducing a strong theme of confession, which he claims is to be seen throughout the Gospel (9.22; 12.42; 13.38; 18.25, 27). But it is not clear that the word translated 'confess' here (ὁμολογεῖν) is a synonym of μαρτυρεῖν, at least in this gospel. As H. Strathmann observes, 'The orientation to evangelisation is what distinguishes the term (μαρτυρεῖν) from ὁμολογεῖν. All μαρτυρεῖν is a ὁμολογεῖν, but not vice-versa. The point of μαρτυρεῖν is that believers should be won.'[1] This positive sense of confession that believers may be won does not appear to belong to the word ὁμολογεῖν in other places where it is used in the Gospel, but rather a more external and technical sense of public acknowledgment or denial with certain juridical consequences. Thus in 9.22 it is said of the parents of the blind man that they said things 'because they feared the Jews', and that the Jews had agreed that if anyone acknowledged (ὁμολογεῖν) Jesus to be Χριστός that person would be put out of the synagogue (this is taken by many scholars to refer to the ban introduced into the Eighteen Benedictions in CE 85). There is no hint of what acknowledgment would be in terms of positive christological confession. Again in 12.42 those of the rulers who believed did not openly acknowledge (ὁμολόγουν) that they did so for fear of excommunication. Similarly Peter's denials (18.15-27) refer to public acknowledgment of discipleship or association. In so far as there is any positive confession of belief in such contexts it is in terms of the Son of Man rather than of the messiah (for example 9.35; 12.23-24). The use of ὁμολογεῖν in the above passages could be relevant to the interpretation of 1.20-27. For it is not necessary to assume that the interrogation of John there is hostile, and that in distinction from the unbelieving hostility of the Jews John is depicted as a confessing Christian. Rather the public affirmations and denials of John could be for the purpose of setting aside certain roles involved in Jewish expectation, and thereby preparing for his positive role of witness as the unique voice, which will be expressed not in terms of messiahship, but in pointing to the Lamb of God and the Son of God.

If Wink is thus judged to have understood 'witness' too narrowly in

---

1. 'μαρτυρεῖν', *TDNT*, IV, p. 497 n. 63.

terms of confessing Christ, the juridical (forensic) view has to be investigated. A.E. Harvey deals in detail with this aspect, and sees it as a major
clue to the whole gospel.[1] With reference to contemporary legal practice
he argues that the main episodes in the Gospel take the form of accusa-
tion, defence and counter-accusation, so that the reader is urged to
consider for himself or herself the 'evidence' concerning Jesus. While
this procedure and analysis frequently illuminate the text of the Gospel
as a whole, they would seem to be deficient in method, at least as far as
the treatment of John is concerned, to the extent that individual statements of the witness tend to be adduced without sufficient preliminary
examination of the whole witness of which individual statements and
phrases are a part. The same lack of any preliminary examination of
their position and function within the whole is regrettable. Thus, while
acknowledging the importance of John as a witness, and correctly
stating that this figure nowhere squares with the Baptist figure in the
other gospels, Harvey does not first attempt to establish where the
testimonies of John precisely begin and end, and what their context,
character and function are in relation to the presentation in this gospel of
this unique figure. Without such precise limits to the material under
consideration a theological understanding of the content of the evidence,
and of the function it is performing, can hardly be arrived at. Thus, in
relation to the witness of John, Harvey translates κέκραγεν in 1.15 with
the emphatic 'he cried aloud', and supplies evidence from classical
Greek usage for a forensic understanding of the word; but he is nevertheless content to describe 1.15b as a 'fragment' of John's evidence,
which he then fills out with isolated statements taken from 1.19, 20, 26.
Is this satisfactory? For not only is 1.15 repeated in a different and better
constructed form at 1.30, thus making 1.15, considered as a fragment,
only an unnecessary introduction for such an important figure as John
the divinely appointed witness; but, also, the relation of 1.15 to the
prologue as a whole and of the contents of 1.15-18 to the Gospel as a
whole is ignored. While Harvey refers to the witness in 3.28 and 3.32 he
does so in isolated fashion, and he does not discuss to what extent 3.27-
36 constitute what some commentators have taken to be the final
witness of John in the Gospel.[2]

---

1. *Jesus on Trial, passim.*
2. *Jesus on Trial*, pp. 23-24 and 94. Harvey does not interpret 3.27ff., though it
is the final evidence of John. Since he appears to hold that Jesus gives evidence about
himself at 3.32, as well as at 3.11 and 8.26, we may assume that, along with Brown,

In his monograph *The New Testament Concept of Witness* A.A. Trites deals with the Fourth Gospel in a survey of the idea of witness in the New Testament as a whole.[1] He claims that as a result of C.H. Dodd's contention for a primitive pattern of apostolic preaching in terms of κήρυγμα and κηρύσσειν there has been a failure to appreciate the significance of μαρτυρεῖν and its cognates for that preaching. After a study of widespread antecedent uses he bases the New Testament concept of witness squarely on the Old Testament concept of 'justice at the gate', and points particularly to the sustained use of juridical language in the controversy material of Isaiah 40–45, where judgment and salvation are set forth in terms of a trial between Yahweh and Israel over against the heathen and their gods. It may be questioned, however, whether this pattern of thought was present to the evangelist, and whether the trial in the Fourth Gospel between the world represented by the Jews and God incarnate in Jesus was modelled on it.[2] The evangelist's language, his particular selection and employment of Old Testament texts and his careful explanation of Jewish customs do not suggest that he was writing for readers cognizant of the ancient Israelite 'justice at the gate'. Further, if the idea of witness is to be taken, as by Trites, in the juridical sense of eye-witness testimony, serving to stress the historical nature of the events reported, which eye-witnessing is said to be the basis for all four evangelists to set forth the life of Christ in the form of a gospel,[3] then it is strange that the Fourth Gospel, which outstrips the others in its use of 'witness', should be so patently unhistorical in comparison with these others. It is strange also that there should be so little correspondence between it and the other 'lives' in matters of historical detail, and that there should be so little evidence in it that apostolic testimony is regarded as authenticating it as history. In that case, the emphasis of the Fourth Gospel on witness is likely to be concerned with the apprehension of the theological and spiritual truth of the events rather than with the events themselves.

While it would seem that both ideas—that of confessing and that of the juridical—have something to contribute, it may be doubted whether either adequately expresses the range of meanings that are present in the

Bultmann and Schnackenburg, he regards the final testimony as ending at 3.30. Barrett, Lindars and others hold that this testimony extends from 3.27 to 3.36.

1. *Concept of Witness*, pp. 78-127.
2. Trites, *Concept of Witness*, p. 226.
3. *Concept of Witness*, pp. 224-25.

Fourth Gospel's use of 'witness'. The juridical sense of 'solemnly testify to someone or something' has been unduly neglected, and has attractive features which can be added to that of confessing. Confession takes into account the Christian exercise of proclaiming Jesus with a view to promoting the faith, but it has little relation to the background of the word itself, and it neglects the situation of alienation and conflict, which is what the juridical sense explains. There is set out first briefly in the prologue a scene of alienation from God, possibly in terms of a cosmic conflict, which existed to such a degree that God determined to put it away by the sending of the Logos-Son to effect the very work of God for humankind. This scene appears in the body of the Gospel not only in theological statements such as 3.16-17, but also in historical scenes of conflict between Jesus and the Jews (cf. 2.18-20; 3.10; 5.18; 8.39-59; 9.13–10.39; 11.47-53) and in declarations of Jesus himself (cf. 3.14-15; 4.34; 5.19-27; 11.50-52; 12.31; 14.30-31; 16.7-11).

But if 'confessing' fails to take account of these elements of judgment and of freely given eternal life which is the right of believers, it may be questioned whether the juridical sense is adequate, if that is held to depend heavily on a background of legal terminology, of forensic practice and the issue of condemnation or rewards. For legal practice can only have meaning within a known and observed set of laws, the infringement of which means prosecution and acquittal or condemnation. But the eschatology of the synoptists, in which God or Christ sits as judge at assize, hearing the evidence against human beings and declaring the verdict, is singularly absent from the Fourth Gospel. Here God acts in love towards the world, which is lacking in the immediacy of qualitatively heavenly life, by sending the unique Son, which effects a situation of self-inflicted condemnation, or of a passing from death to heavenly life. There can hardly be any comparable legal background from law administered by human beings for such a situation. It would seem that in the Fourth Gospel theology has, as it were, 'softened' or deflected previous doctrines concerning the last things, so that a legal setting is hardly adequate.

Nor is it possible to detect in this gospel a Christian moral code, the existence of which would bring with it the need for remission of sins either of commission or omission. The commandments are the theological commandments to believe in God and in the one whom he has sent, and to love in the manner Jesus has loved his disciples. If the context of John's mission as a witness and the theological content of that witness, that is to the Logos-Son Jesus Christ, are examined, it will be seen that not even the forensic material cited by Trites from, for example, Isaiah is really appropriate. Nowhere in Jewish belief and messianic expectation was it ever envisaged that God would act in love in the form of sending his Son in full humanity as a means of restoration to humankind (even while on earth) of an intimacy with God himself. Nor was it envisaged in Judaism that there should descend from heaven a Son figure who was in a filial relation to God before the foundation of the world, but who enters fully into human life. Thus there cannot be here an act of an agent such as was envisaged in Jewish law, a *shaliah*, effecting and interpreting the will of the one who sends him, since this Son is eternally a Son and cannot be other in relation to a Father, whereas a *shaliah* was not such a Son, but an agent for a transaction, and ceases to be such once the transaction is over.[1]

If neither the idea of 'confessing' nor the forensic interpretation is fully satisfactory because neither is sufficiently theological for stating what is at issue in the mission and presence of Jesus, then it could follow that it will be the evangelist's own theology which is likely to determine his use and understanding of μαρτυρεῖν and μαρτυρία. The problem would then not be simply that which faces every translator when the original word covers a wide range of meanings which no one word in the host language can adequately express. The lexicon provides an analysis of usages in extant texts, but these may not suffice, since in the case of the Fourth Gospel the subject matter is held, at least by the evangelist, to be concerned with what is strictly speaking unique and *sui generis*. Undoubtedly something of the previous meanings will still belong to the word that the evangelist has chosen, since otherwise he would not have been able to use it at all; but where a new dimension has enriched the meaning then the author's distinctive uses are the main key to his intended meaning.

We start, then, from those passages where it is clearly expressed that

---

1. For this reason expositions of the Johannine Jesus in terms of agency—as in P. Borgen, 'God's Agent in the Fourth Gospel', in J. Neusner (ed.), *Religions in Antiquity: Essays in Memory of E.R. Goodenough* (Leiden: Brill, 1968), II, pp. 137-48 (repr. in J. Ashton [ed.], *The Interpretation of John* [Issues in Religion and Theology, 9; London: SPCK; Philadelphia: Fortress Press, 1986], pp. 67-78); J.D.M. Derrett, *Law in the New Testament* (London: Darton, Longman & Todd, 1970), p. 52, and K.H. Rengstorf, 'ἀπόστολος', *TDNT*, I, pp. 414-20—are highly debatable.

the witness involved divine sanction to inviolable truths. Thus the works of Jesus (5.36), the writings (Scriptures, 5.39) and the Paraclete (15.26) are all said to 'witness concerning me' (Jesus). What then, it may be asked, is the nature of this witness that is not adequately covered by any of the antecedent meanings of the word? At 5.36 the Son is said to have been given by the Father works to do on earth that he may perfect (τελειόω) them. Their witness is greater than that of John because they are observable human actions which are nonetheless the very works of God himself effected by Jesus, and as such they can only witness to the heavenly truth of the divine origin of the one who is qualified to do them. At 5.39 the witness to Jesus is that of the writings (Scriptures), and the subject matter of the witness is (eternal) life. Devout Jews are said to think erroneously that by searching these Scriptures they may have eternal life. Bultmann maintains that it is the study of the Torah rather than of the prophets that is meant here, since later rabbis asserted that the Torah could give eternal life to Israel.[1] But whether this is so or not, this scriptural activity is not being criticized as such, but from the Johannine standpoint, which he then goes on to state. Eternal life, resident in Jesus (1.4) as the life which has its source in God, and in the heavenly sphere, can only be given to human beings by Jesus, since his origin and his works are divine (5.17-47). Thus the statement 'the Scriptures witness concerning me' imparts as statement the same quality that attaches elsewhere in the Gospel to the works of Jesus considered as *sēmeia*. It is a statement about something in the earthly realm which has its full significance beyond itself in the heavenly realm. Thus this 'witnessing' that the Scriptures actively do is something expressed by means of a verb which, when expressed by means of a noun, constitutes a *sēmeion*. The Scriptures, correctly held to be the encapsulated speech of God, were truly understood only by reference to the divine ordering of things which is made known only by the Logos-Son of heavenly origin (1.5, 18)

The Paraclete similarly bears witness to Jesus, and this is a witness to him by a divine being whose witness is made through the presence of Jesus with human beings. The character of this witness varies according to the character of the recipients. He functions in respect of all humankind, since he will be sent from the Father upon the request of the exalted Son, and believers and non-believers will be placed in their

---

1.　*John*, p. 268 n. 2.

respective groups in their relationship to him. What that relationship is, however, is not unconnected with the vexed question of the meaning of the term Παράκλητος.[1] It can be used for one summoned to the side of another to aid or exhort him or her; also of one who aids by means of comfort. A technical juridical term is 'lawyer', 'advocate' or 'prosecutor'. A further possible meaning derived from παρακαλεῖν in the sense of 'to instruct' is 'teacher'. Apparently the Jews had no word that covered all that a παράκλητος had to do since *Pirke Abot* (4. 11) transliterated the term. A juridical context is suggested by 16.7-11, where the world is being discussed. The world cannot receive the Paraclete (14.26), and he will witness to Jesus (15.26) by convincing or exposing the world in respect of sin, righteousness and judgment. The doctrine of sin here is peculiarly Johannine. It is defined as unbelief in Jesus, and elsewhere in the Gospel unbelief in Jesus is primarily the rejection of his heavenly origin and of his claim to be the Son sent by the Father. Thus for the evangelist and his readers not to know Jesus, and not to believe in him and in the Father, is sin, since it is a total rejection of God and his ordering of things.[2] Therefore attention should be given to the Johannine doctrine of sin in any consideration of the Paraclete as witnessing to Jesus before the world. The same witnessing to Jesus of the Paraclete before the world is said to be in respect of righteousness on the grounds that Jesus departs for the Father and is no longer to be seen. This would appear to mean that the only true righteousness is not only resident in Jesus and active in the world through him, but is so precisely because he returns to God who is the only source of righteousness, and in doing so vindicates his divine claims. The witness concerning judgment consists in the evidence of the Paraclete that the effective working of Jesus is nothing less than the final overthrow by God of his opponents.

The juridical flavour of 16.7-11 is swiftly dropped, and the believers are then considered (16.13ff.). The evangelist has already intimated to the readers that believers have eternal life and will not come into

1. See discussions in the commentaries: Bultmann, *John*, pp. 566-72; Barrett, *St John*, pp. 462-63, and his article 'The Holy Spirit in the Fourth Gospel', *JTS* NS 1 (1950), pp. 1-15; and E.C. Hoskyns, *The Fourth Gospel* (ed. F.N. Davey; London: Faber & Faber, 2nd rev. edn, 1947), pp. 549-54.

2. The evangelist first introduces the doctrine of sin in the body of the Gospel at 1.29; cf. 8.21; 9.41; 15.24; 16.8-9. However, this was prepared for in the prologue, acting as a true prologue, by vv. 5, 10, 11.

judgment, having already passed over out of death into life (5.24). To such persons the Paraclete, as the spirit of truth, will act more as a guide into all truth—that is, into the significance of Jesus, who is himself the Truth. For this reason his speech will have its source not in himself, but from heaven, whence he and Jesus have been sent; and he will speak only what he hears—'the identity of the teaching of the Son and the Spirit being guaranteed by an identity of origin'.[1] The message will be extended to announcing the things to come, which Jesus himself had said he was able to utter but the disciples are as yet unable to receive. In this way he will 'glorify' both Jesus and the Father (16.13-15). In short, the heavenly figure of the Paraclete, who witnesses concerning Jesus, points human beings to their true situation in respect of God, whether they are believers or non-believers. Each will be in relation to God according to his or her response to Jesus. The Paraclete also points human beings beyond themselves to the divine consequences of their responses to that which God freely offered through the Son. The earthly situation is given heavenly significance according to the divine order of things, as it will be effectively at work on earth beyond Jesus' glorification and return to the Father.

The above texts show that a new and consistent feature of the Johannine use of 'witness' is that it covers a variety of functions, which have in common that they act in the way characteristic of a *sēmeion*. What is expressed by way of the noun *sēmeion*, that is, the heavenly meaning of the earthly act, is expressed by way of a verb in the act of witnessing. Thus, although the word retains something of the older meanings of 'confess' and 'testify', that is not where the author intends the emphasis to be placed. Rather, it appears that he intended the reader to understand by 'witnessing' any activity by and through which the heavenly character and origin of Jesus, his actions and his words, are communicated.

An Examination of John's Witness

We come now, finally, to consider the witness of John with respect to two questions: first, how far it illuminates, and is illuminated by, the meaning of 'witness' which I have sought to establish for elsewhere in the Gospel; secondly, to what extent in relation to that witness the

---

1.   Hoskyns, *Fourth Gospel*, p. 486.

prologue prepares as genuine prologue for the rest of the Gospel. There is however, as in the prologue, a preliminary question of determining the extent of John's concluding witness in 3.27-36. As at 1.15-18, so also at 3.27-36, there is support from earlier commentators for the view that the evangelist intended John's witness not to be confined to 3.27-30, but to continue to 3.36. The fragments surviving from Origen and Calvin's commentary support this view. Among recent scholars Bauer, Dodd and Barrett accept this,[1] although there is clearly a certain similarity of thought between the second part of John's witness, 3.31-36, and Jesus' own speech to Nicodemus. On the other hand Bultmann maintains that 3.31-36 is displaced and belongs to the speech of Jesus.[2] There is, however, no compelling reason for supposing a change of speaker here, and John would seem to be the speaker intended by the evangelist to deliver a final witness to Jesus, which in effect summarizes theologically all that has already been stated. Since the style of the evangelist colours all that is said by anyone in this gospel, there is little basis for determining whether John is the speaker on stylistic grounds, and it is irrelevant to discuss it on grounds of historical probability. The real issue is whether the evangelist intended any one person to give an authoritative meaning to the whole at any one point in the structure of the Gospel. If he did so this would be entirely appropriate for John as the divinely ordained witness, and at this point in the development of the Gospel. The theology of Jesus, John and the evangelist are couched in the same language, and are legitimately understood as proceeding from one creative pen.

The witness of John in the prologue is introduced by the solemn word κέκραγεν, which recalls the authority ascribed to John in 1.6-8 as the divinely accredited witness to the Light. It has been argued that it should be considered as extending from v. 15 to v. 18. It falls into three parts (vv. 15-16, 17, 18), each of which is characterized by a negative statement followed by a corresponding positive one. In the first part (vv. 15-16) the negative statement refers to John himself and the positive statement to the one who is superior to him because prior. In the second the negative is about Moses and the law and the positive about Jesus Christ. In the third the negative is about humankind in general and the positive about the only begotten God (Son). How far can these statements be seen as seminal and as acting as genuine prologue in that they determine the Gospel itself in its shape and content?

---

1. See Brown, *John*, I, pp. 159-60 for the discussion.
2. *John*, p. 160 n. 2.

The first statement (vv. 15-16) is a personal one which is negative about John himself, in that what appears to be his superiority in the order of appearance on the historical scene is rendered inferior by the eternal priority of the one who succeeds him in time. But the positive element in this statement is not confined to that priority, but continues with the possibility of human participation in what is called the 'fulness' belonging to this prior figure and communicated by him to human beings. The word πλήρωμα is not easy to interpret. It was a word with religious connotations, and was used in various ways of the divine sphere. Plato regarded the world as the son of God, the *plērōma*.[1] The use in v. 16 is plainly not pantheistic, since it is applied to that which the God of Israel freely gives, but it may be that there is some suggestion here of this fulness being the fulness of God himself, just as what is described in v. 14 as 'full of grace and truth' refers to the divine quality of the unique Son. Here this *plērōma* is defined in terms of abundant grace.

In the three references to 'grace' in this gospel, all of them in the prologue, the word does not stand alone, but has as a continuation 'grace and truth' in v. 14 and v. 17, and 'grace upon grace' in v. 16. Both expressions are without precedent, and both are notoriously difficult to translate. Originally χάρις meant a demonstration or act of goodness seen either from the point of view of the agent or of the recipient. It always had in it the idea of 'kindness' or 'gift' on the part of the agent, and so of 'thanksgiving' on the part of the recipient. In Greek usage before the LXX it was used of the demonstration of divine goodness.[2] In Hellenistic Greek it gained the extra meaning of the gracious power of God, becoming synonymous with δόξα, πνεῦμα and δύναμις. The contexts always decide whether the meaning is 'gracious gift', 'gracious deed' or 'gracious attitude'.

How far are any of these meanings adequate for the three mentions of χάρις in the prologue? In v. 14 'demonstration of divine goodness' could well apply, for it is the glory (i.e. the manifested being) of the unique Son of a heavenly Father which is characterized as being full of grace (and truth). The importance here of the word 'grace' is that it designates what both comes from God and can be seen ('we beheld'), and this cannot happen without the Logos's having fully shared in his own created order. It is thus a term for a divine communication which

1.   Bultmann, *John*, p. 77 n. 1.
2.   Bultmann, *John*, p. 74 n. 1, and BAG, 'χάρις', pp. 885-87.

makes actual contact with and penetration of the world. The communication is of such a kind that it allows the participation by the beholder
through a response called 'receiving'. This doctrine of the divinely
intended participation by human beings in the heavenly state of living
while still belonging to the temporal created order has already been
expressed in the prologue in the references to the light shining (1.9), to
the possibility of people believing through John (1.7) and to those
receiving the Logos through belief in his name (1.12), as a result of
which they are given the right to become children who are begotten
from God (1.13). The opposite state of those who reject the Logos is
described by the negative with the verbs of receiving—
καταλαμβάνειν (1.5), γινώσκειν (1.10) and παραλαμβάνειν (1.11).
It follows that the older view, which saw in the statement in v. 14 simply
sheer theological paradox in the union of the divine Logos with
humanity, fails to set that paradoxical element sufficiently within the
wider context of communication from the divine realm to the human,
which results in a human participation in the former. The participation
can be to the full. This would appear to be what is being stated in v. 16
by 'of his fulness have we all received', along with the other reference
to χάρις in the prologue in the strange and much debated phrase χάριν
ἀντὶ χάριτος.

In interpreting that phrase reference has sometimes been made to
Philo, where in *Poster C.* 145 χάρις and ἀντὶ are found together. In
this passage Philo is concerned with the gifts of God which maintain the
order of the world, one gift replacing another, and with the ever-
changing character of those gifts to human beings in that God mediates
them to the capacities of the receivers. He has been comparing Rebecca
and Hagar as types of this in their manner of drawing water from the
well. Hagar, filling her vessel to slake the thirst of a child, is a type of the
imperfect, indirect teaching through the senses and sensible objects,
which is fitted to the soul in the first stages of its search. Rebecca, in the
manner of her drawing, is a type of the well of the perfection of divine
wisdom which yields direct spiritual instruction from God. Philo then
proceeds:

> Wherefore God ever causes his earlier gifts (χάριτας) to cease before
> their recipients are glutted and wax insolent; and storing them up for the
> future gives others in their stead (ἑτέρας ἀντ' ἐκείνων), and a third
> supply to replace the second (τρίτας ἀντὶ τῶν δευτέρων), and ever new
> in place of earlier boons (ἀιεὶ νέας ἀντὶ παλαιοτέρων) sometimes
> different in kind, sometimes the same.

On the basis of this passage it has been proposed that ἀντί in v. 16 should be translated by 'in place of', and the verse interpreted as meaning that in participation in the fulness of the Logos one kind of grace replaces another. The passage in Philo, however, can hardly be said to elucidate Jn 1.16, to which it stands in marked contrast. The contrast is not only in the general differences between Philo, who allegorizes and spiritualizes the concrete events, and the evangelist, for whom the sensible is the channel for the things of heaven to enter effectively into the lives of believers, but also in the particular difference that Philo draws a distinction between an earlier and lesser grace and a later and greater grace that is to supersede it. This is hardly what the evangelist can mean with reference to any of the graces proceeding from the fulness of the Logos. If 'in place of' is the right translation of ἀντί here, there is nothing in the prologue so far to indicate that a grace belonging to the Old Testament is being replaced by the grace of the Revealer.[1] If v. 17 is to be taken as an antithesis setting grace and truth over against Moses and the law, it could just possibly be that in v. 16 the evangelist is running ahead of himself, and that he proceeds to clarify an obscure antithesis of 'grace in place of grace', though in a minimal degree, in an antithesis between the Old Testament law through Moses and the grace and truth coming by Jesus Christ. This is, however, unlikely; and Bultmann, who refers to Schlatter's interpretation of v. 16 as a radical rejection of a theology of rewards, takes the phrase to mean that the χάρις of the Revealer is inexhaustibly unfolded in an ever-changing variety.[2] If by 'Revealer' here is meant one who actively communicates and enters into the sphere where he communicates, this interpretation would be satisfactory.

One feature common to all the references to grace in the prologue is the heavenly origin and the heavenly quality of this grace. It is the vehicle of communication, solely the property of God, but seen as an activity directed towards human beings. It is present in the Logos-Son, and courses through the lives of human beings through the agency of Jesus Christ. It is received by believers, and as divine eternal gift it must be related to the condition of being born again from God as a source.

The question now to be investigated is whether this part of John's testimony in the prologue (vv. 15-16) has influenced as prologue the contents and sequence of thought of the historical testimony of John

1.   So Bultmann, *John*, p. 78 n. 2.
2.   Bultmann, *John*, p. 78 n. 2.

with which the Gospel narrative begins in 1.19-34, and which is continued in 3.22-36. It is first notable that the evangelist should have begun the Gospel proper after the prologue in precisely this way by giving John such a prominent place in the narrative. It is true that in the Synoptic Gospels John occupies a necessary place at the beginning of the gospel story in preparation for Jesus, in Mark briefly by means of Old Testament quotations and a summary of his baptizing ministry, in Matthew somewhat more fully by the inclusion of John's eschatological teaching, and in Luke more fully still by the inclusion of the story of John's birth. But none of these gives such a prominent place in the opening of their narratives to John as an active figure in Judaism, nor do they, as does this evangelist, introduce him and all he does and stands for under the all-embracing term of 'witness' (cf. 1.19b-34 following 1.19a).

The opening witness in 1.19-34 is itself divided into two parts, 1.19b-28 and 1.29-34. The first part, as the opening statement of the Gospel, is made as a confession—one emphasized as such by ὡμολόγησεν καὶ οὐκ ἠρνήσατο, καὶ ὡμολόγησεν in reply to an official interrogation by representatives of Judaism, described as priests and Levites from Jerusalem (i.e. the cultic aspect of Judaism, v. 19), but also as those sent from the Pharisees (i.e. the aspect of legal piety in Judaism, v. 24).[1] The second part, 1.29-34, is delivered more generally within the context of John as a baptizing figure in Israel.

---

1. ὁι ἀπεσταλμένοι means 'those who were sent [referring to the priests and Levites in v. 19] belonged to the sect of the Pharisees'. In A and B the article is absent; it then means 'Some Pharisees [also?] had been sent' (either included in, or in addition to, the delegation of priests and Levites). The matter cannot be settled by the evangelist's use of 'Pharisee' elsewhere, since there it is not quite the same usage. In 7.32, 45; 11.47; 18.13 they appear to be a corporate organ of administration, who may occasionally call a meeting of the Sanhedrin. In ch. 9 they act as a court with power to excommunicate (9.34), which may not be historically correct. The strict disciplinary functions of priests and Levites at Qumran do not necessarily give meaning to the group depicted here, who are also from the authorities in Jerusalem, which authorities the Qumran sect disavowed. All that is clear is that from the mention of the three groups of practising Jews the reader knows that an all-inclusive audience belonging to official Judaism hears John, and is henceforth in this gospel indubitably cognizant of the divine testimony. The fact is of some importance to the rest of the Gospel, where it is the Logos-Son who alone confronts Judaism, and because 1.19-28 is the first historicization of the negative statement of 1.17a, where Moses and the law are deliberately used. See Bultmann, *John*, p. 87 n. 2, p. 90 n. 7; Dodd, *Tradition*, p. 263; Barrett, *St John*, p. 174.

The first part of the witness takes the form of a confession which begins by being totally negative. In the context of Jewish eschatological hopes John confesses to being himself neither the messiah, nor the coming Elijah, nor the (expected) prophet.[1] But in reply to further interrogation about what his status and function can be if he is none of these things (v. 25) John's entirely negative confession passes over into a positive statement about a figure as yet unnamed, and about whom the authoritative representatives of Judaism are as yet ignorant, but who has already made his appearance on the scene of history, and indeed of Jewish history (v. 26 'amongst you'). John alone knows this to be the case. He also knows that this figure, though making his appearance subsequently in time to himself, is nevertheless eternally prior to him. This picks up, and in part repeats, the statement in 1.15 with which the witness in vv. 15-18 begins, though here the precedence of this figure is stated in terms of an image current in the tradition represented by the synoptists, that John is not worthy to loose the thong of his sandals (v. 27).

It is, however, to be noticed that between these negative statements about himself and the positive statements about this figure who is unnamed and is as yet unrecognized by Judaism, John utters a highly positive statement about himself and his own function. For when the delegation, in the face of his threefold denial, press him further as to his identity so as to have something to report back to headquarters in Jerusalem ('What do you say about yourself...?', v. 22), John replies with an affirmative statement by means of a quotation from Isa. 40.3, 'I am a voice crying in the desert, make straight the way of the Lord'. This Isaianic passage had clearly become attached to the figure of John in the tradition as a description of his preparatory work for Jesus (the Lord), and for this reason it appears in variant forms and ways at the opening of the narrative of the gospel in Mk 1.3, Mt. 3.3 and Lk. 3.4; but nowhere in the synoptic tradition is it made the answer to a question

---

1. The evangelist indicates that there is a distinction between the Christ and the prophet, which is maintained at 7.40. The precise differences between the expectations of Elijah and of the prophet remain unclear. For the different backgrounds, see R. Schnackenburg, *The Gospel according to St John* (3 vols.; London: Burns & Oates, 1968, 1980, 1982), I, pp. 289-90. For a full presentation of the different interpretations, see W.A. Meeks, *The Prophet-King: Moses Traditions and Johannine Christology* (NovTSup, 14; Leiden: Brill, 1967), pp. 17-29, and Dodd, *Interpretation*, pp. 239-40.

as to John's identity, nor does John apply it to himself in this self-authenticating fashion ('I am the voice...', v. 23), prefacing the Old Testament quotation with the authoritative ἐγώ. Those commentators would seem to be in error who interpret 'the voice' here as deprecatory—'a mere voice' being an expression of John's self-depreciation in relation to the one with whom he compares himself. It is, on the contrary, a very positive self-acclamation, an identification of himself with the voice divinely ordained in Scripture, tantamount to the voice of God. Here at 1.23, within the development of the prologue witness of John in 1.15-16, the evangelist would appear to be picking up the positive function of John which had been stated in non-Scriptural terms in 1.6-8, where it is said that he had come (i.e. was sent and commissioned by God) for the purpose of bearing witness to the light.

In the second part of the witness, 1.29-34, there is a development. This is prepared for by a historical notice that John had borne his witness before the Jewish delegation in Bethany beyond Jordan, where he was engaged in baptizing. That is, the context for what is to follow is John in his function as baptizer. Further, the hitherto unnamed figure is now named as Jesus (v. 29), who is said to be coming to John (for baptism?). The witness is now a more general one delivered to an unspecified audience. In this context the previous witness concerning the eternal priority of the one who appears later in time is repeated from v. 27 (which itself refers back to v. 15), but in being repeated it is now applied to Jesus as the unnamed and unidentified person about whom it had previously been spoken. Moreover, it is repeated along with a negative statement that even John himself had at one time shared the ignorance of the Jews as to who Jesus was. Nevertheless this leads to two highly positive statements. The second (v. 31) is when John defines the whole purpose of his baptizing activity in Israel as being that Jesus should become manifest (known) to Israel. The first (v. 29) is that Jesus, named here for the first time, is given his first christological title in the narrative of the Gospel, and is identified by John as the 'Lamb of God', whose function is defined as taking away the sin, not of Israel, but of the world. In this title, which remains the despair of the commentators,[1] the

---

1. 'The Lamb of God' occurs at 1.29, 36 only. Dodd (*Interpretation*, pp. 230-38) refers to four possible backgrounds, none of which is compelling. 1. The sacrificial lamb of the cultus; but in the Old Testament it is the blood of bulls and goats which is said to take away sin, and the scapegoat running free carries Israel's sin into the wilderness. It is unlikely that only here in the Gospel should the idea of

emphasis would seem to be on the words 'of God', which stress in relation to the terminology of 'lamb' its divine origin and divine provision. The statement that this lamb takes away the sin of the world depends for its meaning on what the evangelist understands by 'sin of the world'. It would seem in the light of other passages that this single 'sin of the world' consists in unbelief—unbelief in Jesus and therefore in God.[1]

John's witness to the person and work of Jesus in vv. 29-31 is continued in vv. 32-34. The contents of vv. 32-34 are expressly characterized as witness, and as the climax of the witness of this section, by a fresh introduction, 'And John witnessed saying...' (v. 32). Here, in a witness still in the context of John's baptism and now echoing an element in the synoptic traditions of the baptism of Jesus by John (of which there is no explicit mention in the Fourth Gospel), John refers to himself as the one who was the divinely ordained agent of perceiving the descent from God of the Spirit upon Jesus, and its permanent presence with him. In v. 33 his commission and function are reiterated in remarkable terms, again in a negative and positive manner. Despite the fact that humanly speaking John shared the ignorance of all others of the identity and function of Jesus, God, in commissioning John for his work of baptizing in Israel, has overcome this ignorance. God has given him the capacity to see the Spirit descending on Jesus and abiding with him. In this way he is able to identify Jesus as the one who will effect that baptism of human beings with the Spirit of God. By that baptism alone people may participate in God, the baptism of which John's baptism with water is a *sēmeion*. At this point the testimony of John comes to rest with Jesus as the medium of communication between God and humankind, for that is what Spirit means. This would seem to be picking up the positive side of the witness in vv. 15-16, which refers to the possibility, indeed the actuality, of human beings' participating in God

---

sacrificial expiation be related to the death of Jesus—though the idea is suited to 1 Jn 2.2. 2. The paschal lamb; but there is no evidence that at this time it was associated with sin. 3. The Servant of Isa. 53.7-11; but there 'as a lamb' is only a comparison. 4. The Lamb as an apocalyptic title for the messiah. But this, while probable for the Lamb in Revelation and for what is depicted of it there, hardly corresponds to the thought of the Fourth Gospel.

1.   For example, 8.24, where the plural is used of the sins of the Jews, that is, according to Jewish beliefs; 9.35-41; 16.8-9. The Christian understanding of universal sin is unbelief in Jesus.

by receiving from the *plērōma* of the Godhead and its superabundant grace. The visionary witness to the supernatural activity of the one unnamed in vv. 15-16, but now named as Jesus, is brought to an emphatic conclusion, 'And I saw and have borne witness', v. 34, with witness to Jesus as the divine Son.

In 3.22-36 occurs the final and lengthiest witness of John before he finally disappears from the scene, and it may be asked why there is a repetition of his witness at all, and why it should be made at this point in the Gospel. This second witness shares with the first the fact that it is introduced by a historical note—that Jesus was staying in Judaean territory, and that John was at Aenon near Salem. It also shares with it a context of baptism; in this case a more generalized question raised about baptism as a Jewish practice of ablution is brought up by a Jew. The question raised by this delineation of a contemporaneous baptizing by John and Jesus is that of the character and relative value of each. It is actually raised by John's disciples in the somewhat crude terms of numerical success, which is to be a criterion of judgment of this relative status. In reply John refers to a different criterion, namely, that a person's work is only effective if it is received from God and is commissioned by God, whatever its boundaries and limitations. Because he operates within the divinely appointed framework John interprets his office, which his disciples consider inferior or even a failure, as being what it is precisely because that is what God has ordained it to be, and for that reason it must come to an end. He reminds them, therefore, at this point of the negative criterion that he was not the Christ, as he had previously borne witness (v. 28), and that his divine commission (ἀπεσταλμένος) was to prepare for 'that one'. This testimony is repeated, however, in a way which begins to move over from the negative to the positive by means of parabolic speech about bride, bridegroom and bridegroom's 'friend' (v. 29). The parable is developed in a special way required by the context to yield a picture of one whose proper subordination has positive and joyful results, in that in pursuit of his office of standing in readiness for service to the bridegroom, but chiefly in listening to the bridegroom, hearing his voice and what it says, John completes his commission and sees in advance its fruits. Hence not only has John's 'inferiority' a positive sense when related to the divine purpose, but also in accordance with that divine purpose his position from now on must continue to diminish. This situation, brought about by John's hearing of what Jesus has so far uttered, is epitomized in the

text, 'That one must [by divine will] increase, and I must decrease'
(v. 30). The meaning of this would seem to be that from then on John
must occupy less and less, and Jesus more and more, of the centre of the
stage.

The grounds of this assertion, and the reason why it can be so
confidently made, are then rehearsed by John in his concluding address
(vv. 31-36). These grounds are that with the appearance of Jesus upon
the stage of history there is one who genuinely comes from above, that
is, who is directly from God, and who as such is over all, occupying in
relation to 'all' the position of God. In this he is in distinction from all
others, who, having their origin from earth, can speak only as humanity
speaks within the limitations of earth. As the one who is directly from
God he is able, as is none other, to speak of that which he has seen and
heard in the presence of God, and this constitutes the subject of his
witness to God. It is to be noted that the function of 'witness' to God
through human speech (v. 33), which up to this point has been that
through which John alone has been characterized (and it is his only
characteristic in this Gospel), is now transferred to Jesus, and is so transferred by John himself. In being so transferred it ceases to be testimony
in the sense of the witness which human beings bear to God, and
becomes that which arises from a relationship between Jesus and God
which is that of the Son to God as Father. Out of this relationship God
as Father has given Spirit without limit to the Son, and has handed over
to him sovereign authority on the basis of love for a beloved. This
intimacy of heavenly sonship, and the affirmation by God of Jesus'
function as the one who pours out Spirit, have already been introduced
in John's first testimony (1.33). Here in 3.34-36 for the first time John
declares the results of this Spirit activity for human beings. They will
hear the very words of God, and if by believing in the Son they accept
Jesus' heavenly authority they will already, on the historical plane, have
everlasting life. It is here that the testimony of John comes finally to rest,
even when it proceeds to say negatively that people's unbelief renders
them unable to see (experience?) true life, and therefore subject to the
ultimate condemnation belonging to God.

It has often been observed that there are close similarities between the
final testimony of John in 3.31-36 and Jesus' opening speech to
Nicodemus in the Gospel, 3.3-21. Commentators have tended to deal
with this in one of two ways. It is suggested by some that the parallel
style and vocabulary point to textual dislocation having taken place.

Thus Bultmann comments: '3.31-36 did not originally belong to the sayings of the Baptist, as can be seen from the fact that as far as their form and content are concerned, they belong to 3.1-21, and from the fact that v. 32b does not fit the situation described in v. 26', and he pronounces Dodd's attempt to show that 3.31-36 is the proper continuation of 3.22-30 'highly artificial'.[1] It is suggested by others that the similarity is to be explained on the supposition that much of both speeches is the evangelist's own address to his readers.[2] One or other of these views is held by most to be the only logical explanation of the text. But the matter may be viewed otherwise.

Concluding Survey

It has been argued above that the witness of John in the prologue extends throughout 1.15-18, and that it consists of three statements each containing a positive and a negative (or a negative and a positive) —that is, 1.15 with 1.16, 1.17a with 1.17b and 1.18a with 1.18b. It has also been argued above that these features of John's witness in the prologue reappear in the opening sections of the Gospel to which the prologue is a prologue, and are to some extent determinative of the narrative. Thus, the negative statement concerning the status of John vis-à-vis Jesus in 1.15 prepares for 1.19-28, 30-31 and 33a in John's first historical testimony, while 3.27-30, in his second, works out more fully the significance of these negative statements for John's commission and for his followers, now that the one to whom he has pointed and directed all people has become the central figure of the narrative. 1.16, the positive statement over against the negative of 1.15, asserts that human beings have already experienced the fulness of the *plērōma* in the abundance of heavenly givings of grace. This fulness of grace recurs in John's first historical testimony in terms of the functions of the one to whom he witnesses as taking away the sin of the world (1.29), and in his second in the testimony of Jesus himself to what he has heard and seen with the Father in heaven (3.31-32), and in his making available eternal life (3.36)

1.17 adds three things to 1.15-16: 'grace' is further defined as 'grace and truth'; the gift of this is in some way set over against Moses and the law (this will be considered in detail in the next chapter); and the one who is the agent of these gifts is for the first time named and identified

1. Bultmann, *John*, p. 160 n. 2.
2. Brown, *John*, I, pp. 159-60.

as Jesus Christ. The Logos who is said to belong in the heavenly sphere and to be active in creation, and who as man has radiated the glory of God as befits a Son, is now said to be (in antithesis to Jewish beliefs and practices epitomized as 'Moses' and 'the law') the heavenly agent on earth of grace and truth. So John's first historical testimony is given in the context of Jewish inquisition about Jewish eschatological hopes (1.19-27), and his second is given in the context of Jewish religious practice (3.25-26); and in these contexts one is witnessed to, first as being present but still unknown (1.26), and then as present and now known (3.22-25), and as he who baptizes with God's Spirit, and as the Son of God who utters the words of the truth of God (1.33-34; 3.31-36).

What 1.18a and 18b add to 1.15-17 is a witness from John which extends beyond Judaism to embrace all humankind. Judaism is only one, albeit the most important, of the human approaches to God. The negative statement in 1.18a introduces a universal situation of a total lack of seeing and comprehending God.[1] From that position of universal alienation from God the climax of the prologue is reached in the assertion that the previously mentioned Jesus Christ is the unique God/Son in the most intimate relation to God his Father, and that from this relation he has a mission of being his exegete (the precise meaning of ἐξηγήσατο will be discussed later). This can hardly be said to be reproduced in John's first historical testimony, but it constitutes the essence of the second, where his witness is to the universal supremacy of the one who is the Son, and who as such is sovereign over all things and utters the very words of God (3.27-36).[2]

It may thus be argued that the prologue testimony of John in 1.15-18 is explicated in the historical testimony of John in the first three chapters, and that there is no need to suggest that 3.31-36 is out of place in such a testimony. It still remains a question, however, why there should be two such testimonies of John before he departs from the scene. An answer to this question may be indicated by a consideration of what the evangelist has chosen to put between them, assuming that the text in its present order is original, and that 3.31-36 is meant to be part of John's testimony and not the evangelist's address to his readers. There is first the opening incident of the public ministry of Jesus, the *sēmeion* at Cana, which the evangelist not only chooses to put here but

1. Reformulating 1.10b; 1.11b.
2. These verses require the assertions of 1.1-5; 9-14 to give them true significance.

which he expressly designates the first sign by which Jesus manifested his 'glory' or heavenly status, and through which disciples came to belief in him. It can hardly be doubted that one of the reasons for the evangelist's choice here, perhaps the only reason, is that it was an action of supplying an excessive quantity of wine freely and miraculously given. It was a *sēmeion* of superabundance, a historical action which took as its starting point the water of Jewish ablution, and was a sign of the heavenly truth that human beings received of the 'fulness' of the Son of the Father and of superabundant gifts (1.16).

This is followed by a different public action, probably deliberately placed here at the beginning of the ministry, of the cleansing of the temple, and the confrontation with the heart of Judaism which it implied. Such an act lay beyond the competence of John in his confrontation with Judaism, since his credentials, words and deeds were not of the same calibre. But in the temple, at the heart of Jewish worship and governance, Jesus makes an act of cleansing, the negative aspect of which points to a corresponding promise of the presence of God in the body of Jesus (2.19-22).

Thirdly, there is the first discourse of Jesus, that with Nicodemus, who is the representative of pious Jews. If this discourse is compared with the final testimony of John in 3.31-36 there are links which suggest that there is a deliberate and positive interrelation between these two highly theological proclamations. Both are introduced by way of Judaism, and both move from general considerations to come to rest finally in the will of God as expressed by the Son. Both state the negative and positive situations of human beings in relation to God as a result of their reaction to the Son (3.19-21, 36). There are also thematic links. John asserts that origins, whether from heaven or earth, determine the true content or otherwise of a person's speech. Only the one who belongs in the intimacy of the Father's bosom (1.18) as the Son of God (1.34; 3.35-36) can act and speak in such a way that he truly witnesses to God and to his will for humankind (3.32-33). Jesus says much the same to Nicodemus. The gift by God of the beloved Son out of his love for the world is such that the unique Son alone becomes the place where human beings are restored to God and eternal life sustained (3.16-18); and this is based on the matter of origins, according to which Jesus is able to communicate divine things (3.11-12). And Jesus has already begun to baptize in the Spirit when he announces that to enter into a true relationship with God under his sovereign will a person must receive birth from above, which is to be born of the Spirit (3.3-8).

Thus the final testimony of John is not out of place in relation to the Nicodemus discourse, for only when Jesus has already uttered with the sovereignty of God the truths which are to replace those of Judaism could John bring his historical testimony to a close. His testimony in 1.15-18, and to some extent in 1.19-34, is testimony in advance. Only when Jesus has acted and spoken as in 2.1–3.21 can John's testimony be to that which is now actual, and he can seal his mission and pass from the scene. These *sēmeia* and the accompanying discourse require the attestation of John not only at their beginning in preparation for them, but also at their end to mark their actuality and significance, and John's joy is expressed at the historical fulfilment of his commission. This explains the character of John both in the prologue and in what may be called the historical prologue, in 1.19–3.36. There is no place here for the synoptic John, the eschatological prophet announcing the day of wrath and judgment, for Jesus at the opening of a ministry contemporary with that of John declares that heaven and humanity are already united to God through the mission to, and the presence in the world of, the Son; and by their response to this human beings effect their own judgment (3.19). John's final assertion is that believers in the Son have eternal life already while non-believers remain in the state of being under the judgment not of the Son but of God, and are destined for ultimate death (3.36). Thus John's seminal witness in 1.15-18, it may be maintained, functions as a prologue to prepare for the rest of chs. 1–3 of the Gospel, which themselves form a historical prologue, moving Jesus into the centre of the picture, to remain there throughout the remainder of the Gospel.

Chapter 3

MOSES

The second historical personage to be introduced into the prologue is Moses in v. 17. Or, it would be more correct to say, the second and third historical personages to be introduced are Moses and Jesus Christ in v. 17 of the prologue. For 'Jesus Christ', which recurs in this gospel only in the semi-credal formula in 17.3, is plainly a reference to the Logos made flesh by his historical name, and the similarity of form in the two statements 'the law by Moses' and 'grace and truth by Jesus Christ' indicates that they are two statements making up a single sentence. This introduction is, however, very abrupt, and is unprepared for by anything previous in the prologue; and it is difficult to see why it was made. The two separate statements in v. 17 are made in parataxis, and since there is no connecting particle the relation between the first statement and the second are by no means immediately evident.

Nevertheless, the statement 'the law was given by Moses' is manifestly important to the evangelist, since he has made it part of the first witness of John to all humankind in pursuance of the statement in 1.7 that John came to bear witness that all might believe through him. This makes its occurrence here all the odder in what has so far appeared to be a tightly constructed literary whole. For within the testimony of John in vv. 15-18 the sequence of thought would be clearer if v. 17a were omitted and we would then read 'he was before me'; 'of his fulness have we received and grace for grace'; 'grace and truth came by Jesus Christ'. It is difficult to see what contribution v. 17a makes to this. Moses, in distinction from John as a figure of the present closely associated with the Logos, is introduced as a figure of Israel's past, and is the only one to be introduced. He is introduced without any antecedent preparation in the prologue, especially if, as I have previously argued, 'his own' in v. 11 refers not to Israel but to humankind as the sphere of the universal operation of the Logos; and whereas 17b has been prepared for by 'grace and truth' in v. 14, and by all that has been said about the Logos throughout the prologue, 17a could be removed apparently without loss. Moreover, Moses is introduced along with 'the law', but nothing further is said about this law nor about Moses in his character of lawgiver. Again, in distinction from John, Moses is not mentioned as having a particular mission in relation to the Logos, nor is the law associated with him related to the Logos in the way that the word 'witness' relates John to the Logos. Nevertheless, the evangelist has so written and has so placed the statement, and if it cannot be explained by reference to what has gone before, the only reasonable assumption to take account of the manner in which Moses is introduced in v. 17a is that the statement is intentionally connected with, leads on to and forms some sort of preliminary to the statement in which for the first time in the prologue the Logos, of whom it has been said in v. 14 that he is full of grace and truth, is identified as the person Jesus Christ.

The question will then be what kind of connection is being made between these two statements in parataxis. A frequent answer to this question has been that the statements in v. 17 are antithetical, and further, by isolating the term 'grace' in the expression 'grace and truth', that the antithesis is of the Pauline kind of grace and law.[1] The difficulties of this view appear in Bultmann's comment on this verse:

> The Evangelist is only concerned with the contrast between the two, which is shown as the contrast between their origins... Following v. 14 the new revelation is called ἡ χάρις καὶ ἡ ἀλήθεια, and thus the contrast between νόμος and χάρις is introduced; the contrast is otherwise foreign to John and comes from the Pauline school; moreover vv. 14 and 16 in no way lead us to expect it here.

He then adds in a footnote that 'the antithesis in v. 17 is of a quite different kind to the antitheses of the source vv. 5, 10-11, since in the latter the second sentence always repeats antithetically a term from the preceding sentence'; and he observes of v. 18, the style of which shows it to have come from the evangelist, that the antithesis here 'is of the same type as the one in v. 17... The antithesis here, by which the argument is carried forward, corresponds to countless sentences of the evangelist's, where an idea is developed by preceding it with a negation'.[2]

---

1. See M.J. Lagrange, *Evangile selon Saint Jean* (Paris: Gabalda, 1924), Bultmann, *John*, and Barrett, *St John*, *ad loc.*
2. Bultmann, *John*, p. 79 and nn. 1 and 3.

Thus antitheses can have more than one meaning or form; judged by the form in vv. 5, 10-11, the statement in v. 17 is antithetical but not strictly so. And if on other grounds Bultmann's theory of a source underlying the prologue for such verses as 5, 10-11 be rejected in favour of the view that the entire prologue is the construction of the evangelist, then antitheses of various kinds can be attributed to the author. And if even in the more strictly antithetical statements in vv. 1-14 what is being built up is a step-by-step presentation of the truth about God, the Logos and John by contrast with darkness, ignorance and disbelief in the world and in human beings, in which the emphasis is on the positive and not the negative side of the contrast, it is open to see an antithetical parallelism of this kind in v. 17 also, and to lay emphasis on its constructive side. This is not necessarily, however, to embrace the alternative synthetic solution held by some scholars, whereby a continuity is seen between Moses and Jesus in that it is the grace and truth already found in the law that is found fully in Jesus Christ.[1]

The arguments against the view that v. 17 expresses an antithesis of the Pauline kind are formidable. In the first place, to the extent that the prologue is a tightly constructed whole, the admission into it of an intrusion which does not really belong—which is, in Bultmann's words, 'foreign' and completely unprepared for—is in itself highly suspect. Secondly, if, as I have maintained, the prologue prepares for the main themes of the Gospel, it is notable that the kind of anti-Jewish and anti-law polemic, which in Paul's case was responsible for the prominence of the concept of grace, nowhere makes any appearance in this gospel, and would seem to be not, or no longer, a living issue in the Johannine milieu. Thirdly, what is set side by side with law here is not grace, but grace and truth, and 'grace and truth' is not a Pauline phrase, nor is this a Pauline antithesis. If, however, the idea of a Pauline antithesis between law and grace is rejected, then the question of the place and function of v. 17 within the prologue becomes even more acute, and it may be a preferable procedure to approach the meaning of law and Moses here by way of first attempting to establish the meaning of 'grace and truth'.

Most scholars note that 'grace' in the 'grace and truth' of 17b picks up the 'grace upon [instead of] grace' in v. 16, where it refers to the divine gift which some people receive from the Logos-Son. This itself

1.   See for example Brown, *John*, I, p. 16; A. Loisy, *Le Quatrième Evangile* (Alphonse Picard et Fils, 1903), p. 193, and J. Jeremias, 'Μωϋσῆς', *TDNT*, IV, pp. 872-73.

refers back to v. 14, where the glory of the Logos made flesh is described as being 'full of grace and truth'. This is, therefore, one of the strands running through vv. 14-18 and giving it a certain unity, so that these verses require the previous statements about the Logos and John to give them meaning. Or, to put it the other way round, v. 14 is a bridge verse which does not simply bring what has already been said to a conclusion, but which points forward to what is said in vv. 15-18 about its efficacy for, and appropriation by, human beings. The phrase here, 'grace and truth', is not, however, a natural Greek idiom, and the question is open as to its precise meaning and emphasis. The most common explanation of it is that it is a Hebraism, 'grace' representing *ḥesed* and 'truth' representing *'emet*.[1]

There are, however, weaknesses in this explanation. The actual combination ἡ χάρις καὶ ἡ ἀλήθεια nowhere occurs in the LXX or in any biblical references in Philo, so that Greek readers would be unlikely to recognize it as a Hebraic expression even if they were familiar with the Old Testament in Greek. The frequently cited description of God in Exod. 34.6 is in the LXX rendering of the Hebrew πολυέλεος καὶ ἀληθινός and this can be used as support for the combination χάρις καὶ ἀλήθεια only on Dodd's argument that there is slight evidence in later books of the LXX for *ḥesed* being rendered by χάρις.[2] However, in the four texts in question (Esth. 2.9; 2.17; Ecclus 7.33; 40.17) χάρις means either the favour a woman finds in the eyes of another (her attractiveness), or the kindness and bounty shown by the wealthy to the needy. In these senses it is unlikely to be found in conjunction with ἀλήθεια. It therefore remains open to consider the phrase as a Greek phrase unaffected by Semitic thought, which has perhaps been deliberately created by the evangelist for his own purposes. If so, are they two separate nouns of equal importance, or do they form some kind of compound? If the latter, then which acts as adjectival? Verse 14 does not decide the point, since both grace and truth describe the glory revealed, but the verb in the singular in v. 17, ἐγένετο, would seem to indicate that the phrase is intended to be taken as a compound one. But is it 'gracious truth' or 'true grace'? The element of communication by God and participation by human beings is emphasized in 'grace' by the fact that, whereas 'grace and truth' are twice conjoined (vv. 14, 17), it is only 'grace' that human beings are said to participate in (v. 16), not

1. See Barrett, *St John,* p. 167; Brown, *John,* I, p. 14.
2. *Interpretation,* pp. 175-76.

'truth'. This raises again the question of the reason for the conjunction of 'grace and truth', and of where the emphasis lies in this conjunction. This question is further raised by the fact that whereas 'grace' is confined in the Fourth Gospel to these three mentions in the prologue (1.14, 16, 17) 'truth' and 'true', which are also introduced in the prologue (1.9, 14, 17), are found frequently in the body of the Gospel, and contribute to its structuring in a way that recalls the evangelist's developed use of 'witness' that we have already discussed. What is the significance of 'grace' when harnessed to 'truth'? Is 'truth' something of such a different order that it requires 'grace' as a bridge, a highway of communication for heavenly words and things to enter the earthly sphere, somewhat as envisaged in respect of the Son of Man in 1.51?

The Hebrew word *'emet* had a root meaning of fixing or establishing things. Applied to persons it denoted steadfastness or trustworthiness. In forensic usage it referred to the validity of an enactment, and so came to mean the genuineness of things of their kind, guarantees. It is widely used in the Old Testament and Jewish literature to characterize God, and has been understood to lie behind the word 'truth' in 1.14, 16 by most commentators. S. Aalen, in his article '"Truth", a Key Word in St John's Gospel', reasserts this view, and in so doing rejects the views of Dodd and Bultmann.[1] These latter consider the difficulty of expressing the Hebrew meaning, which had within it a moral category, by a Greek word which had a root meaning carrying within it an intellectual category. The two meanings could on occasion coalesce. If the evangelist wrote in Greek for those who were familiar with the Greek idiom, it could be difficult to tell, except from each context, how far the Hebrew meaning is present in the Greek word. It has been said of a Hellenistic-Jewish student of the Old Testament such as Philo, who nowhere clearly preserves the Hebraic sense, that 'the Hebrew associations of the term have receded far into the background'.[2] If this be the case with Philo, who was steeped in the Old Testament and aimed to present Judaism to the educated Gentile world, it could also be so for the evangelist in formulating a reasoned presentation of Christianity that preserved monotheism in the face of Jewish accusations to the contrary, and did so through a Logos 'Christology' argued to some extent on philosophical grounds for readers who acknowledged a certain indebtedness to the Jews but were no longer in deadly conflict with them, and who were

1. *Studia Evangelica* II (1964), pp. 3-24.
2. Dodd, *Interpretation*, p. 175.

not necessarily well versed in Jewish writings. If this is the background to the Fourth Gospel, then a Greek meaning for 'truth' may be found to suit the Johannine contexts, and an awareness of the difference of meaning between the Hebrew *'emet* and the Greek ἀλήθεια could be vital.

In Greek ἀλήθεια originally signified a content of fact or a state of affairs which could be seen, indicated or expressed. Historians used it of facts over against myths; forensically it was used of the proved state of affairs over against rival claims; philosophers used it of absolute reality. Dodd maintains that something of the Platonic concept of the realm of phenomena pointing as symbols to the real in the realm above is to be found in the Fourth Gospel, a view which finds support in the text in references to 'above' and 'below' (3.7), to being from above or below (8.23) and to the frequent mention in relation to Jesus as Son of Man, or the Son of his descent from God and his return to God. The meaning of 'truth' and 'true' must have something in common with these Hellenistic ideas. Both Dodd and Bultmann understand 'truth' in the Fourth Gospel in the sense of 'reality'.

It could be argued from the frequent occurrence of the terms 'truth' and 'true' in the body of the Gospel[1] that, as with 'witness', their introduction in the prologue (1.9, 14, 17) is in preparation for a content and meaning that the Gospel is to supply. The only instance where the Hebrew idiom is so strong that a Greek reader would find the language strange is 3.21, where there is the expression 'to do the truth'. Dodd, however, renders this by 'to act honourably', which is a possible understanding of the Greek. The statement in 16.13 that 'the Spirit of truth will lead you into all the truth' might at first sight suggest the psalmist's plea to God in the Hebrew text (Ps. 25.5) 'Cause me to walk in thy faithfulness', where the LXX Ps. 24.5 translates ἐπὶ τὴν ἀλήθειάν σου, representing the Hebrew *'emet*, the rectitude that is characteristic of God. This cannot, however, be the sense here, where the leading of believers into all truth is by means of the communication to them of the heavenly things belonging to Jesus, which he has received from the Father, and the announcement to them of things which are future. Thus 'truth', not 'faithfulness', is intended, and this means that things belonging to the heavenly realm are communicated to believers on earth.

1.   ἀλήθεια in the Gospel 5 times, in the Johannine Epistles 20 times (Matthew once, Mark and Luke 3 times, generally in the phrase ἐν ἀληθείᾳ, 'in truth'); ἀληθής in the Gospel 14 times, in the Epistles 3 times (Matthew and Mark once); ἀληθινός in the Gospel 9 times, in 1 John 4 times (Luke once).

In the discourse in ch. 4 the opposite movement of human beings to God in worship is one of the subjects discussed, and here 'truth' appears in a compound expression 'in spirit and truth' which is not unlike that in the prologue, 'grace and truth', especially if, as noted above, 'spirit' could in Hellenistic religion be a synonym for 'grace'. And again the question arises of the reason for the compound, and of where the emphasis lies. The 'true' worshippers are those who worship God 'in spirit and truth'. This can hardly be an appeal to the Hebrew idea of worshippers who approach God with steadfast reliance on him. Since the necessity for worship in spirit is based here on the definition of God as himself spirit, perhaps meaning active in a heavenly way, the addition of 'truth' here may be to indicate that communication from God which enables him to be apprehended and responded to as he is—true worship—is that which is made in 'spirit-full truth'. If so, then what is said of Jesus in the prologue is now said by him of the worship which will be offered to God through the Son after the return to the Father. Bultmann arrives at the same conclusion by a somewhat different route. He recalls that the believers are those who have been born of the Spirit (3.3-8) and who are to be sanctified in truth (17.17), which is God's word, but are 'taken out of this worldly existence and set in the eschatological existence', so that the worship of the coming age which has now dawned is the spiritual worship because it is informed by the reality of God revealed in Jesus the Word.[1] This is the new Christian dimension indicated by 'truth' here, and appears again in the self-acclamation of Jesus, 'I am the way, the truth and the life'.

With respect to the corresponding adjective ἀληθινός there can be little doubt that the meaning 'real' is present in the reference to 'the only true God' in 17.3, and to the one from whom Jesus has come, and who has sent him, as true in 7.28. So also the Logos is the true (real and heavenly) light and Jesus the true vine (15.1). As the Son of Man who has descended out of heaven, and as the Son of God who shares all things with the Father, he gives true or heavenly succour and the bread which is really bread from heaven. Indeed, he is himself the bread which is living because it is true, and conveys life which is qualitatively eternal (6.35, 41, 48, 50, 51). The results of truly eating and truly drinking are life eternal (6.51, 58). Furthermore, the words of Jesus no less than the words of God which will sanctify believers are true because both belong

---

1. Bultmann, *John*, pp. 190-91.

to the realm of that which is true and perfect. Indeed Dodd in his chapter on Truth refers to the address of Jesus to the Jews who had believed in him: 'you shall know the truth, and the truth shall free you' (8.32), noting that it was a commonplace of Hellenistic philosophy that the wise person was free.[1] Thus a concept of liberty through divine knowledge is reflected here. As was shown previously, the prologue also makes the knowledge which understands the divine things an indispensible part of receiving the heavenly gifts through the Son, Jesus Christ. Since the freedom envisaged in 8.32 is stated in the language of Christian thought, it is not surprising that the divine knowledge which is available through the one who is eternally the Son of the Father should set disciples free from servitude to sin (8.32-36).

It is thus difficult to reject the view that the use of ἀλήθεια (ἀληθινός) in the Fourth Gospel rests upon common Hellenistic usage, and that it hovers between the meanings of 'reality', 'the ultimately real' and 'knowledge of the real'.[2] This view cannot be rejected simply on the grounds that it smacks of 'Platonic' or 'gnostic' thought. Rather it would seem to be the case that in his careful construction of a Logos doctrine of creation which issues in the divine functions of the Logos as the true light and makes him the sole vehicle of divine grace and truth, the evangelist has utilized certain current thought forms in the service of the presentation of Christian belief.

In the light of the above discussion the meaning of 1.17b might be put as follows: heavenly power belonging to the reality of the realm of God was bestowed through the agency of Jesus Christ. Thus the functions of the one who at this point is identified as a historical figure, Jesus Christ, coincide with those of the wholly divine figure, the Logos, of the rest of the prologue. It would be logical that the one of whom the most exalted things have been said in the prologue, whose existence was the most intimate possible with God eternally, who performed the very acts of God in creation, who possessed God's glory and was the true light, should be given the function of making God's will and heavenly gifts known as a human being among other human beings. If that is so the Gospel will present a Jesus Christ who is wholly at one with God in words and deeds. That this is indeed the evangelist's achievement will be argued later; sufficient here to say that it may already be indicated in the compressed compound expression 'grace and truth', if this is understood to

1. Dodd, *Interpretation*, pp. 176-77.
2. Dodd, *Interpretation*, p. 177.

mean the 'gracious gift of divine reality'. But then the question remains as to why it should have been introduced by way of a reference to Moses and the divine giving of the law through him. What is the reference to Moses and the law shorthand for, that it should be set either alongside, or over against, 'grace and truth' through Jesus Christ understood in this sense? It is natural for readers of the New Testament (in which the letters of Paul occupy such a prominent part, with their antithesis between the divine but negative and death-dealing law and the divine and life-giving grace through the death of Christ) to approach the statement in 1.17 from the Pauline point of view, even though they have to admit that it is a 'foreign' and intrusive element there.[1] If, however, this is set on one side, it is open to consider whether 'Moses and the law' could mean different things to different people, and could be a shorthand for Judaism as different people understood that Judaism. If in this gospel John is seen to have been a figure reshaped from earlier traditions to serve the theological purposes of this gospel, then it may be asked whether this might not also be the case with Moses.

Which Moses and which Law?

In his monograph *Moses in Greco-Roman Paganism*, J.G. Gager shows both that knowledge of Moses was widespread in the ancient world, and that the estimate of him varied according to the political or cultural viewpoint of the writer who chose to pay attention to him.[2] Thus in his successive chapters he deals with those who hold Moses the lawgiver in a favourable light; those who hold him in an unfavourable light, sometimes considering him as positively evil; those, belonging to literary circles with political and religious involvements, who deal with the Moses of the exodus; and those from unlettered circles, and representing the syncretism of the Christian era, who see Moses as a magician and an alchemist. Thus Hecataeus of Abdera, court historian to the first Hellenistic king of Egypt, Ptolemy I Soter, being concerned with the problem of authoritative government, saw the Jewish system as another example of authoritative rule which could stand alongside Egyptian monarchy, and produced out of ancient Egyptian historical traditions an ideal scheme of education of a Hellenistic kind based on the Mosaic

1. See Bultmann, *John*, p. 79 and nn. 1 and 3.
2. *Moses in Greco-Roman Paganism* (*JBL* Monograph Series; Nashville: Abingdon Press, 1972).

legislative material. In this scheme Moses is described as being of Egyptian origins, as leading into Judaea those foreigners who were not Grecian in an expulsion from Egypt due to the displeasure of the national gods at the practice of alien cults, as a militant leader, and, in conformity with the standards of Greek models, as a wise lawgiver who establishes the distinctive customs of his people. Thus Hecataeus 'shaped the material in accordance with his own philosophical, political and religious ends', and presented the Moses of Egyptian historical tradition in the manner of ethnographic writing as an ideal wise lawgiver and military leader who founded an ideal 'philosophical race'.[1] Strabo, some three hundred years later, also used Egyptian historical tradition and reformulated it for his own purposes. In his *Geography*, Book 16, Moses is an Egyptian priest who leads his people out of Egypt into Judaea—there is no mention of an expulsion or a military conquest—because as a superior theologian he was disenchanted with the Egyptian understanding of deity. He was an influential and wise teacher who established a sanctuary and a cult which did not burden people with expensive contributions and other foolish activities. Gager comments that Strabo 'shows the same penchant for remaking Moses in the image of his own Stoic philosophy'.[2]

Of a different kind, and from a different part of the world, are the observations of the two Roman writers Quintillian and Tacitus. The former refers only once to Moses in his *De Institutione Oratoria* (3.7.21), where, in the context of a series of speeches concerning praise and blame, he states that vice can be denounced in either of two ways, by directing attention to the living or to the dead, and that 'Infamy comes soon after death...we hate the parents of evil offspring; and it is notorious for founders of cities to have brought together a people which is bent on the destruction of others, as for example the creator of the Jewish superstition'. This single allusion, however, is significant as evidence that in Roman literary circles of the first century CE Moses was sufficiently well known to be immediately recognizable; and, if the remarks are not to be taken as an outburst of personal hostility (which is always difficult to judge in a rhetorical work), that the example of Moses was taken from a stock of established *topoi* and set examples for an argument.[3]

1. Gager, *Moses*, p. 37.
2. *Moses*, p. 43.
3. Gager, *Moses*, p. 81. See also F.H. Colson, 'Quintillian, the Gospels and

Tacitus provides much more ample evidence on this score since, in his *Histories*, as a prelude to his account of the fall of Jerusalem, and following the form of a standard ethnographical model, he introduces an excursus on the Jews (*Hist.* 5.2-10). He begins with their early history, recording that at that time there were no less than five theories about their origins in common currency, proceeds to their religion and customs, to the topography of the land and to their more recent history. Tacitus depends on Egyptian historical tradition, which can thus be seen to be a living tradition from the fourth century BCE in Alexandria on into the first century CE in Rome, where it is also known by Josephus, a Jew writing in Greek at Rome after the fall of Jerusalem. Moreover, Gager points out that in Tacitus the Moses of the desert, who is written about in mildly heroic terms, changes abruptly at 5.4 once he becomes the figure who establishes the cities of the newly conquered territory, for he then becomes the 'prototype, historically and symbolically, of Jewish xenophobia and misanthropy'.[1] Moses then 'introduced new religious practices quite opposed to those of all other religions. The Jews regard as profane all that we hold sacred; on the other hand they permit what we abhor' (Tacitus, *Hist.* 5.4). This widespread disapproval of Moses and the Jews was, of course, particularly strong in the anti-Jewish riots in Alexandria in 39–40 CE and during the Roman wars against Judaea in 69–70 CE. With the gradual spread of Christianity in the Roman Empire, when it began to supplant Judaism as the enemy, pagan writers in the first and second centuries could soften their hostile estimate of Moses, and he could be remodelled yet again.

The above material showing that Moses and Judaism were variously estimated under the influence of changing political and cultural trends is drawn from pagan sources. There is evidence, however, that within the confines of Judaism itself (which we now know to be much wider than was once supposed) attitudes to Moses and the law were not univocal. In his article on Moses J. Jeremias documents this.[2] On the one hand was the Moses of Palestinian Judaism, and on the other hand a more Hellenized Moses. As examples of each one can select *Jubilees* and Philo.

Christianity', *Classical Review* 39 (1925), p. 168 n. 4.
    1.   Gager, *Moses*, p. 84.
    2.   'Μωϋσῆς', pp. 848-64. See also T.F. Glasson, *Moses in the Fourth Gospel* (SBT, 40; London: SCM Press, 1963); Meeks, *Prophet-King*; H.M. Teeple, *The Mosaic Eschatological Prophet* (SBLMS, 10; Atlanta: Society of Biblical Literature, 1957).

The former, written by a Pharisee (c. 105 BCE according to Charles), takes the form of a rewriting in the manner of Chronicles of the events from the creation until the giving of the law on Sinai, and does so in order to maintain the absolute supremacy of the law and to defend Judaism from the Hellenistic spirit. It is a Jewish retaliation against pagan estimates. This retaliation could, however, take an opposite form. As H. Chadwick has observed, Philo's exposition of the Pentateuch presupposes that Plato and the Greek philosophers were dependent on Moses, as does Josephus and later Justin Martyr.[1]

The Hellenized Moses stands in sharp contrast with the legalist Moses of the Pharisees. In varying degrees he is endowed with the typically Hellenistic quality of kingship, especially in the romantic legends of Artapanus (first century BCE), who expands the biblical material beyond all recognition, but also in Philo, who keeps closer to the bibical events. In his *Life* Moses conforms to the figure who would represent true Judaism intelligibly to the Gentile proselyte as 'king, lawgiver, high-priest and prophet' (*Vit. Mos.* 2.292), who is 'habitually kind' (a typical Hellenistic characterization, 2.104), as 'incapable of accepting any falsehood' (1.24), and as 'keeping tight hold on the lusts of adolescence with the reins of temperance and self-control' (1.24-25). He 'scorned luxury to exemplify his philosophical creed by his daily actions; for his speech and his actions were in harmony' (1.29). According to Goodenough the Moses of Philo is presented, as are the patriarchs, in such a way as to allow the Gentiles to approach the higher mysteries through him, and, indeed, as a mystic himself.[2]

This evidence—and it could be multiplied—indicates that Moses in the first century CE could be a person with many faces, according to the audience to which he is being presented. Since we do not know for certain in advance who the evangelist is, nor what his audience is, we cannot decide in advance what his or their concept of Moses or of the law was, nor why it should be set alongside grace and truth. And since the prologue itself offers no further description of Moses and the law, the rest of the Gospel has to be investigated for what the evangelist intends his readers to understand by 'Moses' and 'the law'.

1.   *Early Christian Thought and Christian Tradition* (Oxford: Clarendon Press, 1966), pp. 13-14.
2.   E.R. Goodenough, *By Light, Light: The Mystic Gospel of Hellenistic Judaism* (Oxford: Oxford University Press, 1935), esp. ch. 7, 'Moses Presented to the Gentiles', and ch. 8, 'Moses the Mystic'.

C.H. Dodd, in his discussion of νόμος in the New Testament, established a number of different meanings both for the word 'torah' and for νόμος as its Greek translation.[1] He points out that the word 'torah', which was so important in the Jewish vocabulary, changed considerably in the course of time. It was originally used in the sense of 'direction', 'instruction' or 'teaching', and as such covered the three areas of commandments, statutes and judgment by judges, kings and lawgivers. These meanings were similarly covered by νόμος in Greek. The further meanings of 'torah' may be mentioned: 'torah' as the oracular instruction of priests at local and national shrines, and 'torah' as prophetic teaching concerning God and his dealings with, purposes for, and demands upon his people. Both these meanings could be contained within the word νόμος in Greek usage. On the other hand there were some Greek meanings which were alien to the Hebrew understanding of 'torah'. Thus νόμος could be understood as an underlying principle of life and action, or as custom held to be a sovereign power through its established acceptance in civilized society. Dodd refers to the statement of Sophocles that the laws were engendered in the celestial heights,[2] and goes on to observe that the poet here surely refers to the customs of the universe, and not to a code revealed by a deity. If this is correct then clearly nothing like a decalogue can be envisaged. 'They are the eternal principles of right and wrong as immanent in the universe.'[3] The Greeks also developed another line of thought where νόμος referred to legal enactments, whether single or those of a community, given by authorized persons. This narrow legal meaning was common currency in the first century CE, and Dodd refers to the pseudo-Demosthenic work *Contra Aristogitonem* for its fullest expression: 'Every law is the invention and gift of the gods, the judgment of wise men, the correction of transgressions, and the common covenant of the state, in accordance with which all the members of the state ought to live'.[4] However, law in this sense is expressed by the common Deuteronomic phrase 'the commandment(s), the statutes and the judgments', which the LXX translators render by ἁι ἐντολαὶ καὶ τὰ δικαιώματα καὶ τὰ κρίματα. Curiously none of these Hebrew terms is rendered by νόμος, which the translators largely reserve for 'torah'.

1. *The Bible and the Greeks* (London: Hodder & Stoughton, 1935).
2. *The Bible and the Greeks*, pp. 25-26.
3. *The Bible and the Greeks*, p. 26.
4. *The Bible and the Greeks*, p. 26.

'Torah' itself had become a means of referring to the Pentateuch, and later to the body of teaching which was commentary upon the prophetic writings. It could finally be extended to embrace the entire Jewish religion regarded as divine revelation. However, with a later narrowing, the predominantly legal sense came to be applied to 'torah', and this led to a rigid understanding of the Old Testament. From this rigidity an intellectual Hellenizing Jew like Philo had to escape, and to seek a wider religious freedom by a new understanding of the Greek word νόμος. Hence Philo allegorized 'law', and Paul at times appears to be using what looks like a Stoicizing concept of νόμος in his argument that Judaism was a legal religion to be superseded by Christianity as a religion of the Spirit (Rom. 3.27; 7.23, 25; 8.2). According to Dodd, Paul's usage here is explicable by reference to the common Greek meaning of the word as 'principle', and he finds nothing akin to this in the Fourth Gospel.[1]

In the Synoptic Gospels 'the law' is used sparingly and precisely. Mark does not use it at all, preferring ἐντολή, which more accurately renders the use of 'torah' as 'commandment'. Matthew and Luke can use νόμος to distinguish the Pentateuch and the prophets. In the Fourth Gospel the word is used twelve times, sometimes in a more restricted sense and sometimes in a wider sense. Thus in 1.45 it also distinguishes between the Pentateuch and the prophets—'We have found him of whom Moses in the law and also the prophets wrote'. At 7.19, 23, 51 and 8.17 it is used of specific religious ordinances. In a form of introducing a citation from Scripture that is peculiar to the Fourth Gospel, 'It is written in [the, your, their] law', it can be used, even though what is then quoted is not from the Pentateuch but from the Psalms (10.34; 15.25; cf. 12.34). A wider use of 'law' as the community's regulations recognizable by both Jews and Greeks occurs in the trial scenes at 18.31 and 19.7. With reference to the untutored crowds who are ignorant of 'the law' it would appear to have a general sense of written and oral traditions incumbent on Jews (7.49). If this is the background of 1.17 (as Dodd thinks it is), then 'Moses and the law' is to be understood to refer not only to the decalogue and Pentateuchal ordinances, but also to the teaching of authorized successors of Moses, who expanded and interpreted the law for the changing needs of Jews in their religion. By the time of the evangelist 'Moses' (and the law) could be a shorthand for

1.   *The Bible and the Greeks*, pp. 36-38.

the entire system and teaching of Judaism in its manifold varieties, and the context will regulate the meaning which the evangelist intended in his use of the expression.

The Use of Moses (and the Law) in the Body of the Gospel

When one turns to those passages in the Gospel which refer to Moses (and/or 'the law'), it may be observed that at first sight they have the same appearance of being insertions as does 1.17 in the prologue. As I have observed above, the juxtaposing in 1.17 of Moses and 'the law' with Jesus Christ and 'grace and truth' is so odd and awkward that 1.17a could be removed without obvious loss. The same can be said in some measure of the references to Moses in chs. 3, 5 and 6. Indeed, so consistently can they be said to appear as intrusions or redactional additions that it must be seriously considered whether this is evidence of the evangelist's own style and mind in the matter. What he has briefly achieved in 1.14-18 he expands in the Gospel, especially in chs. 5–8, where Jesus is presented as in constant debate with Jews concerning their law.

Thus, the introduction of Moses lifting up the serpent in the wilderness as a type of the lifting up of the Son of Man has struck many as an awkward step in the development of the discourse in ch. 3. Bultmann supposes that it was made by the evangelist, since his source was not interested in establishing any connection here with the Old Testament.[1] Dodd remarks that the reference remains undeveloped.[2] Similarly 5.45-47, with which the discourse in ch. 5 comes to an end, takes an odd turn in the reference to Moses and not Jesus as the one who accuses the Jews before God as those who reject God. It simply reinforces the rejection by Jesus of the Jewish interpretation of Scripture referred to in 5.39, in both of which passages Bultmann again sees an elaboration of an original source by the evangelist. The statement in 6.32, however it is to be translated and understood, reads as unexpected and intrusive. If omitted the text would be: 'Most truly I say to you, but indeed my Father gives you the true bread out of heaven; for the bread of God is the one coming down out of heaven and giving life to the world'. The statement in 6.32 belongs to a passage, 6.32-34, which is so strange in its question and answer format that some scholars have been led to ascribe it to a

1. *John*, p. 152 n. 1.
2. *Interpretation*, p. 353.

Passover haggadah background. If this is rejected and the format
ascribed to the evangelist,[1] then it would appear that the strange intrusive quality of the verse is to be assigned to the evangelist. The question
in 7.19, 'Did not Moses give you the law?', and what follows from it are
so abrupt that some scholars have been led to propose that the passage
is out of order, and should follow 5.47. In that case ch. 5 would have
mention of Moses as the accuser, Jewish failure to understand his
writings, their failure to keep the law evidenced in their desire to kill
Jesus, and then, by way of argumentation from the lesser to the greater,
the invalidation of the whole legal system through circumcision on the
sabbath. It would seem, then, that the awkward and apparently intrusive
character of 1.17a, with its abrupt reference to Moses and the law, has a
certain counterpart in the reference to Moses and the law in the body of
the Gospel. These references may now be examined in a little more
detail.

The first (apart from the formal reference to Moses and the prophets
in 1.45) is in 3.14, and illustrates both this apparently intrusive character,
since it seems to be dragged in to provide a parallel to the lifting up of
the Son of Man, and also the variety in the picture conjured up by the
name 'Moses' in connection with Jesus. For it is not Moses in the
precise sense of lawgiver who is introduced here, but Moses the warrior
leader of the Israelites in the wilderness. He acts here in a way that is
symbolic of the saving death of Jesus, and in his symbolic action confers
a measure of saving healing on the Israelites which points to the complete gift from God of eternal life. The precise purpose of this parallel
puzzles the commentators, and why Moses' elevation of a serpent on a
pole for the Israelites to gaze on and not die should be held to be of
significance remains mysterious. The suggestion that typology is opera-
tive here, and that the serpent is a type of Christ (so Barnabas, Justin,
Tertullian and others), is hardly tenable since the point does not lie in
what was lifted up or who lifted it up, but in the verb 'lift up' itself. This
prepares for, but does not here develop, the exaltation of the Son of
Man; although what is here explicitly stated is the fruits of this for
humankind—that everyone believing might have life in him. This would
be the force of the purpose clause if ἐν αὐτῷ (ἐν now with its strong
support from p75 for this reading, is to be preferred to the variants ἐπί
and εἰς here) is taken not with 'believe', since nowhere else in the

---

1. As by Brown, *John*, pp. 266-67.

Gospel is πιστεύειν found with ἐν (the evangelist's characteristic construction is πιστεύειν with εἰς), but with 'eternal life'. In that case the statement provides an echo of the statement in the prologue that 'life was in him (the Logos)'.

In 3.15 the term 'eternal life' is introduced for the first time in the Gospel, and therewith an eschatology other than that of Nicodemus, a recognized teacher of Israel and representative of Moses, who by implication looked for entry into the eschatological kingdom of God other than by a present and effective birth from above and from the sphere of the Spirit. Whatever the precise reason for this particular parallel with Moses may have been, it is clear that it establishes a qualitative difference between the life which the Israelites received and the eternal life given to the believer, as the difference between what is temporary and imperfect and what is heavenly, eternal and therefore perfect. It may be that the evangelist has made use of Num. 21.8-9 here to make the kind of connection betwen Moses and Jesus as I have suggested is made in 1.17. That is, a curious type of oblique antithesis in which the negative view of Moses is primarily a foil to the positive statement about Jesus Christ is made; but here the emphasis lies on the positive aspect of the relation of the symbol to what is symbolized ('as...so...').

The second reference is in 5.39, 45-47. The analysis of this chapter, which has the first mention of the Jewish persecution of Jesus which is to continue in the following chapters, presents considerable difficulties. Unlike the discourses of chs. 6 and 9, there is no immediately apparent symbolic link between the story of the healing with which the chapter begins (5.1-15) and the discourse that follows. The transition is made awkwardly, and not by means of a statement such as that in Mk 2.27, that the mysterious Son of Man is lord also of the sabbath, but by the positive self-acclamation in 5.17. Lying behind the text there appears to be a theological dispute, related to Gen. 2.1-3, over whether God worked or rested on the sabbath, one solution to which was that the rest from creation did not involve God's cessation from his work of judging.[1] Only from some such debate can the astonishingly abrupt statement of Jesus in 5.17, 'My Father works until now, and I, I also, work', be intelligible. (There is a reverse sequence in ch. 9, where the healing of the blind man is first prepared for by the statement 'We must work the

---

1. Dodd, *Interpretation*, pp. 320-25.

works of him who sent me, while it is day; night comes when no one can work' [9.4], and then in 9.13-41 the issue of the sabbath is raised.)

This statement turns persecution for healing on the sabbath into an intention to put Jesus to death on a charge of blasphemy, which is here introduced for the first time.[1] At this point, which is the starting point of the theological exposition that follows, the reader may perceive that the witness of John in 1.15-18 to Jesus, as the bringer from God of the grace and truth that belongs to God, is being effected historically in Jesus. For he is one who is no mere healer, but one who forgives sins (5.14); and he claims the sovereignty of God as doing God's work *qua* judge on the sabbath as evidence of his uninterrupted union with the Father *qua* Son. But it is the prologue which has first declared the heavenly origin and work of the Logos who is called an only-begotten, unique Son of a heavenly Father (1.1-2, 14b). Indeed this has been the substance of the witness of John in 1.15-18, reiterated with greater precision, and with language to some extent drawn from the climax of the Nicodemus discourse in 3.16ff., in his testimony in 1.27-36. It is notable that in 5.17-32 there is developed the strongest possible state-ment of the equality of Jesus as Son with, but also his subordination to, the Father, and his ability to perform the divine acts because he shares the prerogative of God of having a life which is self-subsistent. From his position of total dependence he performs what he is able to see the Father doing. This performance includes implicitly the work of judgment (5.14), which is made explicit in 5.22; but this itself is in the context of the divine authority and capacity to make alive which is stated in 5.21, and which restates something intrinsic to being the bearer of 'grace and truth', the one who lustrates with heavenly Spirit or activity (1.33b).

Thus, difficult as the analysis of the chapter may be, it would never-theless seem to be a closely woven step-by-step argumentation drawing out positively something of what is meant by grace and truth coming from God into the world by Jesus Christ, the Logos-Son. In theory the evangelist, here as elsewhere, could have written about nothing else than this, and of its results for the world and those who accept. Historically, however—whether we mean by that the evangelist and his readers in their situation or Jesus in his situation—the coming from God of grace and truth by Jesus Christ, the Logos-Son, took place, and moreover had to take place, in relation to an actual religion, the religion called Judaism,

1.   Bultmann, *John*, p. 244 n. 6.

from which the evangelist and his readers are already separated. This accounts for the fact that references to Moses and the law have the appearance of intrusions into an otherwise Christian exposition of theological truth. It also accounts for the way in which the evangelist introduces Moses and the law into his theological exposition, for the Jesus he presents must be seen to disengage himself from Jewish tenets and practice, while at the same time establishing belief in the one God of Judaism; hence the manner in which in ch. 5 the argument introduces both the Scriptures and Moses—both as a foil to Jesus and his work as Son. In 5.39-47, addressing the Jews as those who do not believe in him as the one whom God has sent, Jesus denounces not the Scriptures themselves, but the Jews' use of them in the expectation of finding in them eternal life. The only proper use of them would be to discover in them the witness to himself. The Jews themselves refuse to accept eternal life since they will not go to the Son. But this means that the evangelist is here assessing the Old Testament Scriptures from an already achieved doctrinal position. In no way could it be shown that the Scriptures supply material which resembles anything that the evangelist says here in ch. 5, and elsewhere, about the Johannine Jesus. The statement in 5.39 must be entirely a creation of the evangelist's theology. If so, it may then be asked why it is precisely Moses who is then introduced, and in the positive-negative sense as the accuser of the Jews before God—would not Abraham, or some other figure, have fulfilled this function? It would seem that for the evangelist opposition from Judaism to Jesus set out in terms of the Logos-Son was inevitable, and if Moses stands for Judaism then it is necessary to dissociate him from actual Jewish beliefs and practices, since the Jews' religious understanding of God and the practices which embodied it did not tally with the understanding of the Christians whom the evangelist represents. Moses is their accuser since their beliefs and practices did not, as they would claim, stem from belief in Moses, nor did their use of his writings show a perception that they pointed to Jesus as the Logos-Son. But again it is by no means clear how the Old Testament could be said to point in this way.

Moses is, indeed, a somewhat ambivalent figure in the Fourth Gospel. He is not a figure who clearly evokes antithetical statements about law and grace; yet he is bound up with the relentless opposition from Judaism which historically arose from the life of Jesus itself. Thus, already in 1.17, there is an 'antithesis' which is not completely antithetical, but is rather a statement of tension between what is now seen to be negative and alien when viewed from the point of view of the grace and truth brought by the Son from God, and that to which it is now to be seen as a foil. Is not a tension of this kind inevitable in all Christian theological statements when they are made alongside Jewish beliefs and customs? Hence in the body of the Gospel, wherever Jesus and beliefs about him are in conflict with Jewish beliefs, then Moses is at one and the same time a reputable, even predominant and hallowed authority, who must be shown to under-pin the Jewish case against Jesus, and also an ousted authority in this sense who supplies a basis for the divine case of Jesus against the Jews.

This would seem to be the case in the notoriously difficult passage 7.19-24, where Moses is, as in 5.45-47, introduced abruptly into the argument, and is introduced after an assertion by Jesus that his teaching is true because he comes from God. It has led some commentators to suggest that 7.19-24 originally followed on after the end of ch. 5. Bultmann opens his comment as follows:

> 7.19-24, as it were, tackle the Jews on their own ground and show that Moses is their accuser, as was said in 5.45-47. Jesus' breaking of the Sabbath was the occasion of their attack on him, and in this they believe that they are acting out of regard for the law. But this is a delusion, for Moses, their acknowledged authority, speaks not for them but for Jesus. This idea emerges clearly enough, but the detail of the argument is complicated and obscure.[1]

What is the cause of the obscurity? It is primarily the statement in v. 19. The statement is generally taken as a question, 'Did not Moses give you the law?', followed by a statement 'And [but] no one from among you does the law'. This could imply that it is Jesus and Christians who fulfil the law and do it in contrast to the Jews; but this can hardly be what is meant when the evangelist has already presented Jesus as hostile to the institutions of Judaism and the attitudes of Jews towards him (the temple in ch. 2, rabbis in ch. 3). Or should v. 19a be taken not as a question but as a statement, 'It was not Moses who gave you the law' (cf. 6.32, and 1.17, 'the law was given through Moses'), implying that it was God who had given it, and that they were thus failing to keep the law of God? Whichever way the verse is taken, a difficulty remains of whether it refers to what precedes or what follows. Do the Jews fail to recognize the heavenly origin of Jesus' teaching and the fact that it does not come

1.   Bultmann, *John*, p. 276.

from himself but from the one who sent him because they do not keep
the law of Moses (or the law of God given through Moses)? Or is it the
desire to kill Jesus which constitutes the non-performance of the law? Or
does v. 19 simply effect a transition from the positive self-assertions in
vv. 14-18 to the charge that he has a demon? This charge is met by a
further reference to Moses and the law in respect of circumcision—
though it is correctly pointed out that circumcision did not originate
from Moses and the law but from patriarchal times. In one case it is
necessary to break the law, that of the sabbath, in performing the
demand of the law, that of circumcision. Bultmann concludes his
comment as follows:

> There is only one way in which we can attach any meaning to this con-
> fused speech, in which the Jews are accused on the one hand of breaking
> the Mosaic law (v. 19) and on the other, of breaking the Sabbath in
> compliance with the Mosaic law (v. 23). It must mean that the Jews break
> the Mosaic law, because, even though they act in compliance with the law
> of circumcision, they fail to ask what Moses' real intention was.[1]

Since the whole argument is set in motion by the statements of Jesus
about his heavenly origin and the heavenly source of his words, it would
seem that the evangelist looks upon and evaluates Moses and the law
from the point of view of a grace and truth already present. And the
chief value of Moses (and the law) for him is that he provides an authoritative figure and background for the true monotheism which has been
brought to light in the work and words of Jesus Christ, of whom the
most exalted things were to be said and believed. How exalted these
things were appears in the introduction of Moses in the discourse in
ch. 6.

The introduction of Moses at 6.32 is unlike the references in chs. 5
and 7, though not unlike that in ch. 3, in that there is nothing in it, or in
this chapter as a whole, to suggest that the law is being discussed. Hence
the kind of antithesis which seems to account for the form of statement
in 1.17 is absent. Bultmann, however, claims to find an antithesis in the
fact that 6.32 expresses Jesus' rejection of the deluded view that the
bread once given by Moses could be the true bread from heaven. The
emphatic position of τὸν ἀληθινόν in the sentence makes it an antithetical statement which clarifies the situation by implying that 'all
earthly goods are mere appearances in relation to the revelation'.[2] This

---

1. *John*, p. 278.
2. *John*, p. 228.

revelation is described more fully in v. 33 as the bread of God which (who) comes down out of heaven and gives life to the world. The precise force of the statement in 6.32 and the character of the contrast or antithesis involved are, however, very difficult to establish, since the proper translation is not certain. There would seem to be three possibilities.[1] 1. 'It was not Moses who gave you the bread from heaven [it was God who did so], but my Father [now] gives you the true [real] bread from heaven.' This reproduces the most likely sense of the negative with 'Moses'—οὐ Μωϋσῆς—but it is very harsh, and it is not clear why the statement that God gives the true bread from heaven should be preceded by an assertion that it was he and not Moses who gave the manna. 2. 'It was not bread from heaven that Moses gave you [but physical food]; but my Father gives you the true bread from heaven.' This is unlikely, as it would properly require the negative οὐ to govern the phrase 'bread from heaven' rather than 'Moses', and the required antithesis would be not 'the true bread from heaven' but simply 'bread from heaven'. 3. 'Did not Moses give you bread from heaven? [Yes.] But my Father gives you the true bread from heaven.' A further complication, which affects this last translation, but to some extent the others also, is the force of the expression 'bread from heaven' here. This could be no more than a conventional biblical phrase for the manna in Judaism, in which 'from heaven' does not have the full theological sense it has elsewhere in the Gospel when describing, for example, the origin of Jesus and the character of what he brings. For if it did have this theological sense (as perhaps in 2. above) then the required contrast would be between what was 'from heaven' (i.e. truly from God, as Jesus is) and what was not 'from heaven', and 'the true bread from heaven' would be a tautology, since in the Gospel 'the true' is 'that which is from heaven'. If, as in the translation 1. above, God is the one who has sent both the manna and the Son, then Bultmann's contrast between the manna which belongs to the terrestrial sphere and nourishes terrestrially and is due to perish, and the true bread which nourishes eternally because it is from heaven, does not suffice. The difference, which elsewhere in the Gospel is often established by reference to differences of origin (for instance, 'from flesh or from spirit', 'from earth or from heaven') has to be established on other grounds. And this is what is done in the further development of the discourse here.

1.   See Barrett, *St John*, p. 289.

Thus the 'Mosaic' verses 30-32 are followed by the first of the 'I am' sayings in the Gospel: 'I am the bread of life'. What 'of life' means in this self-acclamation made in terms of bread is expounded in predominantly eschatological terms, though in a way which loosens the fixed time-scale of normal eschatology. It means that the believer receives a final satisfaction of hunger and thirst (v. 35), and is given eternal life by the one whose function it is to confer this because he is the one from heaven who is to do the Father's will on earth, which gift will reach finality in resurrection at Jesus' hands at the last day (vv. 36-41). By the Johannine literary device of misunderstanding (v. 41) the transition is made to further and deeper teaching on the quality of Jesus and his gifts in relation to his and their heavenly origin. In a statement involving the Hellenistic concept of the soul being drawn (ἐλκύειν) to God, the resurrection of the believer at the hands of Jesus is said to be the work of God. This leads to a certain climax in vv. 45-46 with a reference to the promise of Isa. 54.13 of a time when all will be taught (directly) by God. Since already the future eternal life has been said to be a present possession of the believer, it is likely that this promise also is regarded as already in process of fulfilment, in that 'coming to Jesus', which is another way of describing belief in him, is said to be evidence of having been taught by God (v. 45b). There is a similarity here in thought with the final verse of the prologue, 1.18, which has not yet been examined; but if the verb ἐξηγήσατο there is to be rendered by something like 'declares divine truth', which Jesus as the only begotten God (Son) is able to do despite the fact that no one has ever seen God, this would seem to be picked up here in the assertion that the believer is taught by God himself through the presence in the world of the one who has indeed seen God (v. 46; note the similarity between οὗτος here and ἐκεῖνος in 1.18). The pattern of thought would, then, seem to be as follows: Moses was God's agent for the gift of manna for a specific people under specific trials, but how much better the 'bread from heaven' for all people which brings eternal life and a relationship to this same God of the Jews which is complete and unceasing.

The evangelist has not, however, finished with Moses and the episode of manna, but proceeds in vv. 47-51 to secure the claim to a better (true) food with results hitherto unimagined. With a reiteration of the self-affirmation 'I am the bread of life', the bread which descends from heaven is said, in contrast to manna, to secure the one who eats it from death. Eternal life can only be supported by eternal living bread that is quite different in quality and results from whatever may be meant by manna as 'bread from heaven', and from what 'the fathers' may have received through it. The chapter then reaches its further climax when this bread is fully personalized by being identified with Jesus as the Son of Man, who, as a human being among human beings (i.e. his flesh) divinizes human life by virtue of the divine life which he lives along with the living Father (v. 57), and his return by way of death to the Father (vv. 62-63).

What is here set forth in terms of bread and sustenance would thus seem to have been created by the new Christian theological dimension that has already been presented in the prologue. That it arose, as maintained by some commentators,[1] out of the Jewish theological expectation of a second Moses who would give a new manna in the messianic age is highly unlikely; for what is said here bears little or no resemblance to messianic expectations expressed in such terms. Rather do the references to Moses and manna serve as a foil. As in 1.17 the reference to Moses and the law would seem to be made en route to the main point, which is the grace and truth already in existence through Jesus Christ, so here the reference to Moses and the manna is thrown up as a foil to an exposition of Jesus as God present among human beings for their eternal sustenance. In both cases it may be that the point is being made that it is the same God of the Jews who is at work, and that Jewish monotheism is secured in what is believed and said about Jesus.

Something of the same analysis is arrived at, though in a different way, in what is the most extensive modern study of the subject, S. Pancaro's monumental work *The Law in the Fourth Gospel*.[2] Here the material is organized under two headings: (1) the law as a norm which the Jews vainly try to use against Jesus in order to judge and condemn him, and (2) the law as testifying against the Jews and in favour of Jesus. Pancaro, however, would seem to make too much of the material which is there to examine, and does not observe its comparatively secondary and intrusive character. It is doubtful whether he is correct in rejecting, in the end, Bultmann's judgment that the law plays a surprisingly minor role in the Fourth Gospel in favour of the judgment of G. Kittel that the relation of the law to Jesus is one of the basic questions in that gospel. Somewhat surprisingly Pancaro reserves any consideration of 1.17 to the very end of his sizeable volume on the ground that it would be

1. For example Glasson, *Moses*.
2. NovTSup, 42; Leiden: Brill, 1975.

unintelligible apart from recourse to what is said about Moses and the
law in the body of the Gospel. That is, he does not regard 1.17 as a
seminal statement in the prologue functioning as prologue. He holds the
view that in 1.1-18 the evangelist has taken over, and added to, an
already existing hymn, though he does state that the fact that the
evangelist chose to add 1.17 shows that the thought it contains was of
great interest to him. He is, however, on doubtful ground when he
regards this interest as already contained in the rest of the prologue in
that in the background to the concept of the Logos there is Jewish
speculation about the Torah.[1]

The Juxtaposition—Moses and Jesus Christ

In 1.17 the contrast with, or antithesis to, Moses and the law is expressed
as the coming into being of grace and truth by Jesus Christ. This is
curiously formed, since the name 'Jesus Christ' would seem in itself to
be devoid of theological significance, and to be simply the designation of
a historical personage. It may be, however, that the evangelist uses the
formal name to indicate that all that was said of the Logos-Son had
actuality and took shape in what was historically known as Christianity,
as Moses and the law represents Judaism. Or, to put it the other way
round, since it was nothing less than the divine grace and truth that was
to come into being by Jesus, the name 'Jesus Christ' could be a signal
for all that could be said about the Logos-Son. This would seem to be
the case in the only other instance of the name 'Jesus Christ' in the
Gospel. It is found at the opening of the prayer in ch. 17, which on any
showing contains, now on the lips of Jesus himself, a kind of
quintessence of his work and self. And it occurs in an even more formal
way as a reference by Jesus to himself in the third person within what
sounds like a semi-credal formula: 'This is eternal life, to know thee the
only true God, and Jesus Christ whom thou hast sent' (17.3). This would
seem to indicate that for the evangelist the term 'Jesus Christ' combines
a certain impersonality as of a historical movement with a strong
emphasis on the personal; and it is used both in 1.17 and 17.3 in the
context of an assertion of a monotheism which is inclusive of the divinity
of one who is a Son.

Chapter 17 stands in a special position in the Fourth Gospel as both

---

1. *The Law in the Fourth Gospel*, pp. 543-46.

looking backwards over and summarizing the rest of the Gospel, and
stretching forward and acting as a bridge to the passion. Moreover, it is
peculiar in the Gospel not only in some of its thought and language, but
also in being in the form of a single prayer of Jesus to the Father. In his
study of it E. Käsemann takes it as his starting point for an analysis of
the whole gospel, and says of it: 'This chapter is a summary of the
Johannine discourses, and in this respect is a counterpart to the
Prologue'.[1] Hence it is not as surprising as it might have been that the
only two references to 'Jesus Christ' should be in the prologue and here.

What then are the contents and accents of this prayer? In content it
consists of an interlocking of petition and intercession to the Father with
statements of what the Son has already effected and achieved, or what is
already brought into existence through the perfection of the work on
earth that the heavenly Father has given him to do. That is, the prayer is
unique to Jesus, and could not be assimilated to any prayer, for example,
of Moses to God on behalf of his people. For he prays not as Moses, nor
the messiah, nor the prophet, nor the apocalyptic Son of Man who must
be rejected, suffer and die and be vindicated in resurrection by God. He
prays as the Son who makes a return to heaven whence he has come,
and who has perfected the works which the Father has given him to do.
The prayer is also uttered out of an unbroken relationship between
himself and the Father which is called 'being one'.

There would thus seem to be in ch. 17, in the form of a single prayer
summarizing the whole work of Jesus on earth, and in terms of 'giving',
perfection and participation or unity, an exposition of what is meant by
'grace and truth came by Jesus Christ' in 1.17. And behind it is the
permanent living relationship between the monotheistic God of Judaism
and one who is the eternal Logos-Son. Herein is a major clue to the
evangelist's treatment of Moses in the body of the Gospel. For what the
passages in chs. 3, 5, 6 and 7 which introduce Moses have in common is
that he is introduced, with or without the law, from the standpoint of
Christian doctrine about Jesus Christ, and the connection between them
is always a positive one even when it goes by way of a negative. This
means that if the evangelist starts with Moses he must go on to the
positive aspects of Jesus Christ. But he must also go on beyond these
positive assertions, for the Johannine Jesus Christ has been provided
with the divine features of the Christian figure of the Logos-Son,

---

1.   *The Testament of Jesus* (London: SCM Press, 1968), p. 3.

and as such he cannot stand apart from God.

There must be reference to his unity with the Father, whether pre-existently as Son or terrestrially as the Logos-Son, Jesus Christ, or as the ever-present means of communication with believers beyond his return to God. Only thus can a reasoned presentation be made for the Christian claim to be the true worshippers of the God of the Jews without compromising monotheism. In the argument, Moses is pressed into service because his name stood for Judaism in all its varieties and to account for him was a vital part of the Christian case. It is difficult to express the theological difficulty which must have faced the first Christians when they had to justify the incompatibility of their faith with Judaism and at the same time preserve only those Jewish doctrines that were theologically viable in the context of Christian monotheism. It may be that there was a particular historical situation of conflict between the church and the synagogue behind the bitter opposition between the Jews and Jesus in the Fourth Gospel. But such opposition could be understood as inevitable when Christians had claimed to be the true worshippers of God without accommodating most of the antecedent Jewish beliefs and customs; and when Moses was held to point in their direction and away from Judaism.

In conclusion, then, it may be said that the analysis of the text above supports the view that the first eighteen verses of the Gospel were deliberately constructed as a literary whole. That is, they form a prologue designed to introduce, however briefly, items which were vital for readers to know in advance if they were to be prepared for the account of what is to happen when the heavenly and true comes into contact with what is passing and is in opposition to the divine will. In the course of this construction what has been said in vv. 1-16 comes, as it were, to a halt, while Moses and what he stands for are introduced somewhat abruptly and placed in an uneasy relationship with a new figure, Jesus Christ, who represents the historical identity of the Logos-Son of the prologue. This introduction is made by means of a curious antithetical, negative-positive statement, which has already appeared in earlier sections of the prologue, and is a feature of the evangelist's style, albeit in a variety of forms, in the Gospel also. It seems that it is a form of statement by which the evangelist gets from a number of negative situations or beliefs to the corresponding positive claims which the Johannine Jesus enunciates for himself. Nowhere is the negative presented and refuted more consistently in the Gospel than in the

Prologue and Gospel

confrontation of the Jews and Judaism with Jesus Christ as the Son of the Father, in which it is he and not Moses and the law who is the arbiter of what is or is not true. In v. 17 there is a highly compressed and abbreviated statement preparing the reader for this inevitable conflict, but also leaving room for a vital element of Judaism to be claimed by Christians as their own as true worshippers of the God of the Jews. What that ingredient is belongs to the study of v. 18.

This point may be illustrated by comparing the manner in which John and Moses are introduced into the prologue. In vv. 6-8 John is, apart from 'not that light', introduced wholly positively as the bearer of a divine commission to bear witness to the Logos, which is picked up in vv. 15-16. This determines both in shape and content the extent and content of the material devoted to John in the Gospel, which is precisely limited to the carrying out of that commission. And nothing further is developed with respect to him than that positive relationship of John to Jesus. Similarly the material devoted to Moses in the Gospel is already determined by the structure of vv. 17-18 in which he is introduced into the prologue, the distinctive feature of which is that it is antithetical, and thus prepares for the inevitable conflict in the body of the Gospel when-ever Moses is mentioned. Moreover, unlike the verses about John in the prologue, v. 17 has a dual function which is peculiarly its own. For it is not only part of the climax of the prologue in vv. 15-18, but also part of what might be called a bridging summary in vv. 17-18 between the prologue and the Gospel. This summary requires the contents of vv. 1-16 up to 'grace upon grace' to make sense of it—it is the truths about the Logos-Son in his relation to the world which are to be set forth in the body of the Gospel—but in its antithetical form it prepares in advance for what is inevitable when those truths take concrete form with the presence of the Logos-Son, Jesus Christ. For he is not simply in the world, but in the world which belongs to the God of the Jews and of Judaism, and which, for all that, is alienated from him. The conflict arising from this, and the possibility of true belief in the God of the Jews emerging through the presence of the Logos-Son, constitute a consider-able part of the Gospel narrative. The identity of the Logos-Son, Jesus Christ, who by his presence and words both authoritatively opposes Judaism and at the same time establishes its monotheistic belief, is the subject of v. 18.

Chapter 4

THE DIFFICULTIES FOR THE TRANSLATOR OF JOHN 1.18

On either view of the prologue—that it is an original hymn which has been redacted by the evangelist and supplemented by vv. 15-18, or that it is a carefully constructed literary and theological unity from the hand of the evangelist himself—v. 18 is of crucial importance. For if vv. 15-18 are a supplement, it has to be asked why the evangelist thought that the original hymn needed to be supplemented at all, particularly after what some have considered a climax in v. 14; and why it should be supplemented in this way so that vv. 15-18, and in particular v. 18, should not be an anti-climax. And if the whole of vv. 1-18 is the construction of the evangelist it has to be asked why he should have so constructed it that what he had in mind was not completed until the statement in v. 18 had been made.

The meaning of v. 18, its importance for the evangelist and how he envisaged that it should function as the final statement in the prologue, are the subjects of investigation in this chapter. This investigation is, however, by no means easy to carry out, since this single verse contains an unusual concentration of problems of different kinds, which cannot readily be grouped together. As a result almost every phrase in it is controversial. First, the negative proposition with which the verse begins, v. 18a, that no one has seen God at any time, is curious. It does not seem to be connected either with what has been stated in v. 17, or with what is to follow in vv. 19-28, or indeed with the rest of the verse, v. 18b. And, it raises acute questions of the background and origin of such a sweeping and absolute statement. Secondly, the beginning of the positive statement in v. 18b is a commentator's headache, since it contains one of the most complex textual critical problems in the New Testament, over which textual critics remain deeply divided. Thirdly, the translation of the all-important verb ἐξηγήσατο with which v. 18 and indeed the whole prologue comes to rest is highly debatable, though, it would appear, insufficiently debated in the commentaries.

These problems are, however, even more acute in virtue of the fact that v. 18 serves a dual purpose. In the first place it acts as a climax to the whole prologue. As a climax to a literary form known as prologue, and which, it has been argued previously, functions as a true prologue, v. 18 can be expected to contain something which, while it may return to certain earlier statements in the prologue, may also introduce something new that is crucial for the correct understanding of the rest of the Gospel. But it also acts within the prologue itself as the climax of John's testimony in vv. 15-18. The function of this testimony is to give divine sanction through the mouth of his witness to the evangelist's theological propositions in vv. 1-14; and while vv. 15-17 cover some aspects of this—witness to the light, the relation to Judaism, grace and truth—v. 18 introduces within John's testimony a universal aspect, indicating the whole relationship of human beings to God and of God to human beings as located in one who, as μονογενής, is uniquely related to God.

It is generally agreed that v. 17 and v. 18 are from the same hand. What is difficult to see is the connection between the apparently disconnected statements of these two verses. The sudden introduction of Moses and the law followed by the reference to the enigmatic gift of grace and truth, which is brought by one even more abruptly introduced as Jesus Christ, hardly exhibit an obvious sequence of thought. A possible stylistic connection with v. 17 has been suggested if v. 18 is taken as a continuation of the antithetical parallelism in v. 17, where the positive assertion in v. 17a is given something of an implied negative in v. 17b.[1] This is not very convincing, and there is much to be said for taking v. 18 as entirely self-contained, in which the purpose of the very strong exclusive negative in v. 18a is to introduce, and give force to, the very positive assertion of divine uniqueness in v. 18b. When v. 17 had introduced Moses and the law, perhaps in order that Jewish claims to be real worshippers of their God be shown in the Gospel to have been set aside for a universal human right to choose to be recipients of God's eternal gifts, and when v. 17 had ended by naming the exalted figure of the Logos and the μονογενής as 'Jesus Christ', the man who alone conveyed grace and truth, one could think that there was no more to be said. The evangelist thought otherwise, and that to end with 'Jesus

---

1. See Bultmann, *John*, p. 79 n. 3.

Christ' and his bringing of grace and truth would be to fail to establish the full content of the Gospel that is to follow.

The Significance and Meaning of the Negative Assertion 1.18a

In its form v. 18a is not un-Johannine. There are frequent examples in the Gospel of a positive assertion being made by way of a previous negative (cf. 5.22, 30), though generally the positive is asserted as an exception to the previous negative.[1] There are, however, two special points to be noted. The first is that the negative is peculiarly emphatic. This may be illustrated by comparison with the similar statement in 1 Jn 4.12. In both θεόν is emphasized as the first word in the sentence, but in v. 18 the negative is made stronger than in 1 Jn 4.12 by the position of πώποτε at the end: 'God no one (οὐδείς) has seen ever'. Although there is no explicit reference to a 'human being' in the Greek, it is possibly what the Greek intends to convey by οὐδείς; that is, there is already a contrast between human beings in their earthly capacities and the divine capacities of the one who is μονογενὴς θεός. Further, the emphatic πώποτε cannot but be a temporal reference to human capacities in time and history. This is underlined by the perfect tense of the verb, which is also in contrast to the eternal quality of the μονογενὴς θεός (υἱός) being (ὁ ὢν) in the bosom of the Father.[2]

The second point is that the negative assertion in v. 18a is made in terms of 'seeing God', but this is not taken up in a corresponding assertion in v. 18b that the μονογενὴς θεός (υἱός) has seen God. There is a partial parallel to this in 1 Jn 4.12, where the same statement is made as prelude, not now to something said about the capacities of the μονογενὴς θεός (υἱός), but to human capacities to love God. That is,

1.　That is, οὐδείς is followed by the verb and ἐὰν μή or εἰ μή, as in 3.13 and so on.

2.　πώποτε occurs only six times in the New Testament, all, apart from Lk. 19.30, in the Johannine writings, and, apart from 1 Jn 4.12, in the Gospel (5.37; 6.35; 8.33, and here, 1.18a). J.H. Moulton (*A Grammar of New Testament Greek* [Edinburgh: T. &. T. Clark, 1906], I, p. 144) refers to an important category of aoristic perfects 'in which we are liable to be misled by an unreal parallelism in English... There is in fact a perfect of broken as well as of unbroken continuity; in the graph... which leads from a past moment to the moment of speech, the perfect will tolerate the company of adjuncts that fasten attention on the initial point... or some indeterminate point in its course... or on several points in its course... To this category belong perfects with πώποτε, as in Jn 1.18; 5.37; 8.33.'

the denial that anyone has seen God is also not taken up directly in what follows.[1] This constitutes an acute problem in the exegesis of this verse, which has received curiously little attention from the commentators. Thus Brown, in his exegesis of v. 18, makes no comment at all on this opening statement of the verse. Other commentators observe that the position of 'official Judaism' or of later Jewish piety 'was that it lay beyond human capacity to see God'.[2] This, remarks Lindars, the evangelist takes for granted.[3] In that case his statement is bound to be a somewhat lame commonplace. Bultmann has an extended discussion. He denies that this statement of the direct inaccessibility of God is founded either on a 'concept of God as a being of a particular kind' (i.e. unknowable because irrational), or on 'the notion of the inadequacy of human faculties to perceive him'. He rightly understands the reference to the invisibility of God as preparing for 'the revelation of the revealer' referred to in v. 18b, though Bultmann makes it basically a statement about human self-understanding.[4]

There is, however, an exception which places v. 18a in a quite precise context. This is the exposition of Hooker, to which reference has already been made. Starting from the view of Käsemann that the whole of vv. 14-18 is the key to the understanding of the prologue, and from the suggestion of M.-E. Boismard that the Sinai theophany in Exodus 33 is the background to these verses, she suggests, though without argumentation, that 'the subject of vv. 14-18 in John 1 is glory'. This, together with 'grace and truth' (v. 14) interpreted as the equivalent of a Hebrew phrase in Exod. 33.6 'all point us at once to Exodus 33–34'.[5] The alleged antithesis between Christ and Moses in v. 17, and the supposed parallel in Exod. 33.6 to 'grace and truth', have already been examined in the previous chapter, and reasons given for their rejection. Here it may be questioned whether 'glory' is rightly taken as the subject governing vv. 14-18, and not simply as one important constituent

---

1.   Cf. the comment of J.L. Houlden, *A Commentary on the Johannine Epistles* (London: A. & C. Black, 1973), p. 114, that 1 Jn 4.12 'has the air of being misplaced'.

2.   Cf. Schnackenburg, *St John*, I, p. 278, and Lindars, *John*, p. 98.

3.   Cf. also in this sense Barrett, *St John*, p. 169.

4.   *John*, pp. 80-83.

5.   'The Johannine Prologue', p. 53. Cf. Brown, *John*, p. 36, 'Naturally it is the failure of Moses to have seen God that the author wishes to contrast with the intimate contact between the Son and the Father'.

among others. It could be argued that vv. 14-18 comprise a number of separate self-contained statements, each with its own subject, and that they are so arranged as to concentrate the reader on the final verse, and especially on its second half, which is the climax not only of vv. 14-18 but of the whole prologue. But v. 18b is a statement of a universal character and application, and this could suggest that v. 18a, which leads to it, rests on a wider background than simply the Jewish tradition represented in Exodus 33–34.

Vision was indeed a standing feature not only of many religions but also of philosophies. For, as W.L. Knox has observed, philosophy was to the contemporaries of the evangelist a 'theology' in the sense that it was not concerned with the rational discovery of truth, but with the vindication of religion; it was a 'means of explaining away the crudities of popular religion and substituting for them a theology which can claim the allegiance of the wise and learned'.[1] In his classic study K.E. Kirk, having set out Jewish anticipations, classifies pagan anticipations of 'seeing God' under the following heads: Plato, the mystics, the philosophers, Philo and the Hermetica.[2] In contrast to the Hebrew language with its primary emphasis on hearing and doing the will of God, Greek language and literature reflect the high value set on 'seeing', both as sensual and religious perception, and the debate about seeing. This goes back at least as far as Homer.[3] In Greek literature anthropomorphic language of poetry, myth and drama assumed that the gods could be seen by human eyes.[4] On the other hand some Greek philosophers maintained that God was invisible.[5] Thus the Platonic doctrine of ideas contrasted ὁρᾶν and νοεῖν. The world of reality, of ideas, is ἀόρατος, and being only accessible to the νοῦς is νοητός. Yet the Greeks could denote human beings' supreme and purely intellectual striving as a 'seeing'. This was usually expressed by θεᾶσθαι, θεωρεῖν, θεωρία, and for this the Hebrew language has no real parallel. τὸ θεῖον, the

1.   W.L. Knox, *Some Hellenistic Elements in Primitive Christianity* (Oxford: Oxford University Press, 1944), p. 37.
2.   *The Vision of God* (London: Longmans, Green & Co., 1931), pp. 23-54.
3.   See the article (to which I am much indebted here) by W. Michaelis, 'ὁράω', *TDNT*, V, pp. 315-82. In Homer, for example, there is fear and awe when a deity discloses himself (*Iliad* 1.199.24.170), but nowhere in Homer does one meet the idea that seeing a god should result in death.
4.   Michaelis, 'ὁράω', p. 320.
5.   Michaelis, 'ὁράω', p. 321.

divine, was for the Greeks not 'something to be believed or heard; it is something to be seen, something revealed only to contemplation'.[1] In Hellenistic gnosticism it was widely held that God was invisible, though gnostics appended the belief that God was visible to a person who was deified.

Particularly instructive in this respect could be Philo, as an example of a philosopher who is also a theologian in a very special sense, since his material is the sacred literature of the Jewish religion, and his purpose in life was to vindicate that religion in the eyes of intelligent Gentiles. Important for him in this respect is the possibility of human beings' 'seeing God'. This has been studied by H.A. Wolfson,[2] who points out that in those passages to which Philo pays particular attention—where Moses requests to see God or sees him in the Sinai theophany—the translation of the Hebrew text into the Greek of the LXX raised problems for the interpreter.[3] Thus the Hebrew text of Exod. 33.13 reads in translation 'make known thy ways, that I may know thee'. The LXX reads in translation 'reveal thyself to me that I may see thee with knowledge'. Philo, in quoting Exod. 33.13 from the LXX, paraphrases extensively:

> For I would not that Thou shouldest be manifested to me by means of heaven or earth or water or air or any created thing at all, nor would I find the reflection of thy being in aught else than in Thee who art God, for the reflections in created things are dissolved, but those in the Uncreate will continue abiding, and sure and eternal (*Leg. All.* 3.101).

Further, in Philo, as Wolfson shows, to have a vision of God is not confined to Moses, but is open to all Israel. Indeed, Israel can be defined by him in these terms. 'Israel', Philo says, 'means "seeing" God; those are "Israel" whose lot it is to see the best, that is, the truly Existing'. Philo can also contrast Moses with Bezaleel, since Moses alone has a

1. Michaelis, 'ὁράω', p. 322. Pindar, Frag. 137, quoted by Clement of Alexandria, *Strom.* 3.3.17, has 'Happy is he who has seen', which was referred to the importance of the visual in the 'mysteries'.

2. See *Philo: Foundations of Religious Philosophy in Judaism, Christianity and Islam* (2 vols.; Cambridge, MA: Harvard University Press, 1947), II, pp. 82-93, 138-49.

3. Contrast Hooker's assumption ('Johannine Prologue', pp. 54-55) that it was the Massoretic Text of Exod. 33.19 that the Evangelist and his readers had before them.

direct instruction from God, and so alone has a direct vision of God.[1]

Thus a possible background to at least Jn 1.17-18, if not to 1.14-18, could be the type of belief reflected in Philo, where seeing God is not confined to the exegesis of the single passage Exod. 33.13, but is a constituent of a whole religious outlook, which blends Jewish theology with Hellenistic religious philosophy, and is a universal claim for many true and righteous souls. And it is possible that the evangelist has this claim in mind when he opens the prologue with a Logos who is creator and closes it with the same Logos as the only one who is in the position to be the communicator to human beings of the vision of God. It is further to be borne in mind that in this connection, both in Judaism and Hellenistic religion and philosophy, 'seeing God' was closely related to some concept of salvation.[2] In a world which was increasingly obsessed by the search for freedom from death, from the fear of the gods or of fate, and from corruption, many saviours were followed, who among other things promised the vision of God or of immortality. When, then, the evangelist repudiates the belief that some people have seen God, the background to his thought could be far wider than the instance of Moses in Exodus. It could be that the universal 'salvation' explicit at 1.7 and implicit throughout the prologue demanded that 1.17 be developed in 1.18 in terms of an understanding of Jesus' divine work for all humankind and in relation to God.

The use and meaning of verbs of 'seeing' in the Fourth Gospel have received curiously little attention.[3] They do not appear to have an apocalyptic background, at least in the ordinary sense of that term, referring to visions, or to a series of events of ever-increasing chaos and destruction in a recognizable progression of epochs in a history of the last days leading to a final dissolution and judgment. Yet it must be recalled that early in the prologue a situation has been depicted of the created order being in darkness, which is the darkness of imperception. This imperception or failure to grasp the light which is continually shining consists

1. See *Congr.* 51 and *Leg. All.* 3.102.

2. See W.L. Knox, 'The "Divine Hero" Christology in the New Testament', *HTR* 41 (1948), pp. 229-49.

3. See J. Gaffney, 'Believing and Knowing in the Fourth Gospel', *Theological Studies* 26 (1965), pp. 215-41; B. Gärtner, 'The Pauline and Johannine Idea of "To Know God" against the Hellenistic Background', *NTS* 14 (1968), pp. 203-31, where 'seeing God' is dealt with only in passing; and D.A. Hagner, 'The Vision of God in Philo and John: A Comparative Study', *JETS* 14 (1971), pp. 81-93.

in a failure of the created order to know its creator. The true light lightens every human being, but all reject the true light; while those who have made a response to the Logos made flesh have received the right to intimate communication with none other than God. This human alienation from God is stated as real and universal darkness, the word σκοτία being used in a metaphysical sense. Yet the open gift of participating in the things belonging to God remains. This relationship to God involving participation in his gifts could constitute part, indeed a good deal, of what the evangelist means by 'seeing'.

The verb ὁρᾶν is used 30 times in the Gospel, of which three occurrences refer to seeing God (1.18; 6.46 bis), and two to seeing the risen Lord (20.18, 25). Of the remaining 25 instances a visionary experience, which may or may not be intellectual perception, is referred to in 1.50, 51; 3.11, 32; 5.37; 8.38. For the rest, some refer simply to ordinary sight, but in others where this might be so a further element may be involved. Thus ordinary external human perception of actions or events may be indicated when the Galileans have seen all the things that Jesus did in Jerusalem (4.45), when the multitudes saw the signs that Jesus did on the sick (6.2) and when the blind man is told that in seeing Jesus he sees the Son of Man (9.37). However, in these cases there would appear to be a further qualitative element in the seeing. For the Galileans receive Jesus, that is, become his disciples, on the basis of this seeing; the multitudes 'followed' Jesus, that is, became his disciples, because they saw the signs (i.e. they saw the works as significant). An even more religiously pregnant meaning is present when seeing is combined with, and is the fruit of, believing or knowing, as in 11.40, 'If you believe you shall see the glory of God', and in 14.7-9, where the disciples are told by Jesus that if they had known him they would have known the Father, and that from now on they do know him and have seen him. That is, a present knowledge of, and participation in, a heavenly truth is linked to seeing Jesus or his activities. Yet while seeing is essential to believing and knowing, it does not of itself bring about the desired result, and can issue in the opposite, that is, the sin of failure to respond to, and therefore hatred of, not only Jesus but also the Father (15.24). A greater sin than rejection of the works of the Father cannot be envisaged. At 16.16-20 a further question is raised, since θεωρεῖν is used alongside ὁρᾶν in the repeated statement, 'A little while and you no longer behold (θεωρεῖν) me; and again a little while and ye shall see (ὁρᾶν) me'. Here the seeing (ὁρᾶν), which will be the disciples' full sight of the Lord as glorified, differs from the beholding (θεωρεῖν) of him in grief during the historical tragedy of the narrative of the passion. And the ultimate quality of this seeing, which is ultimate in that the Lord will see them as well as they see him, is here described as a rejoicing in their hearts which cannot be removed (16.22). As a result of this seeing and rejoicing they are assured that they will no longer need to question. That is, their knowledge will be perfected, since they will have been taught by God (16.23-33; cf. 6.44-45).

It is not, however, the case that there is an absolute distinction of this kind between θεωρεῖν and ὁρᾶν. θεωρεῖν is used 22 times. It is never used of seeing God or the Lord. Once it is used metaphysically of not seeing death, that is, of eternal life, while in apparent contradiction of 16.16-20 it is used in 14.19 of a beholding of the glorified Lord by the disciples, which, in distinction from the 'not beholding' of him by the world because of his removal by death, issues in participation in the life which is nothing less than the transmitted divine life from the Father through Jesus. Indeed, θεωρεῖν would seem to be used in the same way as ὁρᾶν: people see Jesus' works as signs (2.23; 6.2), and his unique heavenly person as Son of Man (6.62). In some cases it is linked with salvation in a similar way—for example, everyone who beholds the Son and believes in him has eternal life (6.40). In 12.44-45 the belief which results from beholding Jesus goes beyond to belief in the one who has sent him. What is true of θεωρεῖν and ὁρᾶν is the case with other verbs also that are used of seeing. The context on the whole decides the meaning, though even then it is not always clear how far intellectual knowledge or spiritual perception are included in the concept of 'vision'.

With respect to the discussion of v. 18 it could, however, be important to preserve a certain distinction and order. For while, as has already been observed, there has been comparatively little discussion of the concept of 'seeing' in the Gospel, there has been no lack of discussion of the concept of 'knowing' there, and the former has tended to be subsumed in the latter. But this could be contrary to the evangelist's order of thought if the prologue is intended to function as a prologue. For there, while he uses words denoting comprehension, and that with soteriological connotations (καταλαμβάνειν, v. 5; μαρτυρεῖν and πιστεύειν, v. 7; φαίνειν, v. 9; θεᾶσθαι, v. 14), he does not introduce into it the concept of 'knowing' (except negatively in 1.10), and he does have at its climax the concept of 'seeing', though also negatively.

Thus it is somewhat surprising to find that Dodd, in his study of the

leading ideas of the Gospel, refers to 1.18a, 'No one has seen God', only
by way of comment on 17.3, and then almost as an aside at the end of
an extensive chapter on the knowledge of God. He explains the statement in 17.3 on the basis that Jesus is the mediating Logos figure, who
through his relation to God as Son is 'knower and known', and who
therefore stands in place of God reconstituting the relation of human
beings to him. 'Hence it is that the definition of ζωὴ αἰώνιος adds
"Jesus Christ" to the "only real God" as the object of knowledge'
(17.3). It is because of this, Dodd maintains, that the maxim in 1.18a
holds good, because only of such a one can direct vision of God be
predicated (6.46). This knowledge is then said to be vision, which Jesus
mediates (14.9; 12.45). Of 1.14 Dodd also says that the knowledge of
God there is vision also, for human beings have recognized Jesus' glory.
This vision is held to be close to that of the Hellenistic mystic, and the
mediating principle here similar to that of the Philonic Logos and the
Nous of the Hermetists.[1]

But in the Fourth Gospel this mediation is through the Logos made
flesh, identified in the prologue as Jesus Christ, and this could make a
'vision of God' strictly without exact parallel, in which the vision of God
is inclusive of the knowledge of God. The emphatic 'no one' of v. 18a,
with its negation of all human aims and claims for salvation, could prepare for the positive assertion that Jesus has seen God (6.46), since God
was his Father, and for the communication to believing disciples of precisely this vision of the Father through 'seeing' Jesus (14.9), which
vision is closely related to, but is not derived from, knowledge of the
Father (14.7). Likewise to the Jews who are without belief Jesus says
that, despite the witness to him of the Father who has sent him, they
'have neither heard his voice nor seen his form'.

What then is the force of the double negative in v. 18a, 'no one has
seen God' reinforced by the emphatic πώποτε, 'not ever'? Surprisingly
there are only six occurrences of πώποτε in the New Testament, and all
of these have the word in conjunction with a negative.[2] Apart from
Lk. 19.30 all are in the Johannine writings: Jn 1.18; 5.37; 6.35; 8.33, and
1 Jn 4.12 (this last, superficially similar to Jn 1.18, in fact reflects a
development of themes in the Gospel, and uses language not entirely
suited to the evangelist). In 6.35 and 8.33 πώποτε occupies, as in 1.18,
an emphatic position at the end of the clause, indicating a stylistic trait of

1. *Interpretation*, pp. 166-68.
2. Moulton, *Grammar*, I, p. 144.

the evangelist. It is perhaps not a coincidence that all these are passages in which soteriological aims or claims are being dealt with. In 5.37, in the face of the Jewish claim to have eternal life through search of the Scriptures, it is asserted that because they do not perceive the testimony of the Father to Jesus the Jews have neither heard his voice nor seen his form, not ever. At 8.33 it is the Jews who base their salvation (freedom) on the negative assertion that as descendants of Abraham they have not been enslaved to anyone, not ever. This makes way for the irony that they remain slaves to the sin of rejecting the Son of God who offers the true freedom, and so of rejecting God himself. In 6.35 it is said that belief in Jesus is of such a kind that it banishes hunger and thirst for ever. Thus the emphatic use of πώποτε in 1.18 may be doing more than affirming that in history prior to the coming of the Logos, Jesus Christ, no one had in fact seen God. If that were all that were intended it would have been sufficient to say, 'No one has seen God as yet (οὐκέτι) but now the man Jesus Christ is the one who has seen him'. But this is not what the evangelist writes, though 6.46 shows that it was possible for him to write it. In fact he drops the historical name Jesus Christ introduced in v. 17, and proceeds by returning to the predicate μονογενής previously introduced in 1.14 of the Logos made flesh, the true heavenly light. Hence the contrast is not between what human beings have hitherto been unable to do and what Jesus Christ is to do, but between the incapacity of human beings in the created order ever to see God, and the unique salvation and the active presence of God himself to the created order in the person of the μονογενής, who is alone qualified to make available to humankind the eternal gifts of God from God. Whereas previous soteriological aspirations were false, they are now true, since creation has been sanctified by the entry of the creator into his creation.

The Textual Problem in 1.18b

The second major problem in 1.18 is that of the correct text in v. 18b. The variant readings have often been discussed since F.J.A. Hort's magisterial study.[1] The readings are (1) ὁ μονογενὴς υἱός; (2) μονογενὴς

---

1.   *Two Dissertations* (London: Macmillan, 1876). More recently B.A. Mastin's 'A Neglected Feature of the Christology of the Fourth Gospel', *NTS* 22 (1975), pp. 32-51, and P.A. McReynolds, 'John 1.18 in Textual Variation and Translation', in E.J. Epp and C.D. Fee (eds.), *New Testament Textual Criticism: Its Significance*

θεός (ὁ μονογενὴς θεός); and (3) ὁ μονογενής.

The first of these, the 'received' text, was not disputed until the discovery in the nineteenth century of three important Greek uncials which read (2). Indeed Hort could say that his dissertation, which was written after an examination of E. Abbot's argument for the Western text, provided a rare opportunity for a dispassionate study, precisely because the text had not been subjected to centuries of repeated controversial discussion.

(1), ὁ μονογενὴς υἱός, is read by the Byzantine tradition, the chief exemplars of which are A and C (here the third hand), and by all cursives except 33. It was further read by the Western tradition—the old Latin, syr. c h pal—and by what came to be called the Caesarean tradition, fam 1, fam 13. There is also a good deal of evidence for this reading in the Fathers, though patristic evidence is difficult to assess here, since it is seldom clear whether a Father is explicitly referring to, or quoting, Jn 1.18.[1]

(2), μονογενὴς θεός (I shall discuss the significance of the anarthrous expression later), is read by Siniaticus (first hand), B C (first hand) and L. So far as MSS evidence is concerned this reading was further strengthened by the discovery of p66 and p75 (which read ὁ μονογενὴς θεός). It is also read by the Peshitta, the Harclean margin, the Coptic boh., the Ethiopic and the Arabic Diatessaron. The evidence of the Fathers is subject to the same difficulties of assessment as in (1), though it was certainly read by some Gnostics—by Valentinians according to Irenaeus, and by Theodotus according to Clement. Of interest here is the Peshitta, since this generally supports the Western and Byzantine traditions, rather than the Alexandrian. P. Lagrange maintained that it was impossible to justify the definite article in this reading, for 'writing ὁ θεός after θεόν would seem to differentiate the second god from the first'.[2]

(3), ὁ μονογενής, would normally be attractive as the shortest reading; but it has no Greek MS support. Of the ten Fathers who appear to support it only five are consistent.[3] Its originality was maintained by Lagrange and Bousset, but Hort came to reject the view that this

---

for Exegesis (Oxford: Clarendon Press, 1981), pp. 105-18.

1.   McReynolds, 'John 1.18', p. 113.

2.   *Evangile selon Saint Jean*, p. 28.

3.   Mastin, 'Neglected Feature', p. 38. See also McReynolds, 'John 1.18', pp. 107-14.

originality could be supposed if an early accidental insertion of ὅς was postulated between μονογενής and ὁ, which was then altered to θε, a view reasserted recently by J.N. Sanders.[1]

It might have been expected that the weight of the textual evidence for (2)—its presence in p66 (c. 200 CE) tends to undermine the argument against it that it was a product of the Christology of Alexandria in the third and fourth centuries—would have led scholars to abandon the received text, the more so if it is held with Schnackenburg that there is no essential difference of meaning whichever reading is adopted.[2] Nevertheless, without denying the weight of the evidence, some scholars for a variety of reasons prefer (1). It is to be noted that these reasons generally include some judgment on Johannine theology and usage, and on what the evangelist intends by his prologue. The translators of the New English Bible, while acknowledging the strong advocacy of Hort, yet reject (2) on the ground that it does not yield a tolerable sense.[3] Barrett observes that μονογενὴς θεός has better MS support; 'Yet υἱός seems to be required by the following clause, and is in conformity with Johannine usage (John 3.16, 18; I John 4.9; cf. John 1.14)'.[4] Hoskyns considered that the evidence of the MSS offered 'no certain conclusion as to which of the two better readings is original, nor does the Johannine material decide the issue, because "one who is God only begotten" may be taken as complementary to 1.1, and "the only begotten Son" as complementary to 3.16, 18'. His view was that the immediate context settled the issue in that 'who is in the bosom of the Father' required 'only begotten Son'.[5] Schnackenburg writes: 'If μονογενὴς θεός is taken as original...θεός is probably in apposition to μονογενής; "the only begotten one who is divine"; but μονογενὴς υἱός seems preferable'.[6] Lightfoot prefers υἱός on the grounds of internal consistency, translating as 'the only begotten Son'.[7]

1. J.N. Sanders and B.A. Mastin, *A Commentary on the Gospel according to St John* (London: A. & C. Black, 1968), p. 85 n. 1.

2. *St John*, I, p. 279.

3. R.V.G. Tasker, *The Greek New Testament* (Oxford: Oxford University Press; Cambridge: Cambridge University Press, 1964), pp. 424-25. Interestingly NEB in a footnote paraphrases the reading μονογενὴς θεός with 'but the only one, himself God, the nearest to the Father's heart, has made him known'.

4. *St John*, p. 169.

5. *Fourth Gospel*, pp. 153-54.

6. *St John*, I, p. 280.

7. *St John's Gospel*, p. 90.

The position of Bultmann is more complex. In spite of an acknowledgment of the weight of the textual evidence he opts for the reading μονογενὴς υἱός. He does so on the internal consideration that all references in the Gospel to μονογενής, apart from 1.14, are associated with υἱός, and this establishes the evangelist's own usage. But although he connects 1.18b with 1.14—'18.b describes the Revealer as the μονογενὴς υἱός with the title taken from the confession in v. 14'—he makes a distinction between them. The distinction is that in 1.14 μονογενής is used as a title. It is not there conjoined with υἱός as a predicate. The qualification παρὰ πατρός does not denote procession, that is, 'from beside a Father', but is a simple genitive avoiding the ambiguous construction μονογενοῦς πατρός. The anarthrous form of πατρός is here a type of assimilation to the anarthrous μονογενοῦς and is a predicative nominative. The sense is something like 'as befits a Revealer of a Father, a Father's Revealer'. This sense is due to the fact that in 1.14 the evangelist is reproducing his source. The difference consists in the fact that whereas in 1.14 μονογενής is the characterization of the figure who is being referred to, in 1.18 it is 'the attribute and υἱός the actual characterisation'.[1] 'In this way the μονογενής receives the sense commonly found in the LXX of an ascription of value, in which sense it is also clearly used in 3.16, 18; I John 4.9.'[2] If, however, Bultmann's 'source' is denied, and if, as has been maintained, the whole prologue is a deliberate construction of the evangelist, then the singular 'titular' use of μονογενής that he detects in 1.14 is to be ascribed to the evangelist himself. In this case, and if μονογενής in 1.14 is to be rendered by some such phrase as 'the unique one', this itself could supply a reason for choosing the reading μονογενὴς θεός in 1.18. It may be suggested that there is a progression of thought in the prologue with respect to μονογενής. It begins with the bare anarthrous titular sense in 1.14, and is developed in 1.18 with μονογενὴς θεός, which prepares not only for the theme of the unique, only-begotten Son in the Gospel, but also for the work and claims of Jesus who is a divine one, his sonship being one aspect amongst others. He is the concretion of the divine being and divine functions, and as the Logos become flesh is the actualization of God in relation to creation and to humankind.

There have been and still are scholars who accept μονογενὴς θεός as the original reading, and certainly there is more likelihood of scribes

1.   Bultmann, *John,* pp. 81-82.
2.   *John,* p. 82.

changing μονογενὴς θεός to μονογενὴς υἱός than vice versa. Chief of these is F.J.A. Hort. After a full examination of E. Abbot's argument for the received reading Hort decided that 'on grounds of documentary evidence and probabilities of transcription alike...μονογενὴς θεός was the original form'.[1] This reading he considered had intrinsic fitness, was a unique phrase in the New Testament, was part of a unique prologue, and seemed to belong to a single definite step in that prologue.[2] He further maintained that the anarthrous form gave a predicative force which had to be retained in English translation. For this he suggested some such clause as 'one who is...', though, after discussing the difficulties involved in getting an adequate English rendering, he curiously offers in the end 'an only-begotten who is God, even he is...'[3] Reviewing Hort's dissertation Harnack asserted of its conclusion that the reading μονογενὴς θεός 'had been established beyond contradiction'.[4] B.F. Westcott also argued for Hort's view, offering as a translation 'one who is God only begotten, who is...'[5] Lindars, while commenting on 'the only Son' as the text, remarks on the merit of μονογενὴς θεός as the more difficult reading, which can be accepted if 'God' is taken to be in apposition to 'only-begotten one', with the meaning 'who is divine in origin'.[6]

This last observation raises the question of the precise nuance of the word μονογενής. As stated previously with respect to 1.17, the divine origin of Jesus, though an important concept, is not where the stress lies in the prologue. Even in the Gospel itself the heavenly origin of Jesus is primarily the foil in his confrontation with the Jews. If prologue and gospel were written not solely for Jewish consumption and with negative rebuttal of Jewish claims in mind, but in order to make positive and universal assertions of ultimate issues for humankind, how is μονογενής related to this? Brown translates 'God the only Son', insisting that the evangelist does not use the term 'begotten' of Jesus. μονογενής 'describes a quality of Jesus, his uniqueness, not his procession', and he

1. *Two Dissertations*, p. 10.
2. *Two Dissertations*, p. 16.
3. *Two Dissertations*, p. 19.
4. Cited in Westcott, *Commentary*, I, p. 68.
5. *The Gospel according to St John* (2 vols.; London: John Murray, 1908), I, pp. 66-68.
6. *Gospel of John*, pp. 98-99.

translates consistently by 'only Son'.[1] McReynolds argues that neither the argument from etymology, nor that from internal consistency, nor indeed the weight of the textual evidence, have settled the issues. Reviewing English renderings he finds a continuing ambivalence between 'God' and 'Son', and he lists several recent translations which have chosen to conflate 'only-begotten God' and 'only-begotten Son', with an unwillingness to declare a preference in respect either of the documentary evidence or of internal consistency.[2]

What possible meanings of the word would have been known to Hellenistic readers?[3] On a Jewish background *yaḥidh* in the sense of 'only son' is primarily translated in the LXX by ἀγαπητός, but it may be rendered otherwise, for example by μονογενής. This Bultmann takes as the clue to the meaning in 1.18, 3.16 and 3.18, and this determines his preference for the reading μονογενὴς υἱός. Apart from a Jewish back-gound there are three renderings of μονογενής which could be relevant: (1) descending from a single begetter without the aid of a second parent; (2) 'only-begotten', where the emphasis, though this is at a later date than the evangelist, is upon 'begetting'; and (3) unique of its kind.

1. There is no internal reason why 1.14 and 1.18 should not belong in this category, though it would be questionable whether, after the mention of mother and brothers in 2.12, this could apply in 3.16, 18. J. Rendel Harris maintained that the use of μονογενής in this sense, as of Athena, lay behind its use of the Logos in the prologue.[4] In his study of the prologue he regarded as lying behind the Logos there the figure of Sophia, which could itself have rested upon Jesus' proclamation of himself as the Wisdom of God.[5] By an appeal to Paul, and on the basis of his hypothesis of a Book of Testimonies of apostolic authority and antedating both the Pauline epistles and the Fourth Gospel, he sees the belief that Jesus was Sophia as a very early Christology.[6] Clearly the

1. *John*, p. 13, 'Although *genos* is distantly related to *gennān*, "to beget", there is little justification for the translation of *monogenēs* as "only begotten"'. Dodd, *Interpretation*, p. 305 n. 1, holds that μονογενής (from μονός and γένος) does not mean (at this period at any rate) 'only-begotten' (μονογέννητος), but 'alone of his kind', 'unique'.
2. 'John 1.18', p. 117.
3. See Bultmann, *John*, p. 71 n. 2.
4. 'Athena, Sophia and Logos', *BJRL* 7.1 (1922), pp. 56-72.
5. J.R. Harris, *The Origin of the Prologue to St John's Gospel* (Cambridge: Cambridge University Press, 1917), pp. 57-65.
6. *Origin of the Prologue*, p. 62.

gender of the one begotten of a single parent was not restricted, so that at 1.14, where the masculine Logos (who is also the neuter true Light) is said to become human, neither sonship nor daughtership is of significance. However, once the Logos become flesh has been named in 1.17 as Jesus Christ, there can be no other kinship to the one parent designated as 'Father' (1.14, 18) than that of 'Son'. But even sonship may be included in a wider concept, as will be argued later.

2. With regard to 'only-begotten', whether applied to 'Son' or 'God', the etymological argument against it has been noted. In English emphasis is placed on the verb 'to beget', but this is not the case with the Greek. Furthermore, at 1.14 it would be singularly inappropriate, since the result of receiving the Logos who came to his own is the right to become a child of God, 'to be begotten of God' (1.13). It can hardly be the case that a description of believers, that they are begotten of God, should immediately be applied to the unique figure, the Logos become flesh, in and through whom they become believers. This argument would be partly invalidated if the variant reading in 1.13 were accepted which has the verb in the singular, 'who was born', referring to the Logos (so b Iren. lat [Tert.], singular verb with plural 'who' syr cur). However, despite the advocacy of this reading as antedating in the Latin the Greek text of p66 and p75, the earliest examplars of the reading in B and Siniaticus, it is to be rejected, and the plural form of the verb, referring to believers, to be accepted.[1]

3. This rendering, 'a unique one', could be said to be the best suited, precisely because it draws attention to the remarkable statements already made in the prologue about the Logos, that he is creator (1.3-4), and that he radiates the divine glory. With respect to the first, creation, 'only-begotten (Son)' could correspond to the Pauline 'first born of all creation' who is also the agent of creation (Col. 1.15-16), but it would not represent the relation of the Logos to God which is from eternity (1.1-2). And it would blur the distinction between this relation of the Logos to God and the relation to him of believers, who are admitted to intimacy with God only by way of the Logos. With respect to the second, that human beings have seen the 'glory' of the Logos become flesh, which 'glory' is that of one in a special relation to a Father, it is to

1.   Schnackenburg (*St John*, I, pp. 263-64) discusses variant 1.13. L. Sabourin, ' "Who ... was begotten of God", Jn. 1. 13', *BTB* 6 (1976), pp. 86-90, observes that the singular form is to be found in the Jerusalem Bible, perhaps in an attempt to accomodate the virgin birth, which otherwise does not feature in the Fourth Gospel.

be noted that 'glory', if it is being used in a strict theological sense, and not in the more general sense of 'honour', is applicable only to God. The identity of the glory of the Logos become flesh with the glory of God himself would be better conveyed by μονογενής in the sense of 'unique one' than in the sense of 'only-begotten'. This could apply equally to at 1.18, and the more so if μονογενὴς θεός is taken as the original reading. Alternatively, if 'only-begotten' is preferred as the rendering in 1.14, the sonship implicit in the term will have been made explicit for the first time after the naming of the Logos as Jesus Christ by the reading in 1.18 'only-begotten Son', thus preparing for 3.16, 18.

If μονογενὴς θεός is taken as the correct reading in 1.18 the most adequate rendering would seem to be 'a unique one, who is God'. In this creative expression the evangelist would seem to be summing up what has been said in vv. 1-17 in a seminal statement, which not only provided a climax to the whole prologue and to John's testimony in it, but also supplied the reader with a principal clue to what was to be said concerning Jesus Christ, the Logos-Son figure, in the body of the Gospel. It could be objected that, apart from later trinitarian theology, the expression is barely intelligible, and the question is raised both here and at 1.1 why the evangelist did not use the adjective θεῖος, 'divine': 'a unique one who is divine'. The adjective was available as a term for human beings who were deemed worthy of honour (δόξα), and whom other human beings thought fit to deify. But it could be argued that this is precisely what the evangelist had to avoid. For earthly saviours in the ancient world, the deified people of repute and honour, the world of change and decay was the principal threat, and their aim was to be rid of the limitations of earthly life and to aspire to the eternal world of perfection and ideas. The Logos of the prologue, however, is from eternity and before the creation of the world; he is divine and belongs to the heavenly sphere. His function is to be the source of creation itself, to be the source of true life and light to humankind, to be the means of establishing communication between God and the world and to divinize life on earth for those who believe and respond.

The question then to be examined is whether μονογενὴς θεός understood in this sense provides a necessary introduction for what is an essential element in the Gospel. The attractiveness of the reading μονογενὴς υἱός in 1.18 is not only that it is taken up in 3.16, 18, but that it imparts a certain unity and uniformity to a gospel which is so consistently framed around the relationship between the Father and the

Son. Nevertheless this theme, important as it may be, is also limited in its coverage of the words and deeds of Jesus as Son. It is primarily associated with debates about Jesus' sonship, with affirmations that he has been sent from God, and with claims to be intimately attached to the Father so as to know, see and hear him constantly. The reading μονογενὴς θεός would not only round off the prologue itself by returning to the opening statement that the Logos is θεός. It would be a wider designation, inclusive not only of what is said under the heading of Father and Son, but also preparing the reader for those words and actions of Jesus which are the sole prerogative of the God of the Jews: judging, or rather effecting on earth the self-judgment of human beings who come face to face with God; his self-acclamations ('I am') as the embodiment and dispenser of heavenly gifts; his capacity to lay down his life of his own volition and to raise it again; to be alongside God as the sender of the Spirit; and his status as the heavenly Son of Man who descends before ascending, and who brings about the penetration of earthly life with the quality of 'eternal life'. There will be a fuller presentation of this material in the next chapter.

The Problem of Translation of the Verb in 1.18b

The final problem in 1.18 is the meaning of the verb with which it, and indeed the whole prologue, comes to rest as the description of what the μονογενὴς θεός (introduced emphatically as ἐκεῖνος, 'that one') has done. This is a complex problem which seems to have received curiously little discussion. The verb ἐξηγεῖσθαι is nowhere else used by the evangelist; it is in the aorist and it is apparently intransitive, though the majority of translators almost automatically provide an accusative pronoun 'him' (God) as an object, or occasionally the objective genitive 'of God'. There are five other instances of the verb in the New Testament, all in the Lukan writings (Lk. 24.35; Acts 10.8; 15.12, 14; 21.19). In all these an accusative object is supplied, and the contexts are concerned with rehearsing facts, with narrative or declaration. The situation in Jn 1.18 is otherwise; and since this is the sole occurrence the meaning is to be sought not only in antecedent usage, but also in the unique context in which the evangelist has chosen to employ it.

In BAG three meanings are given for the verb: (1) to lead, (2) to explain, interpret, tell, report, and (3) as a 'technical term for the activity of priests and soothsayers, who impart information or reveal divine secrets; also used with respect to divine beings themselves'.

'To lead', 'to take the lead', 'to have the primacy' is the sense in
Homer, and is generally thought not to apply here, but it does take
seriously the intransitive use in 1.18, and has been espoused by two
scholars. The first is J. Rendel Harris, who argued for it on the basis of a
similarity of ideas between the Wisdom Christology of Paul, especially
Col. 1.18 where Christ is πρωτότοκος and is said 'himself to have the
pre-eminence' (πρωτεύων), and a supposed Wisdom background of the
prologue, where ἡγησάμηω and ἐξηγήσατο are an equivalent.
Linguistically he appealed to Ecclus 24.6, where the verb ἡγεῖσθαι is
used intransitively, and which he translates 'in...all the earth, and in
every people and in every race I have the primacy'. But ἡγησάμην is
read only by the seventh-century corrector of Codex Siniaticus, the
Syriac and Old Latin; all other texts have ἐκτησάμην, 'I have obtained
possession'. Nor is the case strengthened by the intransitive use of the
reduplicated verb ἐκδιηγεῖσθαι in Ecclus 43.21 (the same verb is used
transitively in Ecclus 42.15), which may be rendered 'Who has seen him
[God] that he may relate in full'.[1] Thus this is not strong evidence for
the interpretation of ἐξηγήσατο in Jn 1.18, especially if, as I have previously maintained, the Wisdom background of the prologue is to be
called in question. The second scholar to support this meaning is
M.-E. Boismard.[2] To this end, however, he has to emend the text drasti-
cally by inserting εἰ μὴ ὁ before μονογενής and omitting ὁ ὢν before
εἰς τὸν κόλπον, thus making the verse read, 'No one has seen God
except the only begotten; to the bosom of the Father he has led the
way'. But apart from the weakness of the textual support for this, for
such an interpretation the present tense ('he leads the way') rather than
the aorist would be more natural.

The second group of meanings, which expresses the act of declaring
something, rehearsing the facts or narrating, is found in the major
English versions: 'he hath declared him' (AV), 'he has made him known'
(RSV, NEB). Among the commentators Westcott, Hoskyns and Lightfoot
render 'he has declared him', though Westcott found the lack of a direct
object remarkable, and gave as a literal rendering 'he made declaration'.[3]
Hoskyns observed that the use of the aorist and not the perfect tense

1. Harris, *Origin of the Prologue*, pp. 18, 34-41.
2. M.-E. Boismard, *Le Prologue de Saint Jean* (LD, 11; Paris: Cerf, 1953),
pp. 88-95.
3. *St John*, I, p. 29.

indicated that Jesus did once and for all 'declare' the Father.[1] Lightfoot made no critical comment.[2] More recently Lindars has translated 'he made him known',[3] and Brown 'who has revealed him'.[4] Bultmann, after drawing attention to the intransitive meaning 'to give divine knowledge (secrets)', supplies an objective genitive and translates 'he has brought knowledge of God'.[5] Schnackenburg renders by 'he has brought good tidings'.[6] The following objections may be raised against these renderings. First, they are all forced to supply a direct object to the verb, which apparently the evangelist did not find necesary to convey what he wanted to say. Secondly, it may be asked whether 'to declare' in this context makes sense. Normally one declares a thing, or a statement, not a person, and Westcott in effect acknowledged this by giving the verb a substantival sense with 'he made declaration', though it may be questioned whether this has meaning. This translation would thus be a very weak equivalent for the emphatic statement with which the prologue ends, ἐκεῖνος ἐξηγήσατο. A special treatment of the meaning 'to declare' is to be found in J.P. Louw's article 'Narrator of the Father'.[7] In this article, which is primarily devoted to establishing 'Narrator of the Father' as a christological title for Jesus, he insists that the meaning to be given to ἐξηγεῖσθαι is that which 'conveys verbal action, communicating information, in a context which usually requires a detailed account', such as is to be found in the instances in Luke–Acts. He contends that 'in John 1.18 the obvious meaning envisaged by ἐξηγήσατο is that of narration'.[8] But apart from the objection that this explanation by appeal to the Lukan parallels also involves supplying the verb with an object, it may be questioned whether 'narrate' makes any more sense than 'declare'. Normally one narrates a story or rehearses facts concerning a thing, an event or a proposition; one does not narrate a person, God or the Father.

The English word most commonly used to translate the verb when taken to belong to the third group of meanings is 'reveal'. In the end

1. *Fourth Gospel*, p. 153.
2. *St John's Gospel*, p. 78.
3. *Gospel of John*, p. 99.
4. *John*, p. 4.
5. *John*, p. 83 and n. 3.
6. *St John*, I, p. 279.
7. *Neot* 2 (1968), pp. 32-40.
8. 'Narrator of the Father', p. 35.

Bultmann comes to rest entirely on this. Having said of the preceding phrase 'in the bosom of the Father' that it expresses the unity of the Father and the Son, and that it is central to the evangelist's concept of revelation, he proceeds to claim that

> His function of Revealer is denoted by ἐξηγεῖσθαι... used in a technical sense for the interpretation of the will of the gods by professional diviners, priests and soothsayers, but which can be also used of God himself when he makes known his will. This, then, is the final characterisation of the Revealer that he 'has brought knowledge of God'.[1]

In other words the semantic value of the word is determined largely by an already established 'Revealer Christology', which is in turn connected with the hypothesis of a 'Revelation Source' as used by the evangelist. Similarly Schnackenburg argues for a 'Revealer Christology', though he pays careful attention to the variation in meaning dictated by the cultic background. In pagan Hellenism the word was used of the disclosures from the gods in prophecy, while in Judaism it was used of the interpretation of the law by rabbis. He concludes that 'the action of Jesus Christ as the revealer is here designated "ἐξηγεῖσθαι". And, with reference to Ecclus 43.31, where it is said that the pious sage has seen but a few of the works of God the creator, that John 1.18 is concerned with "salvific revelation".'[2] I. de la Potterie also opts for 'reveal', but since he takes very seriously the absence of an object with the verb, and considers it illegitimate to supply one, he is forced after long reflection to replace the verb by a noun and to render by '*il fut lui, la révélation*' ('he is himself, the revelation').[3] But this has the same weakness as Westcott's 'he made declaration' or as Louw's suggestion of 'the narrator'.

It hardly makes sense to say of a person that he is 'the revelation', since what are revealed are things, secrets or situations, not persons. At best 'he is the revelation' can only mean that he reveals himself. Otherwise 'God' or some other object is still required. Further, if 'reveal' and 'revelation' are being used in a strict theological sense, and not as vague general terms for the Christian gospel, serious objections can be raised against their use with reference to the Fourth Gospel. Apart from the one instance in 12.38, where the evangelist quotes

1. *John*, p. 83.
2. Schnackenburg, *St John*, I, p. 279.
3. 'Structure du Prologue de Saint Jean', *NTS* 30 (1984), p. 363. See *idem*, *La Vérité dans Saint Jean* (AnBib, 73; Rome: Biblical Institute Press, 1977), pp. 227-28.

Isa. 53.1, neither the verb ἀποκαλύπτειν nor the noun ἀποκάλυψις
is used in this gospel. The reason for this could be that they have too
strong apocalyptic overtones to serve the evangelist in his theological
exposition. They require contextual support from doctrines inextricably
bound up with apocalyptic, such as belief in a Fall, with its inevitable
consequences for humankind, a particular doctrine of sin and salvation
and of historical epochs with their catastrophic portents and a final
assize. But the prologue does not refer to such doctrines. It makes the
positive assertions that creation is by the divine Logos, and there is no
reference to a Fall. Rather the light has always been within the world,
since the true light lightens every human (πάντα ἄνθρωπον) coming
into the created order. Human beings have preferred to remain in a
metaphysical darkness and ignorance, and thus in alienation from God
and outside the divine life. It is into this situation that the Logos was
destined to come. Moreover, the John of the prologue is not
commissioned to proclaim the nearness of the kingdom or of wrath and
the final judgment; nor does he exhort human beings to repent with a
view to the remission of sins, for where there is ignorance and a
continuous availability of true light the doctrine of sin as envisaged by
the synoptists is inappropriate. John does, however, both in the prologue
and in the Gospel support and enlarge upon the highly exalted claims
about the Logos, so that what the Logos says, does and is becomes
uniquely sacrosanct and sanctifying. It may be suggested that
ἐξηγήσατο in 1.18, as a summary of what the Logos does, is to be
translated by a word which expresses and accommodates such thought.[1]

Consequently we may turn to the meaning the verb could bear, which
is referred to by F. Buchsel and Bultmann although not in the end
adopted by them.[2] This is the meaning: 'to communicate divine things'.

1.   This emphasis has been maintained in some forms of Christian piety, for
example the Franciscan, which teaches that the 'incarnation' was decreed from
creation, and was not occasioned by the Fall and the consequent need of redemption.
This would seem to represent the Johannine view. Incarnation was divinely determined from before the foundation of the world, and it was implicit in the act of
creation itself that the creator should enter his creation, and permanently establish a
clearly discernible communication of all the divine gifts and concerns for humankind.
2.   For Buchsel, see 'ἐξηγεῖσθαι', *TDNT*, II, p. 908, quoting the Pollux text, for
which see also BAG, *s.v.* For Bultmann, see *John*, p. 83. Buchsel in the end considers
1.18 to be a direct answer to the question raised in Ecclus. 43.31, 'Who has seen him
that he may tell thereof?', and Bultmann considers this a possibility. But apart from
the fact that the verb is a different one (ἐκδιηγεῖσθαι), used intransitively, though

The principal text for this is Pollux, Onomasticon, VIII, 12: ἐξηγηταὶ δ' ἐκαλοῦντο οἱ τὰ περὶ τῶν δημοσιῶν καὶ τὰ τῶν ἄλλων ἱερῶν διδάσκοντες: 'They were called "exegetes" who teach the things concerning the signs of the gods and of other holy things'. This points to a verb which can be intransitive, and which, without any object expressed, can mean in itself 'to communicate divine things'. This is preferred by Barrett, who rejects the translation 'recount a narrative' in favour of 'explain or publish divine secrets'. He comments,

> it is not without significance that the prologue closes with this word, characteristic as it is of Hellenistic religion. The notion of revelation is of course biblical as well as Hellenistic... but clearly John means to use language intelligible and even familiar to readers accustomed to Greek literature rather than to the Bible.[1]

The question then to be asked is whether this meaning of ἐξηγήσατο is taken up by, and can best account for, what is said about the status, functions and utterances of Jesus in the body of the Gospel. This will be the subject of the following chapter, but a certain observation about it may be made here.

This concerns the tendency of some scholars in their exegesis of 1.18 to combine 'reveal' and 'revelation' with an appeal to the Greek word Λόγος taken in the sense of the Latin *verbum* and the English 'Word'. Thus Lindars comments: 'the verb [i.e. ἐξηγήσατο in 1.18] implies the revelation of God by human speech, which fittingly represents the activity of the one who is the Word of God'.[2] Bultmann writes that the function of the revealer is denoted by the verb ἐξηγεῖσθαι: 'The evangelist shows that it is in his word that he is the Revealer'.[3] But it may be questioned whether it is legitimate to translate Λόγος by 'Word' and then pass from this titular use to the act of speech contained in the idea of revelation by the Revealer or Word. For, as E.R. Goodenough has observed,

---

used transitively in Ecclus 42.15, and that the question is a rhetorical one, the context of the search for a wise person who has seen God and can relate the experience for the wise and godly, is a very different one.

1.   Barrett, *St John*, p. 170. Louw ('Narrator of the Father', p. 33) would stress διδάσκοντες in the Pollux text, and wishes to define the 'exegetes' by their teaching function, but this appears to be mistaken. The emphasis is on what they teach.

2.   Lindars, *Gospel of John*, p. 100.

3.   Bultmann, *John*, p. 83.

> Logos has for centuries been translated by the English 'Word', following
> the Vulgate Latin 'Verbum'; but of all the scores of nuances in the Greek
> term, that is one of the few meanings which Logos never has… A reader
> of Philo or of early Christian thought must first of all wipe that meaning
> from his mind and use the untranslated term Logos as he would use a new
> term in chemistry… Logos means primarily the formulation and expression
> of thought in speech, but from this it took on a variety of associated
> meanings… Logos, then, is almost anything except the English 'word'.[1]

This could suggest that the starting point for investigating the meaning
of Logos in the prologue is less a supposed background in the Wisdom
literature or an Old Testament doctrine of the Word of God than the
evangelist's own statement that the Logos was θεός (1.1), which is
recapitulated in the closing statement that the Logos, who as Jesus
Christ is μονογενὴς θεός, 'has communicated divine things'.[2] For it is
not only Jesus' speech that is covered by this statement. Jesus does
more than speak. He performs significant acts, which along with his
speech convey the divine glory, grace, truth and light. In him was life,
and his self-acclamations, which are more than apocalyptic vision or
metaphorical expression, link him to the very stuff of divine life, which
through him is conveyed to human beings to penetrate their terrestrial
life. And even his speech is said to be not a revelation of God, but the
speech of God himself. Hence a meaning that will cover all these things
is required for ἐξηγήσατο, and of the available meanings for the verb
'to communicate divine things' would seem to accommodate them best.

Is the content of 1.18, so interpreted, corroborated by and explicated
in the Gospel; and if so, how?

1.   E.R. Goodenough, *An Introduction to Philo Judaeus* (Oxford: Basil Blackwell,
2nd rev. edn, 1962), pp. 103-104. See also the observations of R. Williamson, *Jews in
the Hellenistic World, Philo* (Cambridge: Cambridge University Press, 1989),
pp. 103-104:

> Part of the complexity of Philo's Logos doctrine is due to the extremely wide range of
> meanings which the word *logos* may have in Greek. Of these many meanings the one
> that it definitely should not have—despite the Vulgate's *verbum* and some English
> translations of the Prologue to John's Gospel—is the meaning 'word'…The primary
> meaning of Logos, as it was used in Philo's world, and by Philo, is more than, to quote
> one definition, 'the spiritual Mind of the transcendent God'. Logos means, among other
> things, the rational thought of mind expressed in utterance or speech. It is something
> present within the total reality of God himself, within the natural order of the universe,
> within man himself.

2.   R. Culpepper, 'The Pivot of John's Prologue', *NTS* 27 (1980), pp. 1-31.
Without necessarily agreeing with his elaborate chiastic structure one may accept his
presentation of 1.18 as a recapitulation of 1.1-2 in general, if not in all its details.

Chapter 5

CHRISTOLOGICAL EXPRESSIONS IN THE FOURTH GOSPEL:
THE SON OF MAN

In the examination in the previous chapter of 1.18 as the climactic statement of the prologue the reading μονογενὴς θεός was preferred, and the translation suggested was 'the unique one, who is God has communicated divine things'. It now needs to be considered whether the verse thus translated is the climax of a prologue acting as true prologue, preparing the reader by what it says of the Logos, Jesus Christ, for what is to be said about his person and work in the body of the Gospel. What is said there is not in terms of the Logos, which is confined to the prologue, but in terms of certain christological expressions—Son of Man, ἐγώ εἰμι and Son (of God)—which, paradoxically, are almost entirely absent from the prologue itself. The question will be to what extent the christological statements in the Gospel are consistent with, even crucially dependent upon, what has been said already concerning the Logos for their meaning? The issue raised thereby will be whether the evangelist deliberately provided those expressions with his own distinctive theology which the readers are to understand as explication of the prologue's assertions. To put it another way, do the cryptic statements of the prologue establish the irreducible core for this evangelist's presentation of the life and work of the Logos, Jesus Christ, and at the same time do they demand theological development and explanation? If that be the case then it may be suggested that the evangelist is, in accord with known religious and literary practices, re-presenting to a universal readership a reasoned case for the veracity of Christian beliefs and claims.

The first expression to be considered is 'the Son of Man'. It is introduced dramatically as the climax of the first 'christological' section of the Gospel, 1.37-51, and by means of it certain crucial statements are made in the first part of the Gospel (it is absent from chs. 14–21) in addition to 1.51 at 3.13, 14; 5.27; 6.27, 53, 62; 8.28; 9.35; 12.23, 34 (bis); 13.31. The question here will be how far these important statements show links, however obscure, with what has been delivered to the readers by the prologue. It would be simplistic to say that the Logos, Jesus Christ and the Son of Man are one and the same. For that would fail to explain why the evangelist bothers to introduce not so much the figure designated by the term 'Son of Man' but the term itself, since he clearly saw no need to introduce it into the prologue, and could hardly have done so without great difficulty.

The origins, uses and meanings of the term 'the Son of Man' in the Gospels as a whole (and in its only occurrence in the New Testament outside them, Acts 7.56) remain among the most hotly disputed questions in New Testament study.[1] Moreover, it is not necessarily the case that what could be established for the term in the synoptic tradition would necessarily be valid for its use in the Fourth Gospel.[2] The term in this gospel deserves to be studied on its own, in its own right, and with an open mind. A notable example of such a study is that of F.J. Moloney, *The Johannine Son of Man*.[3] The author opens with a survey of scholarly opinion on 'the Son of Man' as a christological term in the Fourth Gospel, and notes a marked absence of consensus. He distinguishes six types of interpretation: (1) that which finds in the Gospel no explicit Son of Man Christology, since the term means the same as the Logos; (2) that which sees the term as referring to a Jewish or Hellenistic ideal man; (3) that which sees the evangelist as building on the synoptic tradition; (4) that which postulates the Johannine tradition as being older than the synoptic; (5) that which considers the evangelist to have been aware of the synoptic usages, but to have developed his own conception to suit his particular Christology; and (6) that which maintains that a completely new conception is to be found in this gospel.[4]

The first saying containing 'the Son of Man' (1.51) is clearly, by its context, manner and content, of great importance. It is in the context of

1. See for example B. Lindars, *Jesus, Son of Man* (London: SPCK, 1983, and I.H. Marshall, 'The Synoptic Son of Man Sayings in Recent Discussions', *NTS* 12 (1966), pp. 327-51.

2. See the discussion in F.H. Borsch, *The Son of Man in Myth and History* (London: SCM Press, 1976), ch. 7.

3. Biblioteca di Scienze Religiose, 14; Las Libreria Ateneo Salesiano, 1976.

4. Moloney, *Johannine Son of Man*, pp. 21-22.

a section, of which it is the finale, where the first disciples offer Jesus Jewish messianic roles, which he does not necessarily accept: 'the messiah', 1.41; 'him of whom Moses in the law and also the prophets wrote', 1.45; 'the Son of God, the King of Israel', 1.49.[1] It is introduced by the first occurrence of the double ἀμήν,[2] and is the first pronouncement of Jesus in the Gospel. It takes the form of a prophecy. Jesus has just addressed Nathanael as a true Israelite, and now promises that he will see 'greater things' (1.50). What these greater things are to be is presumably the content of 1.51. Indeed, J.H. Bernard maintains that the double ἀμήν never introduces a saying unrelated to what has preceded.[3] However, it has to be admitted that to some extent v. 51 following after v. 50 appears to be explaining one conundrum by another, itself needing explanation. Moreover, it has been argued that v. 51 has the manner of an isolated statement, and that it is intrusive here.[4] In favour of this view is the fact that the address to Nathanael in v. 50 is in the second person singular, while in v. 51, while still an address to him, it is in the second person plural, as though directed to humankind in general.

The promise is twofold: that the heavens will be seen to have been opened, and that angels (messengers) will be seen continually ascending and descending on the Son of Man. These two are often taken as a single promise, but this is to be questioned, since the tenses of the participles are different. In the first part the tense is the perfect passive (ἀνεωγότα), with the meaning either 'You will see that the heavens have been opened', or 'You will see that the heavens are open'. In the second part the tense is the present, which denotes the ascending and descending as continuous and permanent activity.

Nevertheless the two are closely related. The comprehension—something more than vision is suggested—that the heavens have been opened need not refer to a single event of divine disclosure, such as, for example, the baptism of Jesus as depicted in the synoptics, or even the event of the incarnation itself referred to in 1.14. Rather it will be understood that divine communication with human beings has been made available, and has been made available by God himself—that is the force

1. So F.J. Moloney, 'The Fourth Gospel's Presentation of Jesus as the Christ', *Downside Review* 95.321 (Oct. 1977), pp. 239-53.
2. Bultmann, *John*, p. 105 n. 2.
3. *John*, I, p. 67.
4. For this, see the discussion in Brown, *John*, pp. 88-91.

of the perfect participle passive. The permanent and present outcome of this is expressed by angels (messengers) ascending and descending upon the Son of Man. The language of ascending and descending to express communication between heaven and earth (or heaven and earth as in communication) almost certainly derives in the end from Jacob's vision in Gen. 28.10-17. However, in distinction from Gen. 28.12 this communication is said to be not upon the ladder set up between earth and heaven, but upon the Son of Man himself. This is a new thought, and the evangelist's theological construction; and it does not necessarily have any connection with the Jewish exegesis evidenced in *Genesis Rabbah* where the ladder is identified with Jacob.[1] The preposition ἐπί must be given its full weight here in the sense of 'upon', and those who see the Son of Man as the permanently available route of intercommunication between heaven and earth are probably correct.[2]

Since, however, the interconnection is through messengers ascending and descending upon him, the Son of Man must be given the basic meaning of 'man', 'the human' or 'manhood', for they can only descend upon and ascend from one who is on earth. This is not the heavenly Son of Man in the eschatological sense, who is to come on the clouds for judgment and salvation. Upon such a one angels cannot ascend and descend. Nor is it the Son of Man in the simple sense of 'man' in the Synoptic Gospels, where it is used of Jesus in his humiliation or humility. It would seem, therefore, that in his opening use of the term the evangelist, wherever he has derived it from, has made it a vehicle for expressing what he has said in the prologue in different terminology: that Jesus is of divine origin, and communicates verbally on earth and to humankind divine things. Moreover, this very different Son of Man, by virtue of things as yet untold, is to be perceived as the eternal passage for communication between God and humankind.

1.   Moloney, *The Johannine Son of Man*, pp. 26-32, reviews the suggested backgrounds in Jewish exegesis, with special reference to H.T. Odeberg, *The Fourth Gospel Interpreted in its Relation to Contemporaneous Religious Currents in Palestine and in the Hellenistic-Oriental World* (Stockholm: Almqvist & Wiksells, 1929), pp. 33-42. Knox (*Hellenistic Elements*, p. 59 n. 1) observes that for Philo Jacob's ladder symbolized either the air or the soul, through which, in man the microcosm, the divine logoi passed, and concludes that by analogy the ladder in the macrocosm is the divine Logos. He notes the presence of cosmic ladders in Greek thought.
2.   H. Maillet, ' "Au-dessus de", ou "sur"? (John 1. 51)', *ETR* 59 (1974), pp. 207-13, who argues for *sur*, 'upon', as the proper rendering of ἐπί here.

What is thus stated in compressed form in 1.51 is continued and developed in the next two Son of Man sayings in 3.13 and 3.14. The accredited teacher of Israel, Nicodemus, becomes the foil for the first piece of extended instruction from Jesus, the subject of which is the necessity for a true relation with God, for a new or spiritual birth. The stage is thus set for the supreme teacher to utter authoritatively, from his position of communicating between heaven and earth, the heavenly things which humankind at large fails to understand. This would seem to be the logic of the abrupt change of person in the middle of 3.11—'I say to thee [Nicodemus] we speak what we know, and bear witness of what we have seen, and you [plural] do not receive our witness'; and the plural continues in 3.12. As the basis of the claim to be conveying to humankind heavenly things both heard and seen, a further step is taken from 1.51. Jesus is more than the instrument of communication, the ladder upon which heavenly messengers ascend and descend. He is himself in his destiny the communicator, and he is this in his own person as the Son of Man, the ascender because first the descender. What is striking here is that this truth is stated by means of a curious negative construction, 'no man has ascended into heaven', with which may be compared the similar negative to introduce the positive statement in 1.18. (In this context the emphasis in οὐδείς is possibly better reproduced by 'no man' than by 'no one'.) That is, communication between heaven and earth has not been, and cannot be, established from the human side. Here perhaps the evangelist is ruling out all religious, especially Hellenistic, concepts of saviours of humankind storming heaven (for example Prometheus). But the negative serves a positive affirmation. There has been an ascent of a human being to heaven, but only through the Son of Man in virtue of his previous descent from heaven to be man. Communication has been established in a human being in virtue of his heavenly origin and his descent from his existence with God. Thus 3.13 states in this negative-positive way in terms of the Son of Man what is said positively of the Logos-Light in the prologue, that he was a heavenly figure who became a human being (1.14a).

The following verse, 3.14, continues with a statement about the Son of Man: 'As Moses lifted up the serpent in the wilderness, so must the Son of Man be lifted up'. This is puzzling in several respects. First, it does not appear to have any logical connection with the preceding statement in 3.13, or to develop its thought. Secondly, the point of the comparison is not at all clear. The construction 'As...so...' is deceptive, since apart from the use of 'to lift up' of both the snake and the Son of Man there is nothing to indicate what is, and must be, common to them. Some interpreters would press the context and content of the story in Num. 21.6-9 to provide the point of comparison. The gazing of the Israelites upon the elevated serpent which healed them is an Old Testament type of the believer who turns to the Son of Man so that he or she may (not perish but) have eternal life (3.15).[1] If this is the evangelist's intention it is exceedingly obscurely expressed, since there is no reference to any contemplation of the Son of Man to attain belief and eternal life, but simply the necessity of his being lifted up. In the context it might be better to take as the evangelist's primary concern this divine necessity of the Son of Man's being lifted up with the consequent possession of eternal life by the believer, and to take 'lifted up' as a cryptic synonym, to be developed later, for the ascending of the Son of Man in the previous verse. The comparison would then be a comparatively superficial one with an incident in the Old Testament (the only one?) which involved a 'lifting up'. It is then as the heavenly one descending into humanity so that he may ascend with humanity to God that he is the Son of Man, and this ascent is to be brought about by an action in the human sphere, his being lifted up. 'To lift up', 'to hoist up' or 'to elevate' (ὑψοῦν) is peculiar to the Fourth Gospel's theological presentation of the death of Jesus. Along with other words, it expresses this evangelist's distinctive understanding of the life and death of the Logos, Jesus Christ. Chapter Eight will draw together these features.

There are three further Son of man sayings in which the term is connected with 'to lift up', 8.28, 12.23 and 12.34, and these may be considered here. In ch. 8 Jesus is in fierce debate with the Jews following his self-acclamation 'I am the light of the world', and his claim that his followers will by no means walk in darkness, but will have the light of life (living, true light, 8.12). The Pharisees take up the cudgels and there follows a series of accusations arising from the exalted claims made by Jesus for himself and the theological fruits for believers. The dispute is predominantly in terms of Jesus' sonship, with previously stated themes reiterated in slightly different ways—light, his heavenly origins, the Father who sent him, dying in one's sins. It is in this context that suddenly at 8.28 the Son of Man is mentioned, with the statement to the Pharisees, 'When you shall lift up [future] the Son of Man you will

---

1. See, for example, Dodd, *Interpretation*, pp. 306-307.

know that I am [he?]'. The term, once introduced, is immediately dropped, and the dispute continues in terms of sonship and the absolute authority of the one who does nothing of himself, but speaks only what he has been taught by the Father. What distinguishes the statement in 8.28a is that through it the Pharisees, the leaders of current Judaism, are placed in the dock, and are told that they will themselves effect whatever is ordained by the necessary lifting up of the Son of Man, and that by this they will come to a certain knowledge of Jesus. What this knowledge is, however, is obscure in the text. What is meant by ἐγώ εἰμι here? Should one provide, as do most translators and commentators, a predicate 'he', 'you shall know that I am he'? If so does 'he' refer to the Son of Man? Does the text mean that only as one lifted up from earth to heaven, of which the Jews will be the human agents in the crucifixion, can the Son of Man be recognized for who he is? Or does 'he' refer to what has been the main bone of contention in the dispute, 'the Son' (of the Father)? Is the meaning that in the lifting up of the man (i.e. his ascent to God) his abiding relationship with the Father will become evident? On the whole the second seems preferable, especially as the statement continues, somewhat awkwardly, with 'and I do nothing from myself, but as my Father has taught me'.[1]

Some would deny any necessity for a predicate, and would see as an adequate background the Old Testament usage of 'I am', which indicates that God is meant.[2] In favour of this is the fact that it undoubtedly appears in this form as the conclusion of the dispute with the assertion 'before Abraham existed I am' (8.58). This would not say more in terms of a dispute of this kind than the statement in 1.18, 'the unique one, who is God'; and if the assertion in the prologue of the Logos becoming man (1.14a) has a corresponding statement in terms of the ascent of the Son of Man in 3.13, so the definition of the Logos-Jesus Christ in 1.18b may have a corresponding statement in terms of the Son of Man, that as a result of his exaltation through death his 'divinity' will be seen. Further, it may be noted that the context of 8.28 is a dispute arising from the claim 'I am the light of the world', and that the followers of Jesus will not walk in darkness but will possess the living (true) light, and that this has been prepared for in the prologue with the Logos as the true light

---

1.   Bultmann, *John*, p. 349, comments that Jesus' answer to the question 'Who are you?' 'shows immediately that everything that he has claimed for himself is gathered up in the title "Son of man"'.

2.   So Brown, Barrett, Dodd and Schnackenburg.

(1.9) who is not overcome by the darkness. Further, the true light illuminates every human being, and this may be reflected in the remarkable statement that the lifting up of the Son of Man will be the act through which, and the moment at which, they perceive the truth.

The context in ch. 12 is very different from that in ch. 8, being concerned not with the Jews but with the Gentile world personified in the Greeks. This world approaches with the request to 'see' Jesus. This request does not receive a direct response, but is met with the statement that the hour has come for the Son of Man to be glorified, that is, to be invested with 'glory', which denotes the divine and heavenly existence. The 'hour', which up until now has been said to be 'not yet', is now said to be present. That this is the hour of death is clear from what follows about the corn of wheat which must die to be fruitful and about the troubling of the soul, which in the synoptics belongs to the scene in Gethsemane. In this context Jesus prays to the Father to glorify his name, to show himself as the God he is. He is assured by the Father himself through a voice from heaven—the only instance of this device in this gospel—that he has done, and will do so. It leads to a repetition of the original statement, though now in terms not of the Son of Man but of the person of Jesus, and not of glorification but of being lifted up: 'I, when I am lifted up ἐκ τῆς γῆς, will draw all men to myself' (12.32). The evangelist then adds one of his theological comments, that in this Jesus was speaking symbolically of his death. The crowds also understand 'lift up' to mean death, since they introduce a comparison with the doctrine they have been taught that the messiah, with whom they equate the Son of Man, 'abides' for ever, and therefore question what kind of a messiah the Son of Man can be who is to be lifted up in death. So glorification or entry into heavenly existence, and being lifted up from the earth, or the death of one who is human, are identical for Jesus. But in the context something of great importance is added. Not only is this the case with Jesus as the Son of Man, but it has consequences for humankind. These are expressed by the use of the forceful verb ἐλκύειν, 'to drag'. The word is, apart from Acts 16.19, confined to John in the New Testament, and in John is used only here and in 6.44 (of the action of the Father) in a figurative sense. Bauer cites passages from Greek authors and the LXX where the term refers to 'the pull on a person's inner life'. Thus the Son of Man is not only the communicator of heavenly things, he claims for himself the function of dragging, forcibly hauling at things belonging to the inner life; significantly, the discourse then returns in 12.35-36 to talk of light and illumination. So Jesus is the man who through his lifting up to glory in death is able to draw human beings to the source of the heavenly things he communicates and to take them to God. And this he is able to do for all humankind—the most universalistic statement in this Gospel.

It has already been noted that the theme of light or illumination, introduced in the prologue almost as a synonym for the Logos, is associated in the Gospel with the Son of Man (1.51, 'you shall see...', 3.19-21; 12.35-36). This theme comes to a head in ch. 9 after the previous statement in 8.12. Here it is developed with heavy irony. Those in authority among the Jews, those who by right should see and know the truth, are shown to be those who are blind and obtuse with respect to it. The occasion is the miraculous sabbath healing of a man whose blindness is said to be for the purpose that 'the works of God may be made manifest in him' (9.3). As a result of his healing and his subsequent interrogation by the authorities the man is, as a presumed disciple of Jesus, excommunicated from the synagogue. The story, however, does not end here, and his actual discipleship is secured by a further encounter procured by Jesus, who abruptly and surprisingly asks, 'Do you believe in the Son of Man?' The man replies, 'Who is he, sir, that I may believe in him?' This is obscure. It could mean either that he did not know what the term 'the Son of Man' was referring to, or that he knew and asked for him to be identified. On his being identified as Jesus whom he was now able to 'see' and who was talking with him, the man professes that belief and worships Jesus. It is not clear whether 'worship' here means the kind of reverence evoked in similar stories in the synoptics, or that which in the strict sense is due to God alone (cf. 4.20-24), and so here an apprehension of the divine in the gift of sight from the Son of Man. Historically this is a curious ending to the story. Theologically, however, it is appropriate in leading to the following words with which Jesus himself concludes the episode: that he has come into the world (from heaven) for the purpose of judgment (discrimination), with the result that it is the (hitherto) blind who are able to see (the truth), and it is those who think they see it who are shown to be blind.

So far the Son of Man sayings have been relatively isolated in their contexts in discourses conducted largely in other terms, and the problem has been to explain their occurrence. This is not the case in the discourse in ch. 6 on the subject of divine sustenance, where there are three such sayings (vv. 27, 53, 62); here they are not isolated but come at crucial points, and could be said to articulate the discourse. This chapter is notoriously difficult to interpret, as it raises questions about the relation of the text both to the synoptic tradition and to the liturgical tradition of the eucharist.[1] Here it must suffice to leave these questions on one side and to attempt to understand the sayings in their context, with attention to what, if anything, they add to the Son of Man material examined so far.

The day after the miraculous feeding the crowds search for Jesus, which is said to be due not to their having seen a miracle but to their having been satisfied with a unique bread (6.26). They are told not to toil for food that perishes but for food that endures in respect of eternal life. This 'the Son of man will give; for this one God the Father has sealed' (6.27). By itself this could be a statement couched in the language of an earlier eschatology. The miraculous food itself becomes a sign or foretaste of a food which is (1) abiding or heavenly, and (2) concerned with eternal life. It will be given some time in the future, and will be connected with participation in the life of the coming age. Its giver will be the Son of Man, the agent in the coming age. The discourse, however, does not stop there, but moves forward; and does so by way of a discussion of the manna, which the Jews adduce as the instance of God's gift of heavenly food to Israel. This claim is denied; the interpretation of 6.32 is difficult.[2] Over against the manna is 'the true bread from heaven'; which is almost a tautology, as 'true' and 'from heaven' are synonymous. This, which the Father gives, is the bread of God, which is further defined, somewhat strangely, as 'that which comes down from heaven', its purpose being to give life, not to Israel but to the world (6.33). The force of that definition then appears when Jesus defines himself as this bread of life, and as being so because he in truth comes down from heaven (6.38). When the Jews object, the claim is reiterated and underlined. The bread he gives is himself, in that he is the one who veritably comes down from heaven (6.50-51). More specifically it is his flesh, that is, his humanity, supplied to give life to the world. It is with this mention of humanity that the Son of Man is reintroduced. When the Jews object, 'How can this man give us his flesh to eat?', they are met with the insistence that 'except you eat the flesh of the Son of Man and drink his blood you have no life in you'. This has been taken as a reference to the eucharist, but that may be questioned. It is to be noted

1.   For a discussion of the interpretation of this chapter, see Hoskyns, *Fourth Gospel*, pp. 304-307; Moloney, *Johannine Son of Man*, pp. 89-100.
2.   Barrett, *St John*, pp. 289-90 for a discussion.

that 'flesh' and 'blood' are spoken of and not the eucharistic 'body' and 'blood'. Flesh and blood together denote humanity. Their separation into 'flesh' as 'true food' and 'blood' as 'true drink' is no more than a somewhat artificial way of insisting that the 'flesh and blood' (the humanity) of the Son of Man is true, heavenly and divine sustenance.

Finally, these statements cause a grave crisis, not now among the Jews but among the disciples. To assist them Jesus asks, 'What if you were to see the Son of Man ascending where he was before?' This seems to mean that it will be possible to grasp, to comprehend, that Jesus as the Son of Man can through his humanity give the food of eternal life. This will be possible if the disciples perceive that same Son of Man, who has veritably come down from heaven as none other has, returning to his place of origin. His words are 'spirit and life' because it is these things that consistently link heaven and earth, earth and heaven, flesh and spirit and spirit and flesh. As the Son of Man coming from God (spirit) and returning to God he holds all life, including his own, to its origin in the Creator, and is thereby the communicator of the life of heaven to the life of the world of human beings. Thus the life of the Son of Man is related to the Creator, who at the outset in the prologue has been identified as the Logos (1.3), in whom also was life (1.4).

There remains to be discussed the saying in 5.27, 'And he [the Father] gave him [the Son] authority to do (ποιεῖν, 'execute') judgment because he is "son of man"'. This again appears suddenly in a discourse primarily concerned with the relation of the Son and the Father and the participation of the Son in the life and activity of the Father. Its immediate context in 5.25, 28-29 is a reference to a coming hour (which is also said to be present) when the dead will hear the Son of God's voice and will live; and, more specifically, when even the graves will deliver their dead to a resurrection either to life or to judgment (condemnation). It is easy to understand this as a piece of Synoptic-like eschatology in which Jesus functions as the Son of Man, the divine agent, in a future apocalyptic assize. Against this, however, are the following considerations.

First, elsewhere, but also in a measure here, the Johannine doctrine of sin and judgment is that human beings judge themselves for death or eternal life, and that they do so in the present by their response, or lack of response, to the light, that is, by their belief or unbelief in Jesus. Those who do so believe have eternal life already, and do not come into judgement because they have passed from death to life (5.24). And those who reject the Son, or the Son of Man, by disbelief remain in their sins

(8.24; 9.41; 16.9). The phrase 'to execute judgment' in 5.27 is not necessarily identical with the activity of the future judge at the final judgment. To effect judgment could mean here to bring about a situation in which human beings are forced to choose (between belief and unbelief), and in so doing bring judgment on themselves.

Secondly, the statement that the dead will hear the voice of the Son of God could refer not to the final judgment and resurrection but to the effect of the death of Jesus, which is said to be the judgment of the world (12.31), and of his exaltation, through which human beings are drawn to where he is (12.32)—a Johannine equivalent to the tradition about the death of Jesus in Mt. 27.51-53. If that is so, to whom does 'son of man' refer in 5.27? Is it the Son of God of 5.17ff., or must the reader wait until it becomes clear that it is the crucified and exalted Son of Man?

Thirdly, there is a solution which takes seriously the fact that 'son of man' is anarthrous here.[1] Translated literally, the statement would then read 'The Father has given authority to him [i.e. the Son, 5.26] to effect judgment because he is man'. That would correspond to the statements that Jesus had come into the world not to condemn it but to save it (3.17) and that final judgment and eternal life are available now by his presence as man in the world. This could be an equivalent in the Gospel to what is said in the prologue about the Logos-Son becoming flesh (1.14). This already confers on man a divine quality in the creation which owes its existence to the Logos-Son who is eternally with God. Thus the divine quality in man, which in the prologue is indicated by the Logos becoming flesh, is in the Gospel indicated by Jesus the heavenly Son operating, and in the end dying, 'as a man'.

The above survey leads one to suggest that, no matter whence the evangelist may have derived the expression 'Son of Man', he has developed it in accord with his own presentation of the case for belief in the Logos figure of the prologue. The Johannine Son of Man figure complements that of the Logos. His work establishes the permanent availability of eternal life, and the provision of himself as divine sustenance for believers. Such teaching develops, albeit through very different language, what is said of the Logos, Jesus Christ, in the prologue and stated pithily in 1.18. The death of the Logos was not directly mentioned

---

1. See E.C. Colwell's dictum, 'Definite predicate nouns which precede the verb usually lack the article' ('A Definite Rule for the Use of the Article in the Greek New Testament', *JBL* 52 [1933], p. 20).

there, but it could be argued that it was deliberately omitted so that a full explication could be more profitably developed within the sphere of the ongoing drama. Since there was a familiar title to hand, namely Son of Man, the evangelist could exercise at 1.51 the same literary freedom as had been exercised at 1.1 with the abrupt presentation of the figure of the Logos. Thus introduced the figure, whose very title contained within it the concept of humanity, was also given divine status. The readers would know that Jesus' authenticity was guaranteed by the vision and affirmations of the ordained witness, John. Similarly, what is to be claimed for the Johannine Son of Man is given authenticity in this gospel through the affirmations of Jesus who is himself the divine Logos.

The question now raised is whether the evangelist wished to invest Jesus' death with the aura of a *sēmeion*. At various points he uses distinctive theological language about that death, referring to the ordained hour, Jesus' being lifted up, his ascending to his place of origin and his glorification. The mention of 'glory' and its cognates leads one to reinvestigate the significance of that word in 1.14. It affirms that human beings perceived Jesus' divine status during his earthly life. But his very God-status was emphatically proclaimed at the outset; so why introduce at this juncture in the prologue a new word, 'glory', packed with meanings? Could it not be the case that the evangelist has deliberately so written, and moreover placed it in close proximity to the assertion that the Logos had become flesh (fully human), because he intended to give it and its cognates a deep significance in the body of the work? Does the 'glory' used here (1.14) of the 'flesh' of the Logos hint at, even prepare for, the frequent use of the verb when there is mention of Jesus' flesh at the point of death? The phrase 'was glorified' in the Fourth Gospel, alone among the New Testament writings, is frequently synonymous with the death of Jesus whether it be in respect of the Son of Man or concerning the Son (of God). It seems better, therefore, to include in any understanding of 1.14 the view that within the very word 'glory' in the prologue resides a seminal allusion to the death of the Logos-become-flesh. Later the verbal form is undoubtedly used to give a new and significant meaning to the human death of Jesus. The statement that 'the unique God has communicated divine things' in 1.18 requires both the 'flesh' and the 'glory' of 1.14 before the body of the Gospel is begun.

Furthermore, those figures who act as foils to the extensive teaching by Jesus and give contexts to Son of Man sayings also demonstrate the existing state of affairs by their non-comprehension, unbelief and outright rejection of Jesus *qua* Son of Man. Thus the cosmic proportions of alienation, first stated in the prologue in connection with the Logos, are reformulated as those confronting the Son of Man. Significantly, the coming of the enquiring Greeks—that distinctive Johannine episode with its very Hellenistic theological contents—puts into the mouth of Jesus *qua* Son of Man the most explicit affirmation of universalism in the Gospel. In this way the universalistic nature of the mission of the Logos in 1.3-5, 9-13 has been given authoritatively to the Son of Man also.

Finally, reflection upon the triple reference in ch. 6 may be in order here. It is the Son of Man whom God has sealed, who will give imperishable food which is eternal, true, heavenly, because it is none other than himself which he gives for humankind. He himself came down from heaven and has to be appropriated by believers. The phrase 'flesh and blood' expresses his very humanity, while the necessity of devouring them (totally appropriating them) as the source and sustenance of true life effecting an intimacy or an indwelling for believers, is very Hellenistic. This is pure Johannine material and it lies alongside the prologue assertions that the Logos was intimately available as the source of eternal life, which is enlightenment for all believers. Nor is it to be ignored that the coalescence of life and light, darkness and ignorance, in the prologue receives deeper consideration in ch. 6, where those who partake are said to live for ever and to be taught of God. As in the prologue, so here, the fruits for believers are life, which issues in knowledge of the things pertaining to God. It appears, then, that the language built up within the Son of Man theology is the chosen vehicle to express how and when the universal communication of divine things was irrevocably established. In answer to the earlier question—why introduce the Son of Man at all?—it would appear that the evangelist deliberately avoided the commonplace of Hellenism that a god in human form was rescued from the experience of human death. The Logos, unique God and creator, as a son of man (5.27) dies; as divine Son of Man is glorified; returns to the heavenly sphere dragging with him all devotees. Thus he establishes himself not only as the highway for communication between heaven and earth but also as the source and sustainer of life eternal. Nothing has been said which contradicts the prologue's assertions or diminishes the figure and functions of the Logos. However, a good deal more has been said about the manner in which the Logos-μονογενὴς communicates divine things. Furthermore, the factuality of that death has been given a 'symbolic' theology involving the tailor-made Johannine Son of Man.

Chapter 6

CHRISTOLOGICAL EXPRESSIONS IN THE FOURTH GOSPEL:
ἐγώ εἰμι

The present chapter will examine how the prologue was explicated by
way of the second christological expression ἐγώ εἰμι. It may be asked
why the evangelist chose to use it at all, for no other evangelist shows
any degree of awareness that such a 'Christology' was appropriate. That
observation raises a further question, namely whether this expression,
like 'Logos' and 'Son of Man', was universally known, and known,
moreover, to belong to the speech of deities among whom the God of
the Jews was but one.

The expression is highly distinctive of this gospel, being almost
unknown in the Synoptic Gospels.[1] It appears in two forms. The first is
the absolute use ἐγώ εἰμι. This is found in 6.20; 8.24, 28, 58; 13.19; 18.5,
6, 8; (4.26). The second is ἐγώ εἰμι followed by a predicate. It is the
latter which will be the main consideration in the question of possible
connections between the Gospel and the prologue, and especially with its
compressed concluding statement in 1.18.

Either form presents the problem that, except in establishing identity,
'It is I', the expression ἐγώ εἰμι is completely unidiomatic. In Greek the
personal pronoun is contained in the verb and is not separately stated;
the Greek for 'I am' is εἰμι. Hence in any occurrence of ἐγώ εἰμι,
whatever its origin, the ἐγώ is presumably intended to be emphatic; 'I
am (he, she, it)'. In the view of E. Norden, who was the first to research
its presence in ancient literature in general, it was a standardized stylized
expression belonging to religious speech, generally in the mouth of a
divinity; and in the second form, that with a predicate, the ἐγώ was
emphatic over against the claims made by others, with the sense 'It is I
who am'.[2] The matter is complicated both grammatically and
theologically by the Old Testament. In the LXX ἐγώ εἰμι occurs a

1. Only in Mk 6.50 (Mt. 14.27);13.6 (Lk. 21.8);14.62.
2. *Agnostos Theos* (Leipzig: Teubner, 1913), *passim*, and esp. pp. 143-63, 177-
86, 188-93.

remarkable number of times.[1] It does so both on the lips of God and on
the lips of human beings. In the view of E. Schweizer, however, this is
due to a relatively mechanical rendering of the underlying Hebrew *ani*
or *anokhi*, and does not provide adequate grounds for concluding either
that the ἐγώ is intended to be stressed or unstressed (it may be either),
or that the formula is a sacred one. Any sacral character is to be derived
from the context and theological content of the passage concerned; for
example in Isa. 45.19, ἐγώ εἰμι ἐγώ εἰμι κύριος translates *ani* YHWH; in
Isa. 43.25, ἐγώ εἰμι ἐγώ εἰμι ἐξαλείφων renders the different Hebrew
anokhi.[2] A different interpretation of such texts is to take ἐγώ εἰμι ἐγώ
εἰμι not as a simple duplication, but with the second ἐγώ εἰμι as a
rendering of the sacred name.[3] This is questionable, as it requires that
what is duplicated is not the verb but the tetragrammaton, which is
rendered first by ἐγώ εἰμι and then by κύριος. Questionable also is the
widely held view, linked with this, that ἐγώ εἰμι as the sacred name
depends on the text of Exod. 3.14, since the Hebrew text there contains
neither *ani* nor *anokhi,* nor is it *ani hū*. It is constructed in the simple
Hebrew form of the verb 'to be' followed by a relative pronoun and the
verb 'to be', which construction would cause difficulty for any translator. It may be that the LXX rendering here—ἐγώ εἰμι ὁ ὤν (bis)—is
one which was rather more acceptable to the Greek mind. Indeed this is
demonstrated by Philo's frequent use of ὁ ὤν as a title for God.

The Absolute Use of the Expression in the Gospel

To examine first the use of the absolute formula in the Gospel, it would
appear on a first reading that at 6.20 and 18.5, 6, 8 it is a matter of
simple identification—'It is I'; but on closer examination of the setting
another level of meaning may be said to appear. At 6.20 the setting is
Jesus walking upon tumultuous seas towards a boat in which are

1. See the figures in E. Schweizer, *Ego Eimi: Die religionsgeschichtliche Herkunft
und theologische Bedutung der johanneischen Bildreden, zugleich ein Beitrag zur
Quellenfrage des vierten Evangeliums* (FRLANT, 38; Göttingen: Vandenhoeck &
Ruprecht, 2nd edn, 1965), pp. 21-27. According to him the formula occurs 212 times,
which is increased to 367 times when those instances are included where ἐγώ stands
alone with a predicate.
2. Schweizer, *Ego Eimi*, pp. 22-23 includes those passages where ἐγώ εἰμι is
followed by μὴ φοβοῦ as the language of epiphany.
3. So Dodd, *Interpretation*, p. 94.

terrified disciples. He identifies himself and enters the boat, which then miraculously reaches the safety of the other shore. The narrative and language here possibly suggest that Jesus is the master of the chaotic deep and delivers his followers to safety. Deeply rooted in Semitic mythology is the belief that the sea is the abode of monsters and chaos, and is to be feared as having power to upset the right ordering of the cosmos, being itself evil and the source of evil. The incident is set between the miraculous feeding and the search for Jesus by people who have tasted the heavenly banquet. The latter becomes the 'historical' peg for the mention of loaves and for the development by a series of oblique references of the highly complex discourse on bread. The discourse itself centres on the positive presentation of Jesus as the giver of heavenly nourishment, which he himself is. It would therefore be fitting as a preparation for this if the ἐγώ εἰμι at 6.20 were more than a simple self-identification, and rather conveyed the presence of one who is from heaven itself.

In 18.5, 6, 8 the 'historical' context is the pending arrest of Jesus. The inability of the Jews to effect this earlier (8.20, 59) has been due to the divine plan for him. His hour had not yet come (7.30; 8.20). When, therefore, Judas, already under the power of the devil from the time he has determined to hand Jesus over to Jewish authorities, is allowed to effect the arrest, there is no doubt in the reader's mind that he and those with him belong to the realm of darkness and evil. They come— apparently a whole cohort of Romans—from the high priests and Pharisees, armed and equipped for the arrest of a violent criminal. Jesus, on the other hand, is the one who has just finished uttering the statements of chs. 13–17, and has been consistently presented as speaking and acting totally in accord with God and his heavenly will. He would not be arrested but would lay down his life at the appointed time of his own volition acccording to the Father's will (10.17-18). Therefore he has authority over life and death, including his own. The problem for the evangelist and his readers is how it is possible for such a one to be arrested and taken into the power of others. The evangelist's method is to employ the ἐγώ εἰμι formula, this time as a literary device with a heavy irony. Confronted by the representatives of darkness Jesus, the supposed malefactor, turns the tables and takes control of the whole event, procuring his own arrest. He asks 'Whom do you seek?', and identifies himself with ἐγώ εἰμι. Faced by the Truth and the Light of the world, by the Logos Jesus, the opponents representing Judaism (even if

Roman soldiers) fall to the ground at this as at a theophany. This reaction is deemed by the evangelist to be a perfectly suitable response by human beings facing the 'I am', the one who gives eternal life and heavenly succour, namely the heavenly figure of the prologue, to whom such exalted things have been ascribed in the Gospel. Because of the powerlessness of his opponents Jesus is forced to repeat his ἐγώ εἰμι, but now as a means of carrying out his previous claim that he would not lose a single disciple, and as the one in command he allows his arrest solely on the condition that they go free.[1]

In both the cases so far examined the ἐγώ εἰμι formula is part of, and crucial to, an event, and imparts to that event a theological meaning which involves the idea of a heavenly, unique figure among human beings, to whom the quality of the divine is to be attached. Its use in 13.19 is also closely related to the arrest, not as a public event but on its interior domestic side as being set in motion by the betrayal of Judas. Whereas the problem of the arrest itself was how one who, by his status and nature, is in complete control was to be taken into the power of sinful men, the problem on its internal side was how this could come about through one of the inner circle of disciples. In 13.12-19 Jesus expounds the meaning of the footwashing for his disciples, but makes an exception in the case of Judas the betrayer. This betrayal, however, does not lie outside the knowledge of Jesus, their Lord and Master, and he informs them in advance of the events so that when these come to pass they may know that 'I am', that his divine foreknowledge is in divine control.

The remaining uses of the absolute ἐγώ εἰμι occur not in relation to events but as part of theological discourse in 8.24, 28, 58. The starting point for this is the statement in 8.12, 'I am the light of the world', and what is said in 8.13-28 as exposition of this. The statement is said to mean that Jesus gives the light of life, that is, the light which comes from, and is a constituent of, eternal life (cf. 1.4).[2] He does this as the

---

1. The theme reappears at the trial, when Pilate is told that he has no power to influence the decision about Jesus' death except it be derived from heaven, and the reader already knows that the outcome of events can only be according to God's determined plan—a feature of Greek dramatic writing. Jesus' final word 'It is completed' (19.30) demands a previous gradual build-up of him as the one with total authority and alone given the work of God to complete to perfection.

2. N.R. Petersen, *The Gospel of John and the Sociology of Light* (Philadelphia: Trinity Press International, 1993), pp. 10-14. It is a matter of considerable debate that

one who knows his origin in God and his return to God, and who in his judgment is the constant companion of God, in contrast to his opponents who do not know him nor his Father. In this context the assertion is made that they will die in their sins, that is, unenlightened by the light of the world and ignorant of the Father, unless they believe that 'I am', that he is divine (v. 28). The recognition of this divine quality in 'I am' will be made possible by this act of lifting him up, which will be the means of showing that quality in his return to his divine origin, which is the Father (v. 28, cf. v. 21). But since, as we have seen, it is frequently the Son of Man who is said to be lifted up the statement in v. 28 implies the divine status of the Son of Man and of Jesus as the Son of Man.

So far the absolute use of ἐγώ εἰμι would seem to refer to a divine figure of some sort who will be recognized as such by the reader. One problem in this is whether it is entirely based on the Old Testament texts where God reveals himself by the ἐγώ εἰμι formula, and is entirely limited to the confines of Jewish thought. This problem is particularly raised by 8.58. As the climax of a bitter controversy over freedom and truth in relation to Abraham, Jesus solemnly asserts that those who keep his word will not see death; that is, his speech is equivalent to eternal life. The Jews then, on the basis of the fact that Abraham, to whom both sides appeal, is dead, raise the question of who Jesus is making himself out to be. It is in reply to this, and to maintain a common glory with the Father who is the God of the Jews, that Jesus makes the statement 'Before Abraham was I am'. Bultmann, who in relation to vv. 24 and 28 acknowledges some background in the Old Testament, regards the ἐγώ εἰμι in v. 58 as of a different kind. He comments: 'The world's conception of time and age is worthless when it has to deal with God's revelation, as is its conception of life and death...The ἐγώ which Jesus speaks as the Revealer is the "I" of the eternal Logos, which was in the beginning, the "I" of the eternal God himself'.[1] In this instance Bultmann links the formula with the opening verses of the prologue and with the Logos who is in the closest intimacy with God. There would seem to be evidence of how this could come about, to which Bultmann does not refer, in the Philonic interpretation of Exod. 3.14, which is the ultimate source of the sacred use of ἐγώ εἰμι. This is elaborated by

'God', 'the Word', 'the Light' and 'the Life' are four synonyms. Here it is pertinent to note that in Jn 1.4 the 'Light' is a constituent of 'the Life'; and the phrase 'Light of men' is a verbal noun. (So also the term 'light of the world'.)

1.   *John*, p. 327.

Knox, who shows that the Jewish exponents of the Torah to the Greeks found the language of Exod. 3.14 particularly attractive, since through it they were able to prove that the God of the Torah was really the God of philosophy, and was pure being. In this way Philo was able to give respectability to Judaism in the eyes of the Greek enquirer. In *Mut. Nom.* 11ff. Philo uses Exod. 3.14 to prove that, except as pure being, a notion impossible to rabbinical Judaism but possible in Platonism, God is ineffable, and the Logos is ineffable. Knox continues, saying that at 8.58 'Jesus practically proclaims himself the Logos of the God of pure being'.[1] There can be no question of a direct connection between the Philonic conception of the Logos and the Logos of John, in whom is combined flesh and the divine glory, glory being the Jewish equivalent of the Greek idea of pure being. The question is how far Philo illuminates current concepts of Logos, which may also be reflected in the Johannine understanding, and whether the fourth evangelist is using techniques similar to Philo's to commend Christianity to educated Greeks.

Such an interpretation as that given by Knox of 8.58 would certainly allow full weight to be given to θεός at 1.1, 18, and that verse so interpreted would provide a particularly strong climax to the argument throughout ch. 8. In that case Jesus has the last word. He would be reaffirming that he spoke with the veracity and authority of the divine communicator, the Logos who in Christian thinking is as God. As such and as the light of the world he passes untouched through the midst of his opponents, with no one laying hands on him because his ordained hour of arrest had not yet come.

The case with 4.26 is more ambiguous. In the conversation with the woman at the well, who has asserted that when the eschatological (Samaritan?) messiah comes he will announce all things, Jesus says, 'I am the one speaking to you'. This could be a self-identification: 'I am he (messiah), the one who is speaking to you'. But it is doubtful whether all the themes introduced in this discourse can be contained within the Samaritan concept of messiahship. The 'historical' event of the discourse is the drawing of water from Jacob's well, into which are injected highly theological, if indirect, self-acclamations about the gift of God, which is living water. Further, the conversation with the woman prepares the stage for the first prolonged teaching to disciples (4.31-38), where Jesus

1. *Hellenistic Elements*, pp. 70-71 (esp. p. 70 n. 2).

asserts that his food is not earthly victuals but is doing the will of the one who has sent him and to bring his work to completion. He is not only the source of living water but is himself nourished by doing the will and work of God. This would seem to require a wider background than Samaritan messianic expectations for the status of Jesus as the source of authoritative speech about ultimate things, and for his exalted origin, of which the reader has already been informed.

There is a similar self-acclamation in 8.18, 'I am the one witnessing concerning myself'. Jesus has claimed to be the light of the world (8.12), a claim which is immediately challenged by the Jews. In reply the claim is defended by making himself one witness to the truth and God the other, and in this way satisfying Jewish legal requirements. Thus in the only two places, 8.18 and 4.26, where ἐγώ εἰμι is followed by a participle in the nominative, claims are made which require for their meaning previously supplied information about the divine origin of Jesus and his speech.

In summary, thus far, all the instances of the absolute formula may be said to require a theological content. The wider cosmological setting for the readers which the prologue implies throughout is not narrowed even at 8.58, as if that were addressed to readers steeped only in rabbinic thought forms. Rather it seems that a measure of Hellenization, which began in Palestine two centuries before Jesus, contributes to the evangelist's distinctive thought forms, and may explain his peculiar use of the Old Testament.

The Predicative Use of the Formula

We now turn to the use of the formula ἐγώ εἰμι with a predicate. This is found in the text as follows:

> I am...the Bread of life (6.35, 48); cf. I am the living bread, the one
>> having come down from heaven (6.51; 6.41). In connection with
>> these may be taken 'but my Father gives you the true bread out
>> of heaven' (6.32b) and 'the bread of God is the one coming
>> down out of heaven and giving life to the world' (6.33).
> I am...the Light of the world (8.12, cf. 9.5).
> I am...the Door of the sheep (10.7, 9).
> I am...the good Shepherd (10.11, 14).
> I am...the Resurrection and the Life (11.25; 'and the Life' is absent in
>> p45, a, l*, Cypr Or pt; the shorter text is defended by O. Merx).
> I am...the Way the Truth and the Life (14.6).
> I am... the true Vine (15.1, 15.5).

These self-proclamations in the mouth of the Johannine Jesus—the fact that there are seven is probably without significance—constitute the most extraordinary set of claims in the whole of the New Testament, if not perhaps in all extant religious literature. Their origin and background have naturally been a matter of intense discussion. Some scholars have sought to place them entirely on an Old Testament background. Thus Bernard maintains that these similitudes by which Jesus describes himself are in the Old Testament style of deity, as in Isa. 51.12; 44.24; 44.6, and that such a compound formula would have been appreciated immediately by readers familiar with the LXX. He further notes that the only other places in the New Testament where Jesus utters 'I am' with a predicate are in Revelation (1.17; 2.23; 22.16), where an Old Testament background is evident.[1] On the other hand Schweizer states categorically that there is no instance in the Old Testament of the Johannine form of expression, that is, of a metaphor which is determinative and without addition along with the verb 'to be': 'I am the (shepherd)'. The Old Testament has only the form 'I am a (shepherd)' or 'I am your (shepherd)', generally followed by an addition 'who...'. And, significantly, Bernard goes on to state that the style would also have been familiar to readers acquainted with the phraseology of Egyptian cults, citing as examples sentences beginning with 'I am' placed in the mouth of the dragon in the *Acts of Thomas* (2.32), self-declarations in Isis inscriptions (one given by Plutarch), in Egyptian magical papyri and in the first century Mithraic liturgy.[2]

This line of enquiry was instigated by Norden, who adduced evidence for the widespread use in the East (though not in the West) of ἐγώ εἰμι followed by a predicate without further addition as a fixed and stylized form of religious utterance, which he designated 'a soteriological type of

1. *John*, I, p. cxviii. The weakness of this is that the statements of the apocalyptic figure of the risen Christ in a vision of the last things are very different in respect of literary genre, style and theology from the statements in the Gospel.

2. *John*, I, p. cxix, quoting largely from A. Deissmann, *Light from the Ancient East* (London: Hodder & Stoughton, 1910), pp. 135-36, 138-39. Brown, *John*, Appendix IV, pp. 533-34, argues for an exclusively Old Testament background despite this evidence. Schnackenburg, *St John*, II, Excursus 8, pp. 79-80, also adopts this view, though he is forced to admit as a structural influence 'the soteriological type of discourse current in Eastern Hellenism'. Dodd, while maintaining that the Hebrew *ani hu* lies behind the formula, draws attention to certain transitions from Jewish to Hellenistic forms of expression, notably in the use of ἀληθινός attached to the symbol; see *Interpretation*, pp. 93-96, 139, 170-78.

discourse'.[1] This was further extended in a monograph devoted to the subject by Schweizer, who adduced instances from Babylon, Iran, Egypt and even India, and from gnostic literature, with special attention to the Mandaean writings, where the parallels both in form and content are closest.[2] This was summarized, brought to a head and applied as the most likely background to the Johannine formulations by Bultmann in an extensive footnote in his commentary.[3] There he identifies, and copiously illustrates, four distinctive forms of the 'I am' formula.

The first is a *presentation* formula. Here the 'I' is the subject, and the speaker introduces himself in reply to the question 'Who are you?' There are numerous non-religious examples, especially in drama, but it is also a sacred formula for the introduction of a divinity: cf. Gen. 17.1, 'I am El-Shaddai'; the Isis inscriptions 'I am Isis, the lord of the whole land'; *Corp. Herm.* 1.2, 'I am Poimandres'.

The second is a *qualificatory* formula. Here the subject is 'I', and the question 'What are you?' receives a reply in terms of 'I am that and that' or 'I am the one who...'. A non-religious example is when the speaker says 'I am a philosopher'; examples in religious literature are in Isa. 44.6, 'I am the first and the last, and besides me there is no God'; the statement of Isis, 'I am the lord of war, the lord of the thunderbolt'; or the Mandaean 'A shepherd am I who loves his sheep'.

The third is an *identification* formula which proliferates in religious syncretism, for here the speaker identifies himself with another person or object, as when the Egyptian god Re says, 'I am he who arose as Chopre'; or Isis says, 'I am everything that was and is and will be'.

The fourth is a *recognition* formula. This is distinguished from the other three in that the 'I' is not the subject but the predicate. It answers the question 'Who is the one who is expected, spoken to, asked for?' with the reply 'It is I who am'. Bultmann cites examples of this in religious literature, and believes that the ἐγώ εἰμι statements in the Fourth Gospel are to be understood as being of this kind.[4]

Schweizer, while accepting Bultmann's categorization as both correct and useful for assessing the available material, also introduces for the purpose a criterion of his own. He attempts to distinguish 'I am'

1. *Agnostos Theos*, pp. 188-93.
2. *Ego Eimi*, pp. 12-14. See also the references in Knox, *Hellenistic Elements*, p. 70 n. 1, to the evidence in R. Reitzenstein, *Poimandres*, pp. 184-85, 245-46.
3. *John*, pp. 225-26.
4. *John*, p. 226.

statements which are statements of revelation from those which are not. Thus statements which list a whole series of predicates, each of which does not convey anything in itself but together say that the speaker is 'all', are not genuinely revelatory. Nor are those in which the emphasis is on the results for human beings. Revelatory statements are those such as 'I am the helper of those who are without a saviour', which issue in the command to give praise and honour to the speaker. In these the emphatic 'I' and the command to praise legitimate the speaker as the only one who has the right to say 'I am', and set him against all others. Schweizer sees the revelatory utterances in the Old Testament such as Isa. 51.12; 45.5-6, 8 as belonging to this category, and raises the question of a possible affinity with the 'I am' statements in the Fourth Gospel. However, to the Johannine formulations, constructed with ἐγώ εἰμι, a predicate noun standing on its own with no addition except sometimes an adjective (ἀληθινός, κάλος), a participle (ὁ ζῶν) or a adjectival genitive (τῆς ζωῆς τοῦ κόσμος, τῶν προβάτων), he finds no exact parallel either in the Old Testament or anywhere else.[1]

Thus far the Johannine ἐγώ εἰμι formulations, though distinctive, may be said to rest on a wide religious usage whereby the speaker asserts, possibly against all others, a 'divine' status for himself or herself, and claims to be the source of whatever belongs to the 'divine' or heavenly realm. This was the language of the religious competition and syncretism that were rife in the first centuries BCE and CE. Its employment in the context of a monotheism where 'I am' was already reserved for the one God who is the source of all things would represent a profound revolution of thought.

In any further exploration of these formulations two questions in particular arise, and especially if Bultmann's categorization of them as identificatory formulae is correct. The first is the question of *Gattung*. What is the character and function of what I have hitherto designated by the neutral term 'predicate', or 'nominal predicate', that is, the nouns 'bread', 'light', 'shepherd', 'vine' and so on? The second is the question of milieu. Whence did the evangelist derive such predicates, and what led him to select these predicates in particular?

How difficult the first question is to answer is shown by the multiplicity and variety of descriptive terms which have been applied to these predicates—for instance, parable, parabolic speech, similitude, figure,

1. *Ego Eimi*, pp. 27-36.

figurative speech, metaphor, allegory, symbol, mystical phraseology—
and, by the fact that none of them has established itself as satisfactory.[1]
Thus it is of the essence of parable that it states its truth by means of a
comparison with someone or something drawn from life: 'As the heart
desires the water brooks, so longs my soul after thee, O God'. A parable
or similitude makes the comparison in the form of a story of the
extended action of someone or something: 'A sower went out to sow...'
The Johannine formulations, which can be introduced abruptly at the
beginning of a discourse, or anywhere within it except the end, clearly
do not fall into this category. For they make not a comparison but an
assertion ('I am'); and the predicate is supplied not by a figure of speech
(a vine), but by what is specified by the definite article (the vine), and in
some cases is further specified by a determining adjective (the true vine).
Even in the single instance when the predicate is developed somewhat in
story form (10.1-6, 11-18) this is not to make a comparison between
Jesus and a shepherd, but to define the good (true) shepherd by reference to what Jesus is and does in coming in through the door, which he
himself is, and giving his life for the sheep.

A metaphor is a figure of speech by means of which the character or
function of someone or something is described: 'The Lord is a (my)
rock'. An allegory is a story made up of a series of connected metaphors which are to be decoded and applied. This also hardly accords
with the Johannine formulations, for they are not parts of an extended
story in which the predicates—bread, light, vine and so on—constitute
the key terms. Further the 'I am' to which the predicate is attached
makes an assertion and not a coded reference, and the predicate with a
definite article, 'the bread', is no longer a pure metaphor.[2]

Perhaps the least unsatisfactory of the terms proposed is 'symbol'.
Symbolism may be defined as the use of elements belonging to the

---

1.   Schweizer, *Ego Eimi*, pp. 6-7, lists more than 40 terms used in this connection
by commentators and exegetes.

2.   On the similar passage, 15.1-10, J. Jeremias (*The Parables of Jesus* [London:
SCM Press, 1963], p. 86) comments: 'The metaphor of the Vine and its Branches...
introduces at once an allegorical interpretation... which has completely absorbed the
interpreted parable or metaphor into itself. From this it may be seen how great a
prominence the Fourth Gospel has given to the allegorical interpretation'. This
comment would seem to illustrate that the category of allegory is out of place here; for
15.1-10 cannot be said to rest on the basis of an interpreted parable, or itself to be an
allegorical interpretation of it or of anything else.

natural order in a transferred sense of corresponding elements in the supernatural order. This was, however, open to variation given the degree to which the symbol retained or did not retain any vital connection with the material world from which it was taken. Thus in Platonism, and even more in the neo-Platonism which succeeded it, the symbols were increasingly abstract, and in the aeons of the gnostic systems were of necessity totally divorced from the material world. This would not accord with John's usage, for example in the prologue, where the Logos, who is characterized in terms of supernatural 'Life' and 'Light', is also the author of creation and becomes flesh.[1] The problem is analogous to that of finding the proper equivalent of the word *sēmeion*, which plays such an important part in John's presentation of Jesus. In calling these physical actions of Jesus 'signs' (2.11; 12.37) the evangelist underlines their symbolic character. They do not stand in their own right as 'miracles', but signify a corresponding supernatural entity, connected with God and now available to human beings. The feeding symbolizes and points to the bread of heaven (of life) which Jesus is and gives; the healing of a blind man does the same for the light (of life, of the world). So also the verb σημαίνειν, 'to signify', means to indicate symbolically: 'to lift up' in v. 32 shows the quality of the cross as exaltation to God (12.32-33). Yet in this the evangelist does not intend to deprive these actions of their physical quality and to make them abstractions. On the contrary he would seem to go out of his way to underline the physicality. The wine at Cana is vast in quantity, the lame man has been 38 years in his condition, the blind man has been born so, Lazarus has been dead four days and is corrupting. Thus if 'symbol' is the right word to use in connection with the thought and language of this gospel, it has to be the type of symbol that retains a relation with the created order from which it has arisen.

The second question, of a possible milieu for such predicates, involves the exploration of religious literature of the time to see whether there is evidence for their use as standing religious symbols. This is the more necessary in that the Old Testament does not suffice to provide an adequate background to them. Although the Old Testament employs a great variety of metaphors of Yahweh and his activity it has only 'shepherd' in common with the Johannine predicates. Yahweh is not

---

1. Cf. the oft-quoted remark of Augustine that he had found the equivalent of all the statements in the prologue in the writings of the neo-Platonists except the statement 'the Word became flesh'.

spoken of in terms of bread, door, vine, resurrection or way, and while truth, life and light are applied to him this is in a significantly different manner from that in which they are applied in the Fourth Gospel.

We turn, therefore, to Hellenistic Judaism, and to Philo of Alexandria in particular as the most voluminous representative of it. Scholars are divided in their estimates of him and his originality, and of his exact status and influence in that city which was the next in importance to Rome at the time. The riddle of the survival of the Philonic corpus has not been fully solved. They are almost the only contemporary Hellenistic Jewish writings to have been preserved. There is no mention of his name in rabbinical writings, though some claim echoes of his teaching there. It may be asked who valued his writings to the extent that they were still available to the early Christian Fathers in Alexandria. Could it have been that, though the writings nowhere refer to Jesus or to Christianity, it was Hellenized Jews who had become Christians who preserved them? One thing is universally agreed, namely that but for the reverence in which his writings and his allegorical exegesis of the Old Testament were held, even providing a model for patristic exegesis in this respect, the corpus would not have survived.[1] Philo and the New Testament writers had in common that they wrote in Greek in a Jewish environment outside Palestine, and were concerned with the interpretation of the Jewish Scriptures, predominantly in the LXX version. Both espoused forms of religion which were incompatible with much Jewish practice and transcended some forms of Jewish expectation. It has become a commonplace to affirm that Philo's words were valued by Christians, but no one has solved the problem of who precisely treasured them in the first century, nor by what route Philo came almost to be canonized.[2]

1. There is no mention of Philo in Jewish literature, except in a few medieval MSS of Jewish philosophy, until Rossi in the sixteenth century, who relegated him to the status of a wise man of the non-Jewish world; see F.N.D. Winston, *Logos and Mystical Theology in Philo of Alexandria* (Cincinnati: Hebrew Union College Press, 1985), p. 9.
2. There is evidence that by the ninth century Philo was accepted as a Christian. In one MS he wears a stole that is dotted with crosses, and a fresco in the cathedral at Le Puy depicts him standing by the cross together with Isaiah, Hosea and Jeremiah. Indeed, until the sixteenth century it was believed that he was one of the Fathers and had taught the doctrine of the Trinity. This was superficially tenable, since the Logos featured often in his writing, and the Fathers, being part of the neo-Platonist world, would readily use his Logos material. Dionysius Petavius was the first to assert, in 1644, that Philo's Trinitarian doctrine was not Christian but Platonic. In 1693 the

According to E.R. Goodenough and S. Sandmel, Philo represented that Hellenized Judaism which was the vehicle by which Christianity spread rapidly in the Greco-Roman world.[1] It would follow from this that one is justified in searching the Philonic corpus for terminology which provides some sort of a background for Johannine thought forms, and in particular for the symbols attached to 'I am'. They must have been intelligible to the readers of the Gospel, since no need is felt to explain them, just as the Logos appears without explanation, apparently as being readily understood. If it is possible to show a Hellenistic background for them and a link with the Logos figure, this would not necessarily be to say that the Logos of the evangelist came by way of a literary dependence on Philo, or that it is doctrinally a parallel to the Philonic logos. It would simply be to claim here in particular what Goodenough and Sandmel have claimed in general.

The Bread of Life
The discourse on bread in John 6 arises out of the feeding of 6.5-14, which is to be understood as a supernatural banquet, the miraculously provided food being sufficient to satiate a huge crowd, who as a result are compelled to pursue and find Jesus (6.24-26). The incident reaches a climax in a negative command not to toil for perishable food, that is, not to work for earthly nourishment, and in a positive command to labour for food (βρῶσις) which remains in respect of eternal life, which the Son of Man, the man who has already been sealed by God the Father,

German classicist Johann Fabricius removed Philo from his supposed Christian roots, showing decisively that he was a Platonist, and from then on he was open to sharp criticism from Christian scholars. E.R. Goodenough in his *Introduction to Philo Judaeus* (1940) was one of the first to approach him sympathetically, and succeeded in showing that he was a bridge from Judaism into Christianity, and that, were there more contemporary literature available, we would have a firmer grasp of his importance, especially with respect to the transmission of religious ideas, where religion was deeply attached to philosophy of the era. See further Winston, *Philo of Alexandria*, and H.A. Wolfson, *Philo: Foundations of Religious Philosophy in Judaism, Christianity and Islam* (2 vols.; Cambridge, MA: Harvard University Press, 1968), whose views are in contrast to those of Goodenough; and S. Sandmel, *Philo of Alexandria* (Oxford: Oxford University Press, 1979), who is in close agreement with Goodenough and who asserts against Wolfson that Philo is thoroughly Hellenized, and, along with Goodenough, that 'Hellenized Judaism' represented by Philo made possible the rapid Hellenization of Christianity.
    1.   See previous note.

will give (6.28). A transition is thus made from physical loaves (ἄρτοι) which have been devoured (vv. 9.13, 26) to heavenly food (v. 27), which is then loosely connected with manna, which God supplied to Israel (v. 31).

The rest of the discourse is about supernatural food, which is variously defined. It is unlike Moses' supply of manna, for it does not perish, being 'true' (ἀληθινός) bread from heaven (v. 32), which a person may eat and not die (v. 50). 'True' here can only have the Hellenistic meaning of 'heavenly', 'perfect', 'everlasting', 'not subject to change'. This is not only guaranteed by its origin, but itself guarantees eternal qualitative life to believers. Here we are clearly into the realm of ideas current in Hellenistic thought and concerned with salvation. The evangelist, however, does not use this term. Rather he takes the ideas he wants, removes them from the complex of pagan beliefs and rites about escape from this mortal life, and uses them to build up a doctrine of participation in eternal life here and now.[1] The self-acclamation 'I am the living bread' (ὁ ἄρτος ὁ ζῶν) is introduced in this form to emphasize the human reality of the man Jesus. The new idea is not that believers partake of divine food, but that the flesh and blood, the humanity, of the man Jesus, who is speaking as the divine 'I am', is to be appropriated, 'eaten' in order that eternal life may be received. The resultant heavenly state is described in terms of indwelling. As the Father has sent Jesus, the Bread, and he indwells God, so also whoever devours and takes into his or her very self that living Bread will similarly live because of Jesus (vv. 51-57).

How far a specific sacramental background governs the choice of words here is difficult to determine. What is clear is that once more we are in a strong Hellenistic milieu as the discourse proceeds in vv. 52-63. Knox maintains that the purpose of this section was 'to proceed from the theology of Jesus as the Logos of whom manna was the type to the evangelist's eucharistic theology'. He notes the double insistence of the evangelist on the necessity of eating the flesh of Jesus as the Son of Man, and the subsequent explication of this in terms of the words of Jesus which are 'spirit' and 'life'. This, he maintains, is a typically Hellenistic explanation of a rite, and quotes from several Greek sources to the effect that to observe a rite and to understand it philosophically

---

1.   Bultmann, *John*, pp. 220-24 illustrates both in text and notes how deeply engrained in many religions was the search for food which had celestial qualities and guaranteed that a believer was in a state of salvation.

was a sure way of safeguarding against superstition and atheism. 'Any...rite in which eating or drinking appeared had to be explained as a symbol of "assimilating" knowledge, virtue, etc.'[1] 'It need hardly be said that the reading of this "spiritual" meaning (sc. in Jn 6) into a received piece of traditional cultus is entirely hellenistic'.[2]

Relevant here may also be the reference in 6.41-52 to the division among the Jews caused by the statements of Jesus. There it is asserted that human beings cannot come to Jesus by their own power; they have first to hear and learn from the Father. This is linked to being 'drawn' or 'dragged' (the verb ἑλκύειν has a compulsive element) by God (cf. the same verb in 12.32 of Jesus' drawing people to himself). It is also an idea found in Hellenistic thought, where gods drag their devotees through the hostile spheres to the celestial sphere. As a result of this dragging, human beings 'shall all be taught of God' (v. 45). This is a quotation from Isa. 54.12-13, with 'all' substituted for 'your sons' to make it universal in application (though it is also reminiscent of Jer. 31.33-34 and the law written on the heart). Thus the eating and drinking of the flesh and blood of the Son of Man are explicated in terms of hearing and learning from, and being taught by, God; and the consequent partaking of eternal life from its source in Jesus who indwells God.

With these features of the discourse in mind we may note how Philo uses the symbols of manna, bread and celestial nourishment. In *Fug.* 137 he writes of those who sought that which nourished the soul that 'they became learners (μάθοντες), and found a saying (ῥῆμα) of God and a divine logos (θεῖον λόγον), from which all manner of instructions (παιδεῖαι) and wisdoms (σοφίαι) flow in a perpetual stream. This is the heavenly food (τροφή)...It says in sacred records, "Behold, I am raining upon you bread out of heaven".'

In *Rer. Div. Her.* 79-80 he writes more specifically of the person of worth, who sees visions, that 'he extends his vision to the ether...he has been trained also to look steadfastly for the manna, which is the divine logos (τὸν θεῖον λόγον) the incorruptible food of the soul'; and in 191 that 'further, the heavenly food of the soul, wisdom, which Moses calls "manna", the divine logos (θεῖος λόγος) distributes to all who will use it equal portions' (cf. *Det. Pot. Ins.* 118: 'Manna is called the divine logos [θεῖος λόγος], the eldest of all existences').

In *Leg. All.* 3.172-73, with reference to the thirsty souls that love

1. *Hellenistic Elements*, pp. 67-68 and n. 1 p. 67.
2. *Hellenistic Elements*, p. 68.

God, Philo writes, 'Also they are filled with the manna, the most generic
of substances...The supremely generic is God, and next to him is the
Word of God, but all other things subsist in logos only'. Further, with
respect to this nourishment of the soul, he writes in *Leg. All.* 3.173, by
way of an appeal to Moses, 'This is the bread (ἄρτος), the food (τροφή)
which God has given to the soul for it to feed on his own utterance and
on his own logos'.

Finally, in *Congr.* 173-74, commenting on the scriptural words, 'He
fed thee with the manna', he refers to God as 'he who provided it, the
food that costs no toil or suffering' and to the recipients of the manna as
those who feed on the divine logoi.

It would appear from the above that Philo was not infrequently concerned with the idea of nourishment for those seeking God, which he
refers to as manna, bread and heavenly food, among other things, and
which on occasions he can identify with the divine logos. It may be
suggested that their application in John 6 to Jesus had behind it an
intention of the evangelist to depict in the Gospel the Logos of the
prologue in operation.

The Light of the World

The use of 'light' in religious thought is widespread.[1] It was from the
religions of the East, especially Persia, that it entered into Western
religions. It became a basic tenet of gnostic systems, and could take the
form of belief in divinized men, who were frequently portrayed as gods
with rays of sun emanating from their heads. The sun itself became less
and less of a god and more a symbol of cosmic light or truth. Light has
first place in the Genesis creation narrative, and Philo (*Op. Mund.* 29-
37) shows how this could be expounded in terms derived from Plato's
Timaeus. It is part of the creation of a non-corporeal heaven and an
invisible earth, an invisible light perceptible only to mind, which came
into being as an image of the divine Logos. Nowhere in the Old
Testament is God identified with light. The rabbis used the term
metaphorically of the law, of individual teachers and of Israel, and God is
referred to as a light or lamp, though this affords no parallel to the
Johannine self-acclamation in 8.12. Philo, however, does take a step
further when he writes,

1.   See Barrett, *St John*, pp. 335-37.

God is light; for there is a verse in one of the psalms. 'The Lord is my
illumination and my saviour.' And he is not only light, but the archetype of
every other light, nay prior to and high above every archetype, holding the
position of a model. For the model or pattern was Logos, which contained
all his fulness—'Light' (*Somn.* 1.75).

Here is an instance of the Logos regarded through the symbol of light as
a cosmic illuminator of human beings. This is found later in the hermetic
literature, where the revealer-god, the one who illuminates humankind, is
the primal light who begins the cosmogony. Something like it would
appear to lie behind those particular cosmological elements which are
selected in the prologue—the true light coming into the world, the
Logos who made all that was made coming into the world which did
not know him.

The Good Shepherd

The self-acclamation 'I am the Door' (10.7, 9) remains a puzzle, both
because it is introduced so abruptly and fits so ill with the following
picture of the shepherd, and because the use of 'door' as a symbol in
this way has no parallel in Hellenistic Judaism or anywhere else. Hence it
is suggested *faute de mieux* that the use of 'door' in Lk. 13.24, Mt. 7.13
lies behind its application here.

On the other hand the shepherd symbol is ancient and universal. It is
frequently used as a designation of kings and rulers. In the Old
Testament God is said to shepherd Israel; Moses shepherds God's
people, and David is an ideal shepherd king. Jeremiah refers to unfaithful
shepherds, that is leaders, who harm their flocks. There are passages in
the New Testament which plainly rest upon this Old Testament background. But, as Bultmann has observed, the particular use of the symbol
in Jn 10.11, 14 is marked more by differences from than similarities to
the Old Testament usage. Thus the contrast is not between good and
bad shepherds, but between the good shepherd and hirelings. There is
reference to a fold and to other sheep not of this fold. The relationship
between shepherd and sheep consists in mutual knowledge, and the
goodness of this shepherd consists in the fact that he lays down his life
for the sheep. This suggests that the use of 'shepherd' in John 10 is a
composition with a background of thought which is not simply that of
the Old Testament.[1] In Hellenistic thought 'shepherd' was also used of
kings and rulers, who could be thought of as in some sense divine by

1.   Bultmann, *John*, pp. 364-70.

virtue of possessing souls which came from the higher regions of the cosmos.[1] Thus Bultmann refers to Plutarch as contrasting the hireling (μισθωτός) with the divine leader (θεῖος ἡγεμών) who is the Logos.[2] In *Agr.* 51-54 Philo uses the term 'shepherd' not only of kings and sages but of God himself. On the basis of Ps. 23.1 he states that the cosmos is a flock 'under the hand of God, its king and shepherd'. He leads it in accordance with right law, setting over it his true word and firstborn son (ὀρθὸν λόγον καὶ πρωτόγονον υἱόν). Here the term passes beyond the messianic royal figure of Judaism and has taken on a cosmic significance. Shepherding means the right ordering of the cosmos by the intermediary figure of the Logos, to whom the sheep belong.

Peculiar to this self-acclamation is the use of the word καλός rather than ἀληθινός, 'true'. Why is this word chosen and what is its meaning? It is a very Greek word lying deep within Greek civilization. Its basic meaning is 'beautiful', and it was used of gentlemen, in particular of the 'beautiful' young men who are the ideal pupils of the teacher, and whose minds the teacher is expected to mould. It does not mean 'good' in the ordinary sense of human moral worth, and the 'good' shepherd is not here contrasted with 'bad' (i.e. false or immoral) shepherds, but with hirelings, who do not own the sheep. Perhaps the least inadequate rendering for καλός here would be 'perfect'. The perfection of Jesus as the shepherd consists in two things. First, he can say as shepherd 'I and my Father are one' (10.30). This, as Knox observes, would be quite irrelevant on a purely Old Testament background of rulers and kings as shepherds. It requires for its explanation the more Hellenistic conception of the shepherd as a divine intermediary. This shepherding is not of an ordinary natural kind, but is defined by who the shepherd is. He is the one to whom the sheep belong by right, and his perfection consists in maintaining the unity between his own sheep and God. It is this which all who have come before him have been unable to do.

Secondly, the goodness of the shepherd consists in his laying down his life for the sheep. Here the symbol has plainly lost all parabolic quality and is now governed entirely by its application to Jesus. It is impossible literally for a shepherd to lay down his life for his sheep—the wolf, having killed the shepherd, is free to pick off the sheep in his own time. The symbol has been twisted here to depict the character of Jesus—that he gives himself in death for human beings—and the supernatural results

1. Knox, *Hellenistic Elements*, p. 71 and p. 72 n. 1.
2. *John*, p. 367 n. 1.

that he effects—he delivers human beings through his death so that they may have life. This is the result of the commandment of the Father, of the unity of mind and will between Jesus and the Father, and is the ground of the Father's love for the Son (10.17-18). Since this sacrificial and liberating death is later to be characterized by the word τετέλεσται, 'it is accomplished (perfected)', the word καλός is best rendered here by 'perfect'. Jesus actually performs that in which the 'true' (divine) shepherding of human beings consists.

The Way, the Truth and the Life

Difficulties in the interpretation of the self-acclamation in 14.6 appear from early times. They arise over the presence of the three nouns in it, and over their relation to one another.[1] Some of the Fathers understood 'the way' as that which leads to a goal. Along this line 'the way' was sometimes interpreted as itself 'the truth' which leads to eternal life as the goal. Augustine took 'the way' as that which leads to a goal, and along with Clement of Alexandria and Origen, possibly under the influence of Platonist thought, related 'the truth and life' as this goal to the Logos in his pre-existence.[2] Maldonatus, appealing to Hebrew idiom behind the Greek text, argued that 'the truth' was to be taken adjectivally; the rendering should be 'I am the true way to life'. Aquinas, interpreting according to medieval thought forms, maintained that Christ was 'the way' according to his humanity, but 'the truth and the life' according to his divinity.[3]

More recently scholars have interpreted the text against a variety of backgrounds: gnostic, Mandaean and Hermetic.[4] Here we find the idea of the ascent of the soul along a way to the heavenly spheres of truth and life.[5] Bultmann reaches a somewhat different conclusion, which is partly due to his view that in the 'I am' sayings the 'I' is not the subject but the predicate. There is an access to God, which can also be referred

1. See Brown, *John*, II, pp. 620-21, and Schnackenburg, *St John*, III, pp. 64-66.
2. See Schnackenburg, *St John*, III, p. 65, and I. de la Potterie, 'Je suis la Voie, la Vérité et la Vie', *NRT* 88 (1966), pp. 907-42.
3. See Brown, *John*, II, pp. 620-21.
4. So Bultmann, *John*, pp. 603-607; Schnackenburg, *St John*, III, p. 66.
5. Cf. 'You are the way of the perfect, the path that leads to the place of light. You are the light of eternity towards which you went, and where you had a place in (every) human heart' (*Ginza*, 271, 26ff., cited by Schnackenburg, *St John*, III, p. 66). Cf. also Bultmann, *John*, p. 603 n. 5.

to as the goal by means of the symbol of 'the door'. Jesus claims to be this, and alone to be it. This goal is further defined as 'the truth', that is, the divine reality, and 'the life', that is, this reality already bestowed on the believer.[1] In this way the three concepts are bound together, which is in keeping with Johannine thought. Others prefer to understand the subject of the verb as 'I' and the nouns as the predicate. They take the first of the two copulas as epexegetical ('that is to say'), and the second as a normal conjunction. The text then reads 'I am the way, that is to say the truth, and the life'.[2]

It may be significant that the self-acclamation here is glossed by a Johannine idiom in which a negative in the form of an emphatic οὐδείς is followed by a positive statement. This has already appeared in 3.13, where Jesus as the Son of Man is said to effect what no human being can do in descending from, and then ascending to, heaven (cf. 1.51, where the Son of Man has been introduced as the highway between heaven and earth).[3] Thus Jesus is the divine communicator; and what he communicates to believers as the things which belong in the divine realm are presented under the symbols of 'light', 'bread', 'shepherd'. This is now reiterated as 'way', 'truth' and 'life'. It may further be noted that this mode of statement occurs first in the prologue with relation to the Logos, when John witnesses that no one has ever seen God, but that the unique God, the one who is always in the bosom of the Father, has communicated the divine secrets. This could suggest that the self-acclamation in 14.6 belongs to the exposition in the Gospel of what has been said about the Logos in the prologue.

The question remains, however, of the origin of the concepts of 'way', 'truth' and 'life'. Some have seen the origin of 'the way' in the Old Testament concept of walking in God's way, an expression for the practical moral behaviour of people who live according to the Torah. Here there is no thought of any ascent of the soul, nor is there any goal in view. The Torah is a source of directives which, if kept, will effect the eschatological day, or will in some way bring Israel into the direct blessing of God, from which they so frequently exclude themselves. This, however, hardly suits Johannine thought and language. Others have seen the origin in Mandaean literature, for example in such statements as

1.   *John*, pp. 603-607.
2.   This is favoured by Brown, *John*, II, pp. 630-31, W. Michaelis, 'ὁδός', *TDNT*, V, pp. 81-82, de la Potterie, 'Je suis la Voie', and others.
3.   Cf. also 1.3, 10, 11, 18; 3.13-14; 6.44, 65, for example.

'You show us the way of life, and let us walk upon the paths of truth and faith'.[1] But apart from the vexed question of the dating of the Mandaean texts, their concept of the path of the soul has no place in the Gospel. That the truth is both the way and the guide, and that Jesus goes to prepare a place for the disciples and leads the way there as well as himself being the way, are not without contacts with gnostic thought; but that this should be through one who had a concrete historical existence has no parallel there. This is not to say that the evangelist did not draw on gnostic language of any kind for his distinctive theology, and here Philo may prove more helpful. He also is concerned with the true moral life, which, he says, with reference to Num. 20.17, Moses calls the 'royal way'. 'For since God is the first and sole king of the universe, the road leading to him is naturally called royal.' This road is then identified with the true philosophy, which is the genuine wisdom (a divine title), and it is called in the law the utterance (ῥῆμα) and word (λόγος) of God (*Poster. C.* 101-102). Similarly, wisdom, which for Philo is identifiable with the Logos, is 'the perfect way of the eternal and indestructible, the way which leads to God...and when the mind's course is guided along that road it reaches the goal, which is the recognition and knowledge of God' (*Deus Imm.* 14.2). As Dodd observes, in Philo 'for those who are still seeking the goal, God is known in and through his Logos', and he refers particularly to *Migr. Abr.* 174, where the promise of Exod. 23.20, 'I send my messenger before thy face to guard thee in the way', is interpreted as a promise that Abraham, as long as he falls short of perfection, has the divine Logos as his leader.[2] It would not be difficult for readers who shared something of Philo's thought world to relate 'the way' to the figure of the Logos, and then to relate 'truth' and 'life' also to the Logos, since, in the popular philosophy with which Philo expounds Genesis, 'life' as the 'breath of God' and 'truth' as 'light' are themselves said to be an image of the divine Logos (see *Op. Mund.* 30, 36).

The True Vine
On the background of this image scholars are divided. On the one hand the vine is used in the Old Testament of Israel, though generally of an

---

1.   Cited by Schnackenburg, *St John*, III, p. 66, referring to *Mandaische Liturgien* (ed. M. Lidzbarski; AGG, 1920), p. 77.

2.   Dodd, *Interpretation*, pp. 68-69. Cf. also Knox, *Hellemistic Elements*, p. 78 n. 2, for 'the way' as a description of the Logos in Philo.

erring Israel that has neglected God's ways (Jer. 2.21; Isa. 5.1ff., Ps. 80.9-16 [LXX]). But this can hardly be responsible for what is said about the Vine here. As Dodd observes, the symbol 'suggests a unity like that of a living plant, in which a common life, flowing from the central stem, nourishes all the branches and issues in fruit'.[1] As in ch. 14 the images of the way, truth and life extend from who Jesus is to the consequences for disciples. As the Way he prepares a place of abode for them in his Father's house, and in seeing him and knowing him they have seen and known the Father. As the Vine he imparts to them life as the branches, and there is mutual indwelling between them. Because this Vine gives life to the branches Bultmann takes the background of the imagery to be the tree of life.[2] The qualification 'true' gives the Vine the qualities of the genuine and the divine, so that the life imparted in and through it is divine life, of which it is the source (Jn. 15.1, 5). The Johannine stamp is, however, pressed on the imagery, since here the life-flow does not refer to the mutual indwelling of Father, Son and believers (contrast ch. 17), but God stands outside it as the vinedresser.

Here again Philo may prove helpful as standing midway between the Old Testament and more gnostic or philosophical thought. For him 'Israel' could mean far more than either the empirical people or that people in its future eschatological state. As Knox observes, Philo interprets the statement of Isa. 5.7, 'The vineyard of the Lord Almighty is the house of Israel', as referring to Israel as the mind that contemplates God and the world, since Israel means 'seeing God', and the house of the mind is the whole soul, which is the holy vineyard that has for its fruit the divine growth of virtue (*Somn.* 2.172-73). And Knox goes on to say that for Philo Israel can mean, as well as the nation or chosen people, the contemplative type of mind, the contemplative soul which is the first-born of God, or the Logos, 'the divine element in the world which has a special affinity with the highest element in man'. It is as such, he concludes, that Jesus 'animates the disciples, that is the Church, which is the true Israel in virtue of that union between God, the Logos, and the disciple which was the theme of the preceding chapter'.[3]

Thus, apart from 'Door' and 'Resurrection', which of necessity have no pre-Christian basis, the symbols in the 'I am' sayings can be seen to have affinities with Philo's statements about the Logos. This is not to

1. *Interpretation*, p. 196.
2. *John*, p. 530.
3. *Hellenistic Elements*, pp. 80-81.

suggest that the evangelist knew and used the Philonic corpus, but only that his readers in a Hellenistic environment would have been in a position to understand that what Jesus acclaims and claims in the 'I am' sayings was made by means of symbols which were already applied to a Logos figure. If this is so, it would strengthen the possibility that the 'I am' sayings in the body of the Gospel constitute an exposition from Jesus of what was said earlier—albeit in a concentrated form—in the prologue in terms of the relation of God, the Logos and believers. To put it another way, if, as is maintained here, the prologue determined the structure and content of the Gospel then the Logos figure could be said to determine likewise the articular nouns (with or without their adjectives) which the evangelist selected as appropriate for his theology. In this case they are the subject of each ἐγώ εἰμι clause and the ἐγώ εἰμι is the predicate.

The attractiveness of this proposition is that the nouns from Hellenistic symbolism become more intelligible, for they take on the nature of a Johannine *sēmeion.* Then each noun, rather than the ἐγώ εἰμι, takes the weight in exegesis. The ἐγώ εἰμι functions to underpin the claims and teachings presented by means of those nouns by the Logos, Jesus, who utters them as a unique one with divine authenticity.

The heavenly things communicated are to be understood as those activities which the noun itself conveys. Thus the Bread nourishes; the Light enlightens or illuminates; the Door is the means by which the Logos goes to and fro (from heaven?), keeping in communication with his own sheep as befits the perfect divine Shepherd who, by dying, supernaturally provides eternal life for his followers. The Resurrection, the Way, the Truth and the Life similarly present heavenly truths about that which is available to believers; while the true Vine is best understood as stated earlier. It has already been pointed out where the prologue has been explicated, for example with references to Life, Light and the provision of a heavenly qualitative intimacy with the Logos and with God. Thus the ἐγώ εἰμι sayings explicate the seminal statements of 1.1-18 which refer to the Logos and his work, particularly 1.18. The Logos μονογενὴς θεός is the divine communicator, that which is communicated and that which established once and for all the eternal stream of divine communication between God and humankind.

This theme of the communication of divine things, and of mutual indwelling which follows from it, reaches its climax, however, in ch. 17, which in the view of Käsemann occupies a position at the end of the

Gospel equivalent to that of the prologue at the beginning. But here the theme is developed in terms of an address of the Son to the Father. To this imagery we now turn.

Chapter 7

CHRISTOLOGICAL EXPRESSIONS IN THE FOURTH GOSPEL:
THE SON (OF GOD)

While important statements are made in the Fourth Gospel concerning
the status and functions of Jesus by means of the term 'the Son of
Man', and by the use of 'I am', the primary christological expression
here is 'the Son of God', if along with it is taken the absolute use of 'the
Son'. In this the Fourth Gospel differs from the synoptics in two
respects. First, these two terms are comparatively rare in the synoptics,
while in the Fourth Gospel they are comparatively frequent, the first
occurring eight (nine) times, the second 18 (19) times.[1] Secondly, in the
synoptics 'the Son of God' tends to be reserved for certain highly concentrated and significant moments which interpret the rest of the
narrative. Thus it is found on the lips of the angel in the birth narrative
(Lk. 1.35), and on the lips of God in the baptism and transfiguration
stories (Mk 1.11 and pars.; 9.7 and pars.); on the lips of demons in
exorcism (Mk 3.11; 5.7), and of the devil in the temptation story
(Mt. 4.3-6, Lk. 4.3-9). These are, however, notable by their absence
from the Fourth Gospel. The declaration of the incarnation of the pre-
existent Logos (1.14) hardly leaves room for a narrative of a
supernatural birth. There is no account of the baptism as an event, but
only an oblique reference to it in John's testimony that God had
prepared him to recognize as the Son of God the one on whom the
Spirit descended as a dove (1.32-34). The theme of the transfiguration,
that the glory of God is revealed in Jesus, is one which permeates this
gospel, as does the theme of the temptation, in the sense that Jesus is

1.   Note also the dominance of these two expressions in 1 John—the former in
3.8; 4.15; 5.5, 10, 12, 13, 20, and the latter in 2.22-24; 4.14; 5.12. And for 'his Son',
see 1.3, 7, 23 ('Jesus Christ'); 4.9 (μονογενής), 10; 5.9, 10, 11, 20.

depicted as in continuing conflict with the prince of this world (there are no specific exorcisms in John).[1]

In John the phrase 'the Son of God' is more evenly distributed, from its first occurrence in a christological confession by Nathanael (1.49) to the evangelist's concluding statement of the purpose of his work (20.31). This is also the case with 'the Son'. As there is in John no single apocalyptic discourse preceding the passion, there is nothing equivalent to the statement that 'not even the Son' but only the Father knows the exact time of the end (Mk 13.32 and pars.), nor is there anything resembling the ecclesiastical injunction to baptize in the name of the Father and of the Son and of the Holy Spirit (Mt. 28.19). The striking revelatory passage in Mt. 11.25-27/Lk. 10.21-22 is dubiously called 'Johannine', for while there are parallels in John to the mutual knowledge of the Father and the Son, the rest of the language in that passage is foreign to the Fourth Gospel. Again, 'the Son' is more evenly distributed throughout this Gospel, from its first occurrence, either expressly or by implication, in the climax of the prologue (1.18) through to ch. 17, which is a sustained prayer of the Son to the Father.

The background and sources of this use of 'the Son' and 'the Son of God' in the Fourth Gospel and the Synoptics—as elsewhere in early Christianity[2]—have been matters of prolonged discussion.[3] They have been found by some in non-Jewish spheres of thought, and the terms seen as evidence of the Hellenization of an original Jewish-Christian Gospel. Dodd sets out widespread and varied uses.[4] In Greek mythology lesser deities were sons of the supreme deity. Hermes and Apollo were sons of Zeus, and this could be interpreted in philosophical or religious terms to mean that they were different manifestations of the supreme deity. Sometimes the union of gods and mortals resulted in 'sons of God' in the sense of demigods or heroes. Each Egyptian reigning monarch was said to be the son of a god worshipped in the household, whether by miraculous birth or ephiphany is not clear. Such ideas were assimilated by Greeks, who raised men of distinction to be heroes, for

1. The centurion's confession, 'Truly this man was the [a] Son of God [a god]', at Mk 15. 39 would be too ambiguous for use by the Evangelist.
2. For example, in Paul, Rom. 1.3-4 (possibly pre-Pauline); 8.3, 29; 2 Cor. 1.19; Gal. 4.4; 1 Thess. 1.10; and Heb. 4.14; 6.6.
3. See especially M. Hengel, *The Son of God* (London: SCM Press, 1976), and Schnackenburg, *St John*, II, pp. 172-86.
4. *Interpretation*, pp. 250-53.

example Alexander, a son of Ammon, in later versions by means of a miraculous birth. Sovereigns in Syria and Egypt inherited divine status; thus Antiochus IV was θεὸς ἐπιφανής and the Ptolemies were entitled θεὸς εἰς θεῶν. Later, Roman emperors, beginning with Augustus, were called *divi filii*, being raised to divinity after death, though in the East this happened during rulers' lifetimes. Characteristic of all these varied, quasi-physical conceptions was that in them the line of distinction between God (or gods) and human beings was a thin one. There is little sense of the separation, which lies at the heart of Judaism and Christianity, between human beings and the God who is transcendent over them as creator and judge.

By contrast the terms 'the Son' and 'the Son of God' are comparatively rarely attested in Judaism, and have there a metaphorical rather than a quasi-physical and quasi-metaphysical sense. They appear first as designations by God himself of Israel (Exod. 4.22; Hos. 11.1) to express the nation's election by the transcendent God to a special relationship of closeness to him and to his will for the world. In the royal ideology in Israel the king can be addressed by God as his son (Ps. 2.7), since he is the representative and embodiment of the people in their vocation, and as such is 'son' by adoption. Opinion remains divided as to whether in the first century CE 'the Son of God' was applied to the future king-messiah. The high priest's question 'Are you the messiah, the son of the Blessed One?' (Mk 14.61) and Peter's confession 'You are the messiah, the son of the living God' (Mt. 16.16) indicate that, at least in some quarters, they could belong together, the one glossing the other (cf. Jn 20.31).[1]

Some have found traces of a divine sonship of a more mediatorial kind in areas of Jewish mysticism (for example Metatron), or in Wisdom theology (the figure of Wisdom), which may themselves have been influenced by Hellenistic thought; but what emerges here is hardly a figure who is predominantly called 'the Son of God', and who is constantly and actively engaged in a relationship with God.[2] Dodd argued that the Son of God in the Fourth Gospel was modelled on the figure of the Old Testament prophet, who is sent from God (Isa. 6.8), who knows God (Amos 3.7; Jer. 9.24), or who is consecrated a prophet in the womb (Jer. 1.4-5): 'John has deliberately moulded the idea of the Son of God

1. *4 Ezra* 7.28-29 has 'my Son the messiah', but the date, provenance and character of this work are much disputed.
2. Hengel, *Son of God*, pp. 48-56.

in the first instance upon the prophetic model...The human mould, so
to speak, into which the divine sonship is poured is a personality of the
prophetic type'.[1] This, however, falls far short of that sending of the Son
which can be referred to as his coming forth from, and return to, God
(Jn 16.28), whose knowledge of God results from his being in the bosom
of the Father (Jn 1.18), and whose mission in and to the world is not due
to consecration in the womb, but to the incarnation of the creator in his
own creation (Jn 1.14).[2] Philo, who combined Jewish and Greek modes
of thinking in a variety of ways, is hardly of assistance here, since his
conception of divine sonship is as diverse as his use of 'Logos'. He can
refer to the Logos as 'the first born son of God' (*Conf. Ling.* 62-63),
but this is one description among many, and not a standing epithet.
Furthermore, 'the son of God' can be applied to angels, to Abraham
and Isaac, and to those who know God. In the end Philo comes down
on the Jewish side, in that he does not assimilate humanity and divinity,
nor does he diminish the idea of creation by God or confuse it with
procreation.

One conclusion to be drawn from the above discussion could be that
'the Son of God' and 'the Son' were relatively unspecific and pliable
terms. They always conveyed the sense of a close intimacy with God,
and in a Jewish context a derived authority which demanded obedience
to the Father-God, who has ultimate authority. They did not, however,
carry in themselves a clear indication of what this intimacy consisted in,
or how it was to operate, as, on one view, 'the Son of Man' denoted in
itself the one who was to bring about the eschatological events. What
being the Son (of God) meant was indicated rather by statements of
what the Son does, or by conjunction with other terms such as the
Christ, the Lord or the Logos.

In his study of Johannine Christology T.E. Pollard states that 'the
master concept of the Fourth Gospel is the Father–Son relationship...its
recurring theme is that as the Son of God Jesus Christ is the only
mediator between God and man'. This general theme is announced in
the prologue, which is 'an overture in which the stage is set'.[3] Whether

1. *Interpretation*, pp. 254-55.
2. Käsemann, *The Testament of Jesus*, ch. 2.
3. *Johannine Christology and the Early Church* (Cambridge: Cambridge
University Press, 1970), pp. 14, 20. The use of the word 'mediator' may be questioned, not only because the word nowhere occurs in the Gospel, but also because it
has connotations in theology which hardly assist the understanding of the Logos-Son

it is the 'master' concept is open to question, although clearly it is an important concept. It is proper to enquire, therefore, how and in what sense is this the case?

The prologue begins with the Logos, who, apart from the parenthesis concerning John in vv. 6-8, remains the subject until the precise identification in v. 17, where 'Jesus Christ' occurs as a proper name. In a number of compressed statements the Logos is said to be 'with God' and to be himself θεός. He exists with God before the creation of all that exists, of which creation he is the author. Further, he possesses in himself the life of which he is the author, and which is the metaphysical 'light' to that part of creation which is called 'humankind'. That light continues to shine in humankind despite a darkness which results from the non-comprehension by humankind of its origins. The divine quality of this light is indicated by the adjective 'true', and its continuing operation by the statement that it enlightens every human being. Thus, *qua* Logos, he was always in the world and yet was not known by his creation.

In the spiral movement of vv. 11-12 a particular coming of this ever-present Logos is stated with a similar double result. It is a coming to those who are his own—possibly a reference to the Jews, whose rejection provides the background for the establishment of the veracity of Jesus' claims and person, but more probably a reference to humankind in general, who in their ignorance and blindness did not receive him. In contrast to this is the reception of the Logos by those who believe on his name (a divine attribute), which constituted them children of God in a manner that goes beyond inheritance, human procreation or self-determination, and is a direct birth from God. In v. 14 a distinction is drawn between those made the children of God in this way and he who brings it about; and it is here that the concept of divine sonship begins to appear. The agent of the re-creation of humanity is the Logos incarnate, dwelling in proximity with human beings and they with him, through

in John. A mediator is one who forms a connecting link, who acts as intermediary for the purposes of reconciliation, as a go-between or agent. Such a description may be fitting for a figure who is subordinate to God, as in much Hellenistic thought, but it does not fit one who is 'with' God before creation, who is never diminished in his intimacy with God as Father, and who out of such unity effects the work of God, so that his works and words are those of God himself, not of an intermediary. This could apply to ch. 17 also, where the prayer is doubtfully called 'high-priestly' or mediatorial.

whom the divine 'glory' or being is made evident. This glory is then
defined in terms of sonship as that which belongs to one who is a unique
(only-begotten?) one with, or from, a father.

The prologue closes (vv. 15-18) with the witness of the John referred
to in vv. 6-8 as having come for witness to the light, in a series of compressed statements with reference to the historical figure Jesus Christ,
who is the source of the fulness of grace and truth. This is further
defined in terms of divine sonship, either explicitly with the reading in
v. 18 'the only Son, who is in the bosom of the Father', or implicitly,
but not less forcefully, with the reading 'the unique one who is God,
who is in the bosom of the Father'. The function of this figure has been
to communicate to human beings the heavenly things. Thus divine
sonship could be said to be a major, rather than 'master', concept in the
prologue to convey who Jesus Christ is and what he does. It is so,
however, not by itself and on its own, but only within the concept of the
Logos μονογενής, whose being and operations it expresses in terms of
a unique filial relationship with the Father God. This Logos-Son has as
his authoritative functions both to be the author of creation and its
perfector in re-creation, and to be the communicator of divine things
from God to humankind.

In the body of the Gospel the themes of 'the Son' and 'the Son of
God' are taken up immediately by means of two repetitions and expansions by John of his witness in the prologue (1.29-34, 3.25-36, cf. 1.15-
18), bracketing the words of Jesus in the opening discourse with
Nicodemus (3.1-21).[1] 1.29-34 is the evangelist's equivalent of the
synoptics' story of the baptism of Jesus, now in the form of an oblique
reference to it by John himself. They have in common John's assertion
of his own inferiority, and the fact that the Spirit is seen to descend on
Jesus as a dove, whereby he is established as the Son of God. Where
they differ is that in the Fourth Gospel the ability to recognize Jesus'
divine sonship has been conferred by God himself on John alone as the
divinely appointed witness to the light. This includes the knowledge that
Jesus communicates the heavenly gifts in already baptizing with the
Spirit.

In 3.25-36 the witness is both repeated and expanded. All gifts and
vocations, including that of John, have God as their source, but he who

1. In 1.49 Jesus is hailed as 'the Son of God...the King of Israel' in a series of
christological confessions on the lips of potential disciples, but these are not
developed, and appear to be displaced by the Son of Man in 1.51.

is of heavenly origin is above all others, for he utters the words of God by witnessing to what he has seen and heard with God, and hence confers the Spirit without limit. This is theologically formulated in 3.35-36. It is out of his love for the Son that the Father, God, has given him authority over the creation, so that the possession of the creation's perfection, eternal life, or otherwise, is dependent on a believing obedience to this Son. Here John's testimony has incorporated something of the language of Jesus' previous words to Nicodemus and the world.[1] There, perception of, and entry into, the kingdom of God—a synonym of eternal life—is dependent on a radically new beginning, described as birth from above (3.3, cf. 1.13), or birth from the Spirit. This is made possible by the descent from heaven of the only one able to communicate heavenly things (3.12). Then it is theologically formulated in terms of the love of God for the world in the sending to it of his only Son, belief in whose (divine) name (3.18, cf. 1.12-13), or otherwise, brings with it the final things—eternal life or divine condemnation (3.16; 3.36). And this, recalling the language of the prologue, is the entry of the light into the darkness (3.19-21, cf. 1.4-5). Thus, by the end of his mission John has repeated and expanded his statements in the prologue: Logos Jesus is the Son of God who has authority over all things, and whose words are heavenly communications. Furthermore, he has introduced the theme of eternal life as a bridge to the teaching of Jesus in the rest of the Gospel, where it plays a large part in the disputes over the veracity of Jesus' words in the face of the opposition of non-comprehending audiences.

In ch. 5 the theme of divine sonship moves into the centre and is further developed. The context is now not the words of Jesus but his healing or restorative acts, which in the synoptics are referred to as 'mighty acts', but in this gospel either as 'signs', in pointing to a corresponding eternal reality, or here, significantly, as 'works'. The occasion is the healing of a lame man, which is the subject of attack because performed on the sabbath. This situation appears also in the synoptics, where the defence is that the law of rest from work on the sabbath may be broken in some circumstances of special need (Mt. 12.11; Lk. 13.15; 14.5). Here the defence is quite different, and is entirely theological and christological. It is related to the sabbath observance itself, and to the God whose sabbath it was at creation. In

---

1. Note the transition from the singular verb in 3.10 (referring to Nicodemus) to the plural verbs in 3.11-12 (referring to the world).

contradiction of a possible deduction from the Genesis text that the sabbath marked a permanent cessation of activity by God after creation, it is stated that the Father (God) is continually at work in relation to creation. And it is in cooperation with this unceasing activity of God himself that, Jesus asserts, his work has been performed and is thus in a direct sense the work of God. It is perceived by the opponents, correctly, as a claim to be on a par with God, and hence as blasphemy. This divine cooperation, which will extend beyond the present act of healing, is now expounded in various ways. It is grounded in a mutuality between the Father and the Son; for on the one hand the Son's actions are not self-determined, but are in imitation of the Father's activities and an unceasing obedience to his will, while on the other hand they can only be so because the Father out of love for the Son constantly shows him what he is himself doing. Or again, 'to have life in oneself', that is, a life underived from any other source, but the source of life to others, is one way of defining the nature of God (cf. 1.4 of the Logos). This is possessed by the Son as well as the Father, though it is so because it has been given by the Father to the Son. As a consequence it will encompass those final activities towards the creation, by which the creation is purified and perfected—judgment, resurrection and the conferring of eternal life. These belong to the Son, having been given him by the Father. Hence equal respect is due to both, to the one who sees God and is sent by him, and to the Father who sends him. This is a form of divine sonship which requires the Logos-Son figure of the prologue as its background.

The discourse in ch. 6 has been discussed already, because it is developed largely in terms of the Son of Man and of 'I am'. However, elements of the Father–Son relationship present in ch. 5 are introduced to establish the heavenly nature of what Jesus communicates, now considered in terms of nourishment. Thus the claim as the Son of Man to be the living bread of God, which comes from heaven to be the nourishment of the world, is based upon a mutuality between the Father and the Son, whereby the Son comes from heaven to do the will of the Father, and the will of the Father is that the Son confers on believers eternal life now, and a consequent resurrection in the end (6.35-40). With this may be compared 3.11-18, with a similar transition from the Son of Man to the Son (of God). Further, in face of the opposition such a claim arouses, it is asserted in language recalling that of the prologue (1.18) that no one has seen God (the Father) except one, the one who is

from God and is sent by him; and for anyone to come to Jesus is itself
the work of the Father (6.44-51). And behind the capacity of human
beings to live, and to have eternal life by reason of Jesus, lies the fact
that Jesus himself as Son lives by reason of the Father who lives (6.57).

In the remainder of the public ministry, chs. 8–12, some of these
truths are repeated and others added. In 8.12-53 the question addressed
is that of origins, implied in the idiom 'son of', and their relation to
character. The claim of the Jews to be sons of Abraham is denied on the
ground that they do not in their actions reproduce the character of
Abraham. Their claim to be sons of God and to have God as their
Father is denied on the ground that they fail to respond to the one who
has come forth from, and has been sent by, God, and whose mission is
to culminate in a return to the one who is, in fact, always present with
him. They are rather sons of, and enslaved to, sin; and permanent freedom from such a slavery they can find only at the hands of the Son,
who continues for ever (8.35), and who pre-exists with God (8.58).

In ch. 10 the theme is the sheepfold and flock of God, of which Jesus
is both the sole entry and the good shepherd, in that his knowledge of
the sheep and theirs of him is a replica of the mutual knowledge of the
Father and the Son. His gift to them of invincible life is the result of this
being given to him by the Father, who is invincible. This is then formulated as 'I and the Father are one' (the neuter ἕν, indicating a unity in
will and operation). In the face of the charge of blasphemy, to which this
statement inevitably leads, this unity in operation is stated as a mutual
indwelling of the Father and the Son.

In 12.44-50 the public ministry is brought to a close in a manner not
uncharacteristic of the evangelist by a catena of compressed and seminal
statements (cf. 1.15-18), which are introduced by the dramatic verb
κράζειν—Jesus 'cried' to them (cf. 1.15). The sequence is as follows.
Jesus is always the one sent from God (the Father), so that to believe in
Jesus (cf. 1.7) and to 'behold' him (cf. 1.12) is to believe in, and to
behold, God as the one who has sent him. In v. 49 this is expressed by
the compressed idiom, possible in Greek but impossible to reproduce in
English, ὁ πέμψας μὲ πατήρ (already introduced in 5.37; 8.16, 18),
where 'having sent me' is placed between the article and the noun, so
that God is known for who he is, and as the Father, in and through his
act of sending the Son. The coming of Jesus from the Father is the entry
of light into the world (cf. 1.4-9), and belief in him is to move out of
darkness; for his mission is one of salvation for the world. Nevertheless,

judgment is also involved. For not to listen to his words and to keep them is to incur a judgment which is ultimate, and which will be exercised by his present speech. This is because his present speech is identical with the speech of God, and exactly reproduces what his Father has commanded him to say. This is summarized as the knowledge by Jesus of the Father's commandment of eternal life.

Some of the contents of chs. 13–17 have already been examined in so far as they were related to the 'Son of Man' and 'I am'. These chapters may now be re-examined in relation to their bearing on the theme of the relationship of the Father and the Son, and the character of that relationship. The chapters form a distinct section of the Gospel with a special introduction and conclusion of its own. They have been called the Farewell Discourses; and while this is appropriate inasmuch as there is repeated reference by Jesus to his departure, it is by no means entirely so, since this departure is to be followed very quickly by a return, and a permanent presence with those addressed either personally or through the Holy Spirit.

Indeed, how far these chapters have literary antecedents is problematic. The literary genre of 'testament', as in the *Testaments of the Twelve Patriarchs*, has been suggested, but they afford only partial parallels. None, for example, concludes with prayer, as does John 17. It may be that these discourses are a fresh creation of the evangelist himself in his handling of the tradition. This question is further raised by the fact that this section overlaps, in general and in some particulars, with the synoptic tradition, for example in referring to a (Passover) meal, the prophecy of Judas's betrayal and of Peter's denial, but is also widely and strikingly different from it, for example containing no 'eucharistic' action or words, but four lengthy chapters of instruction. Dodd has argued that some of the contents of these chapters exhibit similarities with the esoteric eschatological discourse spoken by Jesus in Mark 13 (and parallels) and similar material scattered in the synoptics, with forecasts of the future, of coming tribulations for humankind, and of persecution, rejection, sorrow and vindication for disciples.[1] If this is correct, it follows that the evangelist has handled the tradition with remarkable freedom, refashioning, reformulating and rephrasing it according to his theology, and making it the final instructions and guidance for the present and the future of one who has been, is and will remain omniscient

1.   *Interpretation*, pp. 390-96.

and privy to the total will of God. And this may apply to particulars. The evangelist shares with the synoptists the approach and the arrival of the Passover as the context of the meal and its discourses (13.1, 20); but in the opinion of some this is for him more than a historical or chrono-logical datum, and is a theological sign that Jesus is to be seen in his person and death as the true Passover feast.[1]

The section has in 13.1-3 a remarkably emphatic theological intro-duction, which provides the setting for all that is to follow. It is on the basis of his knowledge (from the Father) that the time has come for him to pass from the world and to rejoin the Father that Jesus (the Son) pro-ceeds to do and say what he does (13.1). This is further underlined by reiteration in 13.3. It is on the basis of his knowledge that his origin has been with God, and, with the plan for his death already beginning to be set in motion, that he is on his way back to the Father, that Jesus acts and speaks. Thus, all that is to follow is given a pre-determined character. It stems from an omniscient participation by Jesus in the will and intention of the Father, and this includes the granting to him by the Father of a universal control (13.3). This applies also to the passion, where Jesus will be shown to be in control of events.

What immediately follows is that, about to leave the world, Jesus loves to the utmost 'his own', whom he had already loved in the world. These are 'the disciples', who are not here, as in the synoptics, to be limited to, or identified with, the Twelve, and who probably here stand as repre-sentative of all believers (cf. 10.3-4, 'his own sheep' of the true, as opposed to the false, shepherd). Their designation here as 'his own' cannot but recall the only other use of the term, in the prologue (1.11), where they are those to whom the Logos comes, but who reject him, thus making way for believers, whom the Logos is able to make children of God by a divine rebirth. The immediate act of loving his own is the footwashing, which is a double symbol, both of the paradox of the Lord and Master who performs towards them the functions of a slave, and which is to issue in the commandment to love one another as he has loved them, and also of their total cleansing from defilement which he is able to secure.

The loving of 'his own' to the uttermost continues in 14.1–16.33 through speech. Although 'the Son' is expressly mentioned only in 14.3,

---

1. Lightfoot, *St John's Gospel*, Appended Note pp. 346-56. After examining all references to the Passover in the Gospel Lightfoot reaches the conclusion indicated in the title of his Appended Note—'The Lord the True Passover Feast'.

there can be little doubt that in these discourses, which contain the word 'Father' 40 times, ten of these being in the phrase 'my Father', it is 'the Son' who is speaking throughout.

In ch. 14 the disciples are given assurance of ultimate achievement (14.12) and of attainment of the heavenly goal (14.1-6). This is grounded in the fact that the speaker is one who, in a manner familiar in Hellenistic religious thought, cuts through the spheres to make a way to the heavenly for his adherents, with the result that there is committed to them truth and life. It is further grounded in the co-existence and cooperation of this figure as the Son with the Father, so that to believe in, 'see' and know the one is to believe in, 'see' and know the other. Into this mutuality the disciples will be taken by the return to them of Jesus himself, or by the coming to them of the Father and the Son, or by the sending to them of the Spirit by the Father in the name of the Son.

In ch. 15 the assurance of achievement is further developed in terms of the disciples' abiding as branches in Jesus the true or heavenly vine, as he himself abides in the Father, the viniculturalist. This abiding, which makes them constantly fruitful, is in his love, his words and his commandments, which themselves reciprocate the love, words and commandments of the Father. Their communication from the Father through the Son, and their reception from such a source by the disciples, constitute the disciples as friends, in contrast to the unbelieving world, which is hostile.

In ch. 16 the theme of the attainment of life by those who have known the truths which the Son has communicated from the Father is continued, but now with particular reference to the future of the disciples, to the coming hatred of them by the unbelieving world, to their perplexities, their bereavement and sorrow, but also to their ultimate recovery and invincible rejoicing. Crucial to this is the activity towards the disciples of the Paraclete-Spirit, whom here Jesus himself will send to them, and whose function as the Spirit of truth is to make the things of Jesus a present reality. But this is to make the Father a reality, since anything the Father possesses belongs to the Son, and whatever the Son possesses he has from the Father. There is therefore reiterated with the greatest possible emphasis, and as the point of comprehension of the disciples in contrast to the world, that Jesus the Son is the unique emissary of God, is the source of the knowledge of 'all things', and that having come from the Father he is leaving the world to rejoin the Father (16.25-30).

Thus far the relation of the Son to the Father, and of both to human beings, has permeated the instruction given in chs. 13–16. That sonship involves an intimate participation in the divine plan for the world, a heavenly activity towards humankind on the part of the Son, who is present as 'man', but uniquely so (1.14). All this reaches a surprising conclusion in ch. 17 in a long, uninterrupted monologue in the form of prayer. This chapter has hardly received from commentators the attention due to it by reason of its position in the Gospel, its character and contents. For there is no parallel to it in the Christian tradition of Jesus' concluding words on earth before his 'passion', nor outside it.[1] Nor is there any prayer recorded which is really like it.

An exception among commentators here is Käsemann, who in his book *The Testament of Jesus* makes ch. 17 the starting point, and a constant reference point, for his study of this Gospel as a whole, his search for its place in early Christianity and for the nature of its Christology, ecclesiology and eschatology. In his view, 'it is unmistakable that this chapter is a summary of the Johannine discourses and in this respect is a counterpart to the prologue'.[2] One may quarrel with the title of Käsemann's book, since it depends on his judgment that in composing ch. 17 'the evangelist undoubtedly used a literary device which is common in world literature and employed in Judaism as well as by New Testament writers. It is the device of the farewell speech of a dying man.'[3] He cites as a parallel Paul's speech to the Ephesian elders in Acts 20 and compares Appendix VI of E. Stauffer's *The Theology of the New Testament*, where the characteristics of this literary genre are set out. But it is notable that prayer is very rare in, or entirely absent from, speeches of this kind, nor is it the case that in this chapter Jesus says farewell to anyone. It is addressed to the Father whom he is soon to rejoin. Indeed, in deference to the actual contents of the chapter, Käsemann is forced to modify his original judgment when he says,

1. Dodd, in his investigation of these Farewell Discourses as a Johannine equivalent of Mk 13 and parallels (*Interpretation*, pp. 390-96) sees no parallel to ch. 17. He suggests as parallel a dialogue concluding with a hymn or prayer in Hermetic writings such as the *Poimandres* or the *De Regeneratione*—see *Interpretation*, pp. 420-23.
2. Käsemann, *Testament of Jesus*, p. 3.
3. *Testament of Jesus*, p. 4 n. 1.

> This chapter is not a testament in the sense of a last will and bequest, but
> rather in the sense of a final declaration of the will of the one whose proper
> place is with the Father in heaven and whose word is meant to be heard on
> earth.[1]

But when the model is modified to this extent it ceases to serve as a
model. Jesus is not saying farewell to anyone in the prayer, but speaks
throughout to the Father in anticipation of his imminent return to him;
and he does not speak as a dying man in the ordinary sense, but as one
who is already the other side of his death. It could be, therefore, that the
chapter has to be viewed as *sui generis*, and as such because it is the
creation by the evangelist of what he thought a fitting conclusion for the
Jesus of his gospel. We have a similar situation with regard to the
contents of the chapter, which constitute prayer of a very unusual kind.
While there are elements throughout of prayer in the ordinary sense of
petition and intercession, these are intertwined with, and are dependent
on, statements by the Son to the Father of the unique relationship
between them, and, as it were, a report by the Son of his stewardship of
the Father's will on earth.

The prayer is addressed to one who is called four times 'Father'
(vv. 1, 5, 21, 24), once 'Holy Father' (v. 11) and once 'righteous
Father' (v. 25). It opens with a deliberate repetition of the opening of the
discourses in 13.1-3, putting into the first person of personal prayer
what was there stated in the third person of narrative. This is that 'the
hour' of departure to the Father had arrived, and that the Father had
given the Son authority over all humankind for the purposes of eternal
life (vv. 1-2). The Son's opening petition, which is for himself, rises out
of this. It is a petition for a reciprocal 'glorification' by Father and Son.
'To glorify' here means something like 'to make evident the divine
quality of'. This the Son has done with respect to the Father, in that his
activity on earth has been throughout the performance of what the
Father intended to be done, and what he had given him to do with the
power to do it (vv. 4-5). This will be shown to have been the case when
the Father gives his glory to the Son, that is, acknowledges his divine
quality (by resurrection or exaltation?). Moreover, this divine quality to
be conferred on him and his work will not be something added to them

---

1.   *Testament of Jesus*, pp. 5-6. For a criticism on this score, as also of other
categorizations of this chapter, see C.F. Evans, 'Christ at Prayer in St John's Gospel',
Lumen Vitae 24.3 (1969), pp. 576-96, to which I am much indebted in this section.

from the divine sphere. It will be given from the being of God himself, and will be manifested as having been there all along, and indeed as his since before the creation itself (v. 5). Such an opening petition only makes sense as that of a Son who, though he is speaking on earth, is pre-existent with the Father; a Son, indeed, who as the Logos-Son was with God and was God, or as God was in the bosom of the Father (1.1-2, 18). As if to underline this reciprocal glorification there is placed between the two parts of this petition something quite incongruous in personal prayer, since it is formulated as an impersonal credal definition, though it continues to be addressed to the Father as God (v. 3). The eternal life which the Father has committed to the Son to dispense for humankind is now defined (v. 3) as consisting in a double but also single knowledge. It is the combined knowledge of the Father as the only and true God, and of the speaker, here named as Jesus Christ, as the sole emissary of this God (cf. 16.27-30; 1.17-18; 1 Jn 5.20-21). Eternal life is now available through the presence, in human form, of divine being in the Son; and behind this is the pre-existent fact that in the Logos was life, and the life was the light of human beings (1.4).

Thus the double knowledge arising from the reciprocal relation of Father and Son is developed in vv. 5-11 with respect to those who possess it, and leads to the second petition of the prayer, which is for them (v. 11). It has its basis in the fact that Jesus, the Son, in his activity and words has made known nothing less than the Father's 'name' which, like 'glory', is almost a synonym for God himself, his being. To know God's name is the equivalent of knowing God himself. In this context it means knowing that everything which the speaker, the Son, possesses so as to be able to give it to others is not his own, but is a gift from, and has its source in, the Father. It is knowing, furthermore, that his words which he has given to human beings are words which have been given to him from a divine source, and that he is indeed the Father's emissary (vv. 6-8). All this, however, has not been received by the world as a whole, but only by some. These are now themselves defined in terms of the reciprocal relationship between Father and Son, and its character of mutual giving. Those elsewhere called 'the disciples' are throughout the prayer defined in terms of the heavenly gift of Father to Son (vv. 2, 6, 9, 11, 24). They are those in the world who are the possession of the Father, and have been given to the Son as evidence of his divine achievement (vv. 6, 9-10). The achievement of the

Son is to have given them knowledge of the name (being) of God, and to have preserved them in it over against the ignorance, based on unbelief, of the world, which refuses this knowledge. As he is about to leave them behind in the world, they and not the world are the object of his petition to the Father that he will keep them in his name, which he has already given to the Son. Since this is a petition to keep them in holiness over against the unholiness of the world, which is unbelief in its creator, he is addressed as 'Holy Father' (v. 11). This state of being is further defined as unity (ἕν, lit. 'one thing'), and is modelled on nothing less than the unity of God as Father and the Son (vv. 9-13). It will bring with it that totality of joy which the Son has in returning to the Father with his work completely done.

As well as the name or being of God, Jesus the Son has also brought to humankind God's word, his utterance which goes out to create and re-create. It is by its nature missionary (that is, it is sent), it belongs to the Son who is uniquely the one sent from God, and now belongs to the 'disciples', whom the Son has drawn into his mission to the world. They have for this reason incurred the same hatred from the world as the Son himself, for they together with the Son have opposite origins from those belonging to the world—one is either from (ἐκ) God, or from the evil one. This word is also called 'the truth', which Jesus has already claimed to be along with 'way' and 'life' (14.6; cf. 1.17-18: truth came by Jesus Christ who is the unique one who is God, in the bosom of the Father). The previous petition for the holy Father to keep the believers in his name (v. 11) now becomes a petition to sanctify them, that is, to keep them from the profanity of the world's unbelief—'in' or 'by' truth.[1] And as the one responsible for having sent them into the world in these conditions, Jesus maintains himself in a state of such sanctification.

The prayer then goes on to include those who will subsequently believe in Jesus through the mission to which he has committed the 'disciples'. The prayer for these is that they may possess that same unity

---

1.   Schnackenburg, *St John*, III, p. 185, cites as a Hellenistic parallel a statement from the *Mandaean Liturgies*, p. 165: 'You are set up and established, my chosen ones, by the discourse of truth that has come to you'; and he would take 'in the truth' here as meaning 'in the sphere of truth'. This local meaning he sees as parallel to the expression in v. 12 'keep in the name (of God)'. In view of v. 19, 'On their behalf I sanctify myself, that they also may be ones having been sanctified in truth', this sphere of truth may be a personal one, like the name of God, and sanctification in truth may be akin to dwelling in the Son and in God.

as is modelled on the unity of Father and Son (v. 11), but this is now further specified as a participation in it, and in the mutual indwelling of the divine life (vv. 22-23). This is stated in the eschatological language of a final goal and its achievement—that they may be 'perfected' into one. That will be the chief evidence to the world of the divine mission to the world, and of the divine love of humankind and of the Son which occasions it.

In vv. 24-25 the evangelist concludes, as elsewhere in the Gospel, with a summary consisting of a sequence of compressed statements. The Son prays that all believers may be where, in anticipation of a work already finished, he already is, that is, with God, and so may themselves see the glory or state of being which the Father, out of love for him, had made his from before creation. The world has not acknowledged the righteous Father, but the Son has, and now also those to whom he has been sent. And this will continue, so that the love between Father and the Son, and the Son himself, may be in them.

It is evident at this point, as indeed from the beginning of the chapter, that the one who addresses the Father in this way, and who prays for others in the context of a rehearsal of the significance of his own actions and words, is the unique Son of God. But more than that, he is the Son who has shared, shares and will share the life and being of the Father (God), pre-existently and before creation. The prayer is thus a prayer which could only be uttered by the Christ, the Son of God, as the Fourth Gospel conceives him and portrays him, and by no one else. In form and content it is governed by that fact. This is also to say that it can only be the prayer of a Logos-Son, who has the origins, qualities and divine activities of the Logos, who is with God, and himself θεός, and who as μονογενὴς θεός in the bosom of the Father communicates heavenly things to humankind.

These truths have been given repeated expression throughout the Gospel in the form of statements by the Son about himself and the Father and the relations between them. In being restated in the form of prayer addressed by this Son to the Father they are given a peculiar intensity, and are shown to be at the divine heart of all things. Indeed, the contents of ch. 17, through the term 'Son', form a theological climax to all that Jesus acclaims and claims as Son. They are, it would appear, the most concentrated form of an authenticated divine explication of 1.18 that can be written.

It remains to be shown that the remainder of the Gospel was similarly influenced both in its construction and content by the prologue, and all that has been developed thereafter concerning the Logos μονογενὴς θεός.

Chapter 8

THE FINAL DAYS IN JERUSALEM OF THE LOGOS, JESUS CHRIST

I have argued throughout this study that the prologue provides the basis for a correct understanding by the reader of the Gospel which is to follow. This discussion has extended as far as ch. 17. That chapter consists of a continuous address to God in the presence of disciples such as could only be spoken by a Logos-Son as found in the prologue. Moreover, to be understood it requires a knowledge of much of the teaching contained in the preceding chapters. Significantly, ch. 17 includes the assertions that the Son has already completed his ordained task of communicating the name, will and glory of the Father-God to human beings, albeit in the face of hostility from, and rejection by, 'the world'; and that he is on the point of returning to the Father-God, at whose hands he awaits his glorification. It now remains to consider how the conclusion of the Gospel in chs. 18–19 (20–21) is related to this.

The prologue itself contains no direct reference to the manner in which the Logos who has become flesh (1.14) will cease to be flesh and will leave the earth. Since his becoming flesh to dwell among human beings was accompanied by 'glory'—that is, a radiance denoting a divine origin and a purpose of communicating divine truth—his exit from the earth, whatever its manner, will presumably be of the same kind, since, among other things, it is a return to the Father-God from whom he has come (17.5, 11), and it will display a heavenly background and convey truth of heavenly origin. This may be examined first by reference to the language which is used about it.

It has become commonplace to use of all four Gospel accounts of the last days of Jesus in Jerusalem the word 'passion'. The origin of this is the Latin word for these accounts, *passio*, which itself renders in noun form the Greek verb πάσχειν. In Greek this verb functioned as the passive of the verb ποιεῖν, 'to do', 'to act', and so had the basic meaning of 'to be done to', 'to be acted upon', that is, to be no longer the agent of one's actions but the recipient of the actions of others.[1] It could be used of receiving good or evil, though later it was primarily used of the latter, and while 'suffering' came to be associated with the experiencing of physical and mental pain, this was not its basic meaning, but being the object of the action of others. The word is used in predictions of what is to happen to Jesus as the Son of Man in Mk 8.31 = Mt. 16.21 = Lk. 9.22; Mk 9.12 = Mt. 17.12. Luke uses it further in an additional prediction (Lk. 17.25), in the statement of Jesus that he greatly desires to eat the Passover with the twelve before he suffers (Lk. 22.15), and in the interpretive statements of the risen Christ that it was the divine purpose that the Christ should suffer (Lk. 24.26, 46).

Along with this word, two other verbs are used to depict the character of this 'passion'. ἐξουδενήσθαι, 'to be made nothing', is found in the prediction in Mk 9.12, and is used of mockery by soldiers in Lk. 23.11; ἀποδοκιμάζειν, 'to reject after scrutiny', as of counterfeit coins, is used in the prediction in Mk 8.31 = Lk. 9.22, and in the citation of Ps. 118.22-23 of the stone rejected by the builders in Mk 12.10 = Mt. 21.42 = Lk. 20.17. Taken together, these expressions serve to portray the death of Jesus in terms of the extreme humiliation of the human messiah at the hands of his enemies (chiefly the Jewish authorities), a figure who is brought to nothing by his accusers, who in fear of what is coming to pass pleads with God for it to pass, but in human faith and piety accepts that God's will be done. None of this language is used of the rejection of Jesus in the Fourth Gospel, whose account of it is not properly called a 'passion narrative'. For it would not be appropriate for the exalted divine figure of the prologue, who alone on earth has heavenly origins and treads the appointed path of life, who never sheds his divine authority, who alone ensures that the work of God is perfected for human beings, and is in control until his final word of consummation upon the cross (τετέλεσται, 19.30).

This is further indicated by those expressions which the evangelist does employ to convey the theological meaning of the death of Jesus. These are peculiar to himself, and they paint a very different picture from that in the synoptics, more in harmony with the thought of the prologue. The first is ὑψοῦν, 'to lift up, to elevate'. This word is used at 3.14 of the hoisting up of the Son of Man (not unlike that of the serpent by Moses), which is performed by others, but is necessary for the

1. For this and what follows, see C.F. Evans, *Explorations in Theology 2* (London: SCM Press, 1977), pp. 37-38.

creation of belief and the consequent possession of eternal life (3.14). The elevation will be effected by human beings, but will result in knowledge of Jesus' divine origins and authority (8.28). Through this elevation, of which the physical hoisting involved in crucifixion is a *sēmeion*, he will draw all people to himself (12.32-33). Then there are the two synonymous verbs ὑπάγειν and πορεύεσθαι with the meaning 'to go on a journey'. They refer to the departure of Jesus from the flesh and from the earth without denoting the manner of it in death, and they impart to that departure its wide and deep theological meaning. For this departure is said to be a journey to the Father-God who has sent him, indeed a return journey corresponding to, and completing, the mission of the Son by the Father and of the Logos by God (7.33; 16.28). Indeed, it is in full knowledge that this is the case, and that he is about to transfer (μεταβαίνειν) from the world to the Father, that Jesus utters the theological truths in chs. 13–17 (13.1). Further, it is through the return journey to the Father of him into whose hands the Father has committed the creation (13.3) that the spiritual truths and powers which the Logos, Jesus Christ, possesses will be released for believers (13.36; 14.4, 12, 28). By the use of these expressions the physical event of the death of Jesus is subsumed in the theological truths to be conveyed. If the becoming flesh referred to so briefly in 1.14 was of such a kind that in it human beings saw the glory of a unique one in relation to the Father, the death of such a one, thought of as a departure or return to the Father, will be unique, not only in its physical character, but in its divinely ordained function.

While making no direct reference to the death of Jesus, the Logos-Son, the prologue does refer to certain negative conditions in which he operates, and which prepare for the hostility and alienation sometimes found in the Gospel as the background of his actions and words. It should be noted, however, that these negative things are largely a foil to the positive affirmations of the heavenly activities present through the Logos Jesus Christ, and of the certainty of their bringing the will of God to completion through him. Thus in 1.5 the light, which has its source in the life which is in the Logos, shines continuously in a metaphysical darkness, which is unable to 'comprehend' (or 'overcome') it. This darkness recurs in 8.12; 12.35, 46 as something by which human beings can always be encompassed and overcome, so that they do not know which way to go, but from which they are delivered by following Jesus, who defines himself as 'the light of the world' or the 'light of life come into the world'. Again in 1.10-12 the Logos, present in his own created order and enlightening every human being, is not recognized by that order or received by his own (that is, humankind, including the Jews). Yet there are those who do recognize, believe and know, who as a result receive a divine birth as children of God. This theme of a universal possession of true or eternal life through belief in and knowledge of God through Jesus, in the face of an unbelieving 'world' which is both judged and saved, recurs constantly through the Gospel (cf. 3.15-21; 5.24; 6.40, 45; 8.12; 9.39; 11.23-24 ; 12.31-32, 46-47; 14.6; 16.33; and 17). Further, it has been argued above that the reference to Moses in 1.17, who acts as a shorthand for Jews and Jewish beliefs, also has a negative function. He is the foil, the *dramatis persona* on the stage, who provides the background of inevitable hostility to, or ignorance of, the 'grace and truth' which is present in the Gospel in the Logos, Jesus Christ.

The first instance of this is in 2.13-22, which is an instructive piece of evidence of how freely the evangelist can handle the tradition to expound beliefs about Jesus. The synoptics use the incident of the cleansing of the temple as that which finally determined the Jerusalem authorities to have him arrested with a view to his death, and portray Jesus as having said something like, 'I will destroy this temple made with hands and in three days will build another not made with hands'. In the Fourth Gospel it is quite otherwise. It is the opening event of the first visit to Jerusalem. In reply to the demand of the Jerusalem authorities for a sign authenticating the action, the reply is, 'You destroy this temple, and in three days I will raise it'. The evangelist interprets 'this temple' here to refer to Jesus' body, and the saying becomes a prophecy of his death at their hands; which death, however, will be negated and reversed by his capacity to raise himself from death. Henceforth, whenever the Jews, Jerusalem or Judaea are mentioned, it will be reasonable for readers to expect the religious authorities to be antagonistic to the very person whom their God has sent.

The next hint of death and the mode of it occurs at 3.14ff. There Nicodemus, an authorized Jewish teacher who has been shown to be lacking in understanding of matters relating to God, is told that the Son of Man—a figure already introduced in 1.51 as alone bridging heaven and earth by an ascent following upon a previous descent—is destined by divine decree to be 'lifted up'. The parallel drawn with Moses' lifting up the serpent is not an exact one; the verb is the real point of the contact. It is only later that the double reference of the verb to 'hoisting aloft' (i.e. in crucifixion) and 'elevation' (to God) is made explicit, when, after saying, 'the hour is come for the Son of Man to be glorified' (12.23), Jesus proceeds with 'I, if I am lifted up from (ἐκ) the earth, shall draw all men to myself', which statement the evangelist himself interprets as signifying the mode of death he was about to suffer (12.32-33; cf. 18.31-32). Here it serves to hint that the Jews (Moses) will bring about this death, and immediately the positive theological thrust is shown when the result of such an elevation is said to be the availability of universal belief in this Son of Man and the consequent possession of eternal life (3.15-21).

Plots of the Jews to kill Jesus occur spasmodically within the largely discourse material of chs. 5–10, and the basis is always some form of the charge of blasphemy, of claiming for himself a relation to God and the authority of God, which the prologue has already given him. Thus the healing in ch. 5 is the occasion of such a plot because it is expounded by Jesus as part of the sabbath activity of God, performed by one who, like God, has life in himself, and possesses the divine prerogatives of judgment and giving life. Opposition to this, and the charge of making himself equal with God, come from those who are false representatives of Moses (5.17-18, 20-27, 44-47). This conflict continues to rumble on throughout chs. 7–8. Jesus remains in Galilee because the Jews have determined to kill him (7.1, 25). When eventually he appears in Jerusalem to teach in the temple, chiefly about his origin and his authority, he is the object of abortive attacks (7.25-30, 32-36, 40-44, 45-52). Conflict finally erupts in an attempt, also abortive, to stone him in the temple for his claim 'before Abraham was I am', and his condemnation of his opponents as illegitimately sons of Abraham (8.48-59). Then, again in Jerusalem, as the result of Jesus' teaching about himself as the good shepherd, and in particular the statement 'I and the Father are one', the Jews make another abortive attempt to stone him on the grounds that although a man he was making himself equal with God (10.29-30, 31-33, 39).

From ch. 11 onwards the character of the narrative changes. It is more continuous, with one event leading to another, and all forming part of an inexorable movement towards the climax of death by elevation. Thus the raising of Lazarus, the last and supreme *sēmeion*, leads directly to an official condemnation to death by the high priest and the sanhedrin (11.45-53), and has repercussions in the two following incidents of the

anointing at Bethany and the triumphal entry (12.1-11, 19), which, with
the following incident of the coming of the Greeks, are probably to be
seen as symbolic of the burial, exaltation and universal sway of Jesus.
After the single discourse, as it were, of chs. 13–17, spoken by Jesus out
of his foreknowledge of the hour of his departure from the world to the
Father, there follows the arrest, a cursory interrogation by the high
priest and an extended interrogation by Pilate, ending in an official condemnation, with subsequent crucifixion. This could suggest a connection
with the prologue of a more general kind, namely, that the prologue is a
prologue to a narrative which increasingly takes on the character of a
drama. As has been noted of this narrative,

> it achieves... more of those unities traditionally required of the drama.
> Thus, there is a unity of time, with the long discourse of chs. 13–17, the
> examination and crucifixion taking place in a single day before the
> Passover. There is a greater unity of place, with so much of the action con-
> centrated at the praetorium, the govenor's residence. There the story has a
> *mis-en-scène* as on a stage, with those who have brought Jesus forced to
> remain outside through scruples about incurring uncleanness for the
> coming Passover, and Jesus inside except when he is dramatically brought
> out for exhibition, Pilate acting as a kind of go-between. There is also... a
> unity of theme. The motif of kingship, which makes a somewhat fleeting
> appearance in the synoptics in the abrupt question of Pilate and in the
> subsequent title on the cross, now becomes the dominant.[1]

There is also, as throughout the Gospel, but especially in this part of it,
considerable use of symbolic language, of paradox, of words with a
double entendre, and of dramatic irony, whereby characters on the stage
speak better than they know, or unwittingly make statements the full
import of which only the audience is in a position to understand.

If it were the intention of the evangelist to cast the story of the death
of the Logos-Son, Jesus Christ, in a form approximating to current
drama he undertook a new and revolutionary task.[2] For on the Greek

---

1.　Evans, *Explorations*, p. 51.

2.　See P.R. Trebilco, *Jewish Communities in Asia Minor* (SNTSMS, 69;
Cambridge: Cambridge University Press, 1991), pp. 159-62. Excavations of the
theatre of the Roman period at Miletus have found named seats for city dignitaries
who were Jews and who would have been aware of Greek drama and its conventions.

See also J.M.G. Barclay, 'Manipulating Moses: Exodus 2.10-15 in Egyptian
Judaism and the New Testament', in R.P. Carroll (ed.), *Text as Pretext: Essays in
Honour of Robert Davidson* (JSOTSup, 138; Sheffield: JSOT Press, 1992), pp. 34-
37, for a recent discussion of the Greek fragments of the Jewish dramatist Ezekiel.

side the mode of death for gods who took human form was to be whisked away by the intervention of Zeus or some other eternal deity. In 1.1 the Logos has been placed in the highest echelon of the eternals, but he, and not some demiurge, is the creator of all that exists, and as a man he has fully entered his creation, to die and to consummate the work determined by the God of the Jews. The view that creation was good, and was not something from which to escape, and that the transience of the flesh and the uninterrupted cycles of change and decay had been given divine approval, was intolerable to the Greek religious mind. That which was incorruptible, perfect and not subject to change was the ideal world for which human beings strove, and in doing so they yearned to shed all that the impermanence of human life forced upon them.

On the other hand, for the Jews the fact that their God had determined to send a Logos-μονογενής as fully human was incredible. Their God was the creator, and the creation had in the first instance been good. The Fall and its ramifications also rendered it apparently impossible for their God to enter fully into human life, even as a Son. Yet the whole Fourth Gospel argues that such is indeed the case. Further, it is only the God of the Jews who gives veracity to the Gospel events and authenticity to Jesus as the source of his divine authority. With the entry of the Logos into his creation as fully a human being, the evangelist has made startling new assertions from which new Christian understandings will grow. That is to say, human life (flesh) and all its experiences are in reality shot through with heavenly things, if human beings could only see, comprehend and receive them. Human flesh is able to be

---

The fragments of *Exagōgē* are probably to be dated in the late third or early second century BC. They are written by a Jew, Ezekiel, in good Greek, in the formal structure of a Greek drama. Barclay makes the following important point: 'That Ezekiel should write a play about the Exodus, with Moses as its central hero and with numerous echoes of the LXX, is a sign of his loyalty to Judaism; that he should be able to master the form and vocabulary of Greek tragedy is a sign of his extensive education in Greek literature. He probably intended both Jews and non-Jews to watch his drama and to experience one way in which Jewish tradition and Greek culture could be made compatible' ('Manipulating Moses', p. 35).

See also R.A. Batey, *Jesus and the Forgotten City* (Grand Rapids: Baker, 1991). Archaeological investigations of Sepphoris, only four miles from Nazareth, have shown that Jesus lived close to the main city of Galilee which was part of a chain of Roman forts. Sepphoris had a theatre and would have provided a fully Hellenized background for Jesus and his Galilean disciples.

'divinized', and is able to enter into a relationship with God as intimate as that of a child to a father. Even human death is to be seen as part of God's plan of life within creation, and through all changes and complexities the qualitatively eternal life endures for believers. How does the evangelist convey these truths in his narrative of the death of Jesus, and his handling of the tradition of it?

The process is set in motion by the raising of Lazarus. This is peculiar to the Fourth Gospel, where it is the last and climactic of the seven signs. It is dramatically told, with the command which brings Lazarus to life as its conclusion, and after a dialogue in which Jesus interprets it as a sign that he is himself the source of resurrection, and that he confers eternal life on those who believe in him (11.25-26). The reaction to it is twofold. On the one hand, many Jews become believers; while on the other hand, the Jewish authorities, fearing that this belief will become universal, and will lead to the destruction by the Romans of Jewish privilege and national identity, gather in council, and in the person of the high priest condemn Jesus to death untried and without a hearing. In this juxtaposition of life and death there is heavy irony, for not only is the high priest of Judaism blind to the divine authority resident in Jesus, but he gives his verdict in terms of the politically pragmatic maxim that it is expedient that one man die 'for the people', that is, that he die so that the people should not. This the evangelist regards as inspired utterance in a sense otherwise than intended, inasmuch as the death of Jesus would indeed be in the divine purpose for the nation's deliverance, and, further, for the gathering into a unity of all the dispersed children of God. Orders are then given by the authorities that anyone who knows of Jesus' whereabouts in the days before the coming feast of the Passover should inform them with a view to his arrest. What follows in chs. 12–17 takes place in the context of a coming and going of crowds, and of Jesus himself from private to public, with the authorities unable to make the arrest until the divinely appointed hour for it, which Jesus alone knows, and by which his actions and words are governed.

Of the remaining days before the Passover three incidents are reported: the anointing, the entry into Jerusalem and the visit of the Greeks, the first two being given a link with the raising of Lazarus (12.1-2, 9-11, 17-19). These two have parallels in Mark and Matthew, though in the reverse order. The change of order could be explained as due to the evangelist's intention to make these events symbolic of what is to come in the burial of Jesus (already condemned to death by

Caiaphas, 11.50), and his subsequent elevation.[1] In Bethany Mary, who
had witnessed the raising of her brother Lazarus, and had addressed
Jesus as 'Lord', in contrast to the actions of the authorities anoints
Jesus' feet in an extravagant act of devotion, which calls forth protesta-
tions of waste. In reply Jesus relates her action to his coming embalming
for burial.

This is followed the next day by the 'triumphal entry'. The evangelist's
account of it has one significant difference from those of the synoptists,
that it is in response to the crowd's acclamation of him as 'the king of
Israel', and presumably as a rebuke to it, that Jesus procures the young
ass in order to fulfil Zechariah's prophecy of the humble king, which is
expressly quoted here. The nature of his kingship and authority will be a
principal subject of chs. 18–19.

There then follows the visit of the Greeks, a story peculiar to the
Johannine narrative and bearing marks of his hand. Their request to
'see' Jesus is presumably to be taken as evidence in advance that
through his death he will 'gather into one the children of God scattered
abroad' (11.52), and perhaps as evidence of the choice of Gentiles to
worship the God of the Jews through the Son. For it is taken as a signal
that the hour of the Son of Man's glorification has arrived, which
glorification is indicated by the parable of the grain of wheat which must
die in order to bear fruit (12.20-26).

It is developed in two ways. First, with language about Jesus' distress
of soul reminiscent of the synoptic agony in Gethsemane, but used with
the contrary purpose of marking yet again the continuing unity of will
between Father and Son; and with an interior dialogue between this
Father and Son so intense that it is said to have exterior manifestations,
it is affirmed that it is for the glorification of God that the hour has
arrived for the expulsion of the world's ruler, and for Jesus' drawing of
humankind to himself through his being 'lifted up'—a reference, the
evangelist notes, to the manner of his death (12.27-33).

Secondly, as if to round off the public ministry and to introduce what
follows, there is a sequence of compressed statements about unbelief and
belief: the unbelief of the Jews and of those too afraid of human judgment to confess belief; and the belief in (and seeing) Jesus as belief in
(and seeing) the Father who has sent him (12.37-50). This summary may
correspond to the statement in the prologue that the Logos 'came to his

1. Lightfoot, *St John's Gospel*, pp. 235ff.

own things (ἴδια) but his own (ἴδιοι) did not receive him' (1.11), particularly as what is to follow in chs. 13–17 is said to be delivered by Jesus to 'his own' in the world, and out of love for them (cf. 1.12).

These chapters consist of authoritative declarations by Jesus to 'his own' of their involvement with the ultimate truth and purposes of God through what he himself has been, is and will continue to be after his departure. They are restated in ch. 17 in the form of a prayer of the Son to the Father. They are introduced with the greatest possible emphasis as spoken out of his foreknowledge of the divinely appointed hour for his departure and return to the Father, and of its arrival (13.1, 3) and of the delivery to him by the Father of authority over creation (13.3). This is also said to govern the utterance and contents of the prayer itself (17.12). That is, the authority of Jesus carries with it, unlike all other human authorities, the quality of omniscience in knowing intimately the mind of God, and a certain omnipotence derived from him.

Omniscience combined with omnipotence is vividly illustrated by the next incident, which sets the process of events in motion to their end, the arrest of Jesus. Here is the height of paradox in the form the evangelist has given to the story, where history is subsumed in theology.[1] For traditionally the arrest is the 'handing over' of Jesus into the power and authority of his enemies, so that he ceases to be a free agent and becomes the subject of the actions of others. Here, however, these others prove to be powerless, and Jesus, who is in complete control, has to do their work for them and bring about his own arrest. When a (mixed?) band (σπεῖρα, 'cohort') of soldiers from the Jerusalem authorities under a chiliarch are led to the spot by Judas (Jesus has not only foreseen this action but has himself prompted it; cf. 13.2, 25-30), and say that they are looking for Jesus of Nazareth, he replies with ἐγώ εἰμι. These are the normal words of self-identification: 'It is I'; but, as the reader knows, they are also the language of divinity. Uttered by

1. This is contrary to the view of M.W.G. Stibbe, for whom a number of details, or more accurately historical clues from an eyewitness tradition, were in front of the Evangelist when he composed the passion narrative (*John as Storyteller* [SNTSMS, 73; Cambridge: Cambridge University Press, 1992], pp. 168-79. Of the passion narrative he writes: 'It has much to commend it as historiography when read in the light of the Synoptic passion narratives...' He (John) is said to 'have created in 18–19 a model of actuality' (p. 178). See by the same author *John* (Readings; Sheffield: JSOT Press, 1993) where the same narrative-critical approach is applied to the whole Gospel.

Jesus at this point they act as such, with the result that the soldiers all fall to the ground as at the epiphany of a god. As a way out of this impasse Jesus repeats question and answer, and so procures his own arrest, though in doing so he lays down his terms that, in the fulfilment of the divine plan, those with him shall be allowed to go free (18.8-9).

The theme of authority (ἐξουσία), with the connected question of origins, has been implicit or explicit throughout the Gospel. ἐξουσία indicates freedom of choice, the right to act. In a stronger sense it conveys 'absolute power, the warrant to do something'. It is generally used of the power of rulers by virtue of their exalted positions, for example of kings or high priests. It can also be used of the rulers of the spiritual world. Within the word, as with its Latin equivalent *auctoritas*, is the idea of sovereign weight, which is exercised in right rule. Perhaps not unconnected is the word 'glory' (δόξα, the Hebrew word behind it, *kabōdh*, having the root meaning of 'weight'). It is applied both to God (5.44; 11.40) and to Jesus as the Logos-Son (1.14; 2.11); and the evangelist uses the verb 'glorify' of their mutual relationship. The Son so acts and speaks that God may be seen to be God, and the Father so acts as to make evident who the Son is (12.27-33; 17.4-5). In 17.1-26 Jesus prays out of the knowledge that the Father, God, has given to him as the Son authority over the whole of humankind. This has been specified in relation to human beings (5.17-29) as an authority delegated from Father to Son (who work together) to exercise the twin divine activities of giving eternal life from the dead and final judgment, which is passed by human beings upon themselves by their attitude of belief or unbelief in respect of the Son. It is specified in relation to himself as the ἐξουσία received from the Father and exercised in obedience to the Father to lay down his earthly life at his own volition, and not under compulsion from human beings, and also to resume his life. The words and actions of Jesus are authoritative and true because they have God as their origin, are the words he has heard from the Father and the works which he has seen the Father doing. They are spoken and done in constant conflict with human authorities, who fail to recognize him, but recognize only those who come in their own name and seek human glory (5.30-47).

The theme of authority now occupies centre stage, but this is not through a direct confrontation with the Jewish authorities. The appearances before Annas and then Caiaphas—who has already consigned Jesus to death (11.49-50)—are perfunctory, and contribute nothing of substance (18.12-14, 19-24). The theme is developed through a judgment scene at the praetorium, the residence of Pilate as the representative of the supreme imperial power, and it takes the dramatic though artificial form of a succession of three-sided dialogues between Pilate, Jesus and the Jewish authorities. This is a theological unity, in which again history is subsumed in theology. It proceeds by stages.

In the first stage (18.28-32) Pilate, addressing the Jews who are compelled by religious scruple to remain outside, proposes they deal with the matter themselves. To this they reply that they do not have the ἐξουσία over the death penalty which is required in this case. This statement the evangelist interprets as dramatic irony, for it is the means by which Jesus is in control, and he will now assuredly die by the means which has already been determined, that is, crucifixion, or 'lifting up', as symbolic of his elevation to the Father through it (12.32-33).

In the second stage (18.33-40), inside, Pilate, now apparently aware of the charge, introduces the theme of sovereignty in terms of it with the question, 'Are you the king of the Jews?' Jesus, after asking whether this is a genuine enquiry, affirms that he has a sovereignty (βασιλεία), but one which does not have its origin from (ἐκ) this world. This is further explicated in more Hellenistic terms as that for which he has been born (as human) and has come into the world (from heaven), namely to bear witness to the truth to be recognized by all who belong to (πᾶς ὁ ὢν ἐκ) the truth. This Pilate brings to an end with the question (purely rhetorical, cynical and dismissive, or genuine and puzzled?) 'What is truth?', but conveys its effect outside with the offer of Jesus as a candidate for the Passover release. The Jews, however, choose the revolutionary Barabbas.

In the third stage (19.1-7), inside, Jesus is scourged on Pilate's orders. The episode takes the form of a charade in which soldiers array him in a royal robe and the palm diadem of Hellenistic kings, ritually buffet him and give him royal acclamation. In this guise since a dummy king he is brought outside and presented as 'the man'. The term is no doubt contemptuous, though also possibly ironical, as the reader may recall that God has given Jesus, the Son, ἐξουσία to exercise judgement because he was 'a son of man' (5.27). The response of the Jews to this is a renewed demand for his crucifixion; and after Pilate's exasperated, because impossible, direction to crucify the innocent one themselves, they shift ground from the political to the religious with the assertion that he merited death by Jewish law because he had made himself the Son of God.

In the fourth and final stage (19.8-16, 19-22), inside, Pilate, apprehensive at the divine title Son of God, raises again the theme of origins with the question, 'Whence (πόθεν) are you?', and to force a reply asserts his ἐξουσία for release or conviction. To this the reply is that Pilate would have no ἐξουσία for this at all without it having been given him from above (ἄνωθεν). At this, Pilate being outside again, attempts once more to effect the release of the innocent Jesus, but the Jews, shifting the ground again back to the political, warn that to do so would amount to treason to Caesar. Therefore Pilate brings Jesus out again (presumably still dressed as a dummy king), and sits on the official judgment seat (the Greek allows the translation 'sat him on the judgment seat', which would be dramatic irony indeed), with the words 'Behold your king!' To renewed demands for crucifixion he asks, 'Shall I crucify your king?' At this, in order to gain their purpose, the high priests commit apostasy. Turning their backs upon the divine vocation of Israel to testify that their God rules in the kingdoms of human beings, they speak like good secularist inhabitants of the Roman Empire, and profess that they have no king but Caesar. At this, the high point of the drama, Pilate hands over the innocent Jesus for crucifixion, though in doing so he continues to bear some kind of testimony to him. For he himself writes the titulus to go on the cross in the form 'Jesus of Nazareth, the King of the Jews', and does so in the three principal languages of the Greco-Roman world for all to read. When asked to modify it he refuses so to do, but affirms, as if adding an official testimony to a document, 'What I have written, I have written'.

The narrative of the crucifixion itself is brief, and is concentrated on Jesus as in control of events, which serve his and God's purposes. He carries his cross unaided, and from the cross makes his testamentary disposition by commending his mother and his beloved disciple to each other. Out of his omniscience he utters the cry 'I thirst' in order to compel the fulfilment of Scripture (which fits him exactly, as in 19.23-24, 32-36, 37), and with his final word τετέλεσται announces to the world the actual consummation which he had announced proleptically to the Father in prayer (17.4, 'I have glorified thee on the earth, having accomplished the work you gave me to do').

A Survey of the Material in Chapters 20 and 21

The question then arises why the evangelist did not lay down his pen
with this final word of accomplishment, but continued his narrative, as
also the question of how much of the present text of chs. 20–21 was
from his pen. What immediately follows is the handing over of the body
for burial to Joseph of Arimathea, who is said to be a disciple, but a
secret one out of fear of the Jews, along with Nicodemus, who as the foil
to Jesus in his first teaching (3.1-21), and as an authority who had
asserted the legal requirement to hear a person before he or she is
judged (7.50-51), is possibly here a representative of those Jews who
were not entirely hostile. This could be for the purpose of stating that
this consummatory death was factual and historical. For in human life
death involves a corpse; and in the Gospel divine communication, if it is
to be through the Logos who is genuinely flesh, involves the dead body
of Jesus. But if the death of the Logos, Jesus Christ, is all that the
evangelist has set it out to be, it also involves what happens to that
corpse. In this way the narrative of the burial may not only look backwards to the historical death, but prepare for, and be for the sake of,
what is to follow in the story of the empty tomb.

In the Johannine version of this story Mary Magdalene comes first
and alone to the tomb, and finding the stone rolled away returns to
Peter and the beloved disciple with the report, 'They [i.e. human beings
of some sort] took away the Lord out of the tomb, and we do not know
where they laid him' (20.2). Thereupon the beloved disciple runs with
Peter to the tomb, enters it, sees the burial clothes and believes. What he
believes is not stated, but it would be in accordance with the absolute
use of the verb in this gospel that on the basis of the empty tomb alone
he believed Jesus to be all that he said he was, including the claim that
he had authority and power to raise himself and to resume again the life
he had voluntarily laid down. If this is so, it is possible that the Gospel
originally ended here, and that what follows, including the statement that
they did not yet know the Scripture that he must rise from the dead
(20.9), were later supplements of various kinds to establish particular
viewpoints by means of the resurrection stories.

Thus 21.24 and 25 appear to be two codicils added by different hands
to bring ch. 21 and so the Gospel to an end, and to validate it as the
work of the beloved disciple. 21.1-23 has been held by a number of
scholars, on literary and theological grounds, to be an addition, perhaps

to show the risen Lord as the author of a universal mission and to rehabilitate Peter as the chief apostle.

In ch. 20 the appearance of the risen Lord to Mary outside the tomb (20.11-18) superficially follows well the visit of the disciples to the tomb, though she is not said to have returned there. It is, however, the core of the incident, Jesus' forbidding Mary to touch him because he has not yet ascended to the Father, which presents the greatest difficulty. The use of the word 'touch' for communication between the believer and the Lord is unique here in the Gospel, and may owe something to the language of the first epistle of John (cf. 1 Jn 1.1). The command seems to imply in the 'not yet' that there will be a proper touching of the Lord by believers when he has ascended, and its point may be to assert that the resurrection of Jesus is still only a stage on his return to the Father, which truth is to be conveyed to the disciples in the message that he is in the process of ascending to their common Father and God (20.17).

In the next story (20.19-23) there are also elements which are not in complete harmony with the rest of the Gospel. The breathing of the Spirit by the risen Lord upon the disciples hardly accords with the teaching in chs. 14–16 about the Paraclete-Spirit, who proceeds from, and will be sent by, the Father and the Son. And the doctrine of sins (plural) in 20.23, while it may correspond with that in 1 John, is not in accord with the Johannine doctrine of sin (singular).

Finally, in the story of the appearance to Thomas (20.24-29) there is the immediate problem that the command of the Lord to touch him (20.27) is in flat contradiction with that to Mary not to do so (20.17), so that some scholars have felt compelled to presume that the evangelist understands the risen Lord to have ascended between the two appearances.

It appears that the Johannine presentation of Jesus' last days in Jerusalem has been prepared for most carefully throughout the entire Gospel. Thus a theology of location in the reordering of Jerusalem episodes was begun with the cleansing of the temple (ch. 2), followed by frequent returns to the city where opposition to Jewish religious authority was the backcloth for Jesus' teachings and claims, and prepared for the universally effective death and glorification of this Logos, Jesus. However, perhaps even more importantly, only this Logos, a divine figure of whom the most exalted things were said in the prologue itself, could have provided the theological meaning of the events leading to the death and resurrection presented in the Fourth Gospel. Only such a Logos-Son, the μονογενὴς θεός Jesus Christ, could have been depicted in chs. 18–19 as in total control of his life at all stages so that he alone effected his own arrest, at the appointed 'hour', according to the predeterminate will of God the Father; he alone voluntarily laid down his life and took it up again, which was an exercise of authority and of the prerogatives of God according to the Jews; he alone was able to effect a return to the intimacy with the Father, whence he had come by that death; he alone could enter into that same glory which was his from before the foundation of the earth.

Without the cryptic structure of the prologue in its entirety, together with its elucidation, the distinctive and truly dramatic theology of the last days of Jesus Christ, the Logos μονογενὴς θεός, could scarcely have been presented in this way.

CONCLUSION

This book has been concerned with two problems connected with the Fourth Gospel. The first was that of its literary form, for which adequate antecedents, including the other gospels, are difficult to find. The second was the relation of the so-called prologue to the rest of the Gospel, on which point scholarly opinion has ranged from the view that the prologue is integral to the Gospel to the view that it is only loosely attached to it.

The development of the concept of 'prologue' in Greek and Roman literature, its form and function, were briefly examined. Emerging in ancient religious drama, and continuing in some form into the first century CE, the prologue was intended to inform the readers (or audiences) in advance about the drama to be unfolded. In highly compressed statements it announced past events, intimated the present situation and its cosmic proportions, and introduced the main characters, who were about to fulfil the ordained will of God (the gods), other characters being part of the scenery and necessary background to the execution of the events divinely ordained. The prologue, then, set forth cryptically in advance the religious and philosophical truths which were to be unravelled and explicated in the body of the work.

This concept of prologue was then applied to the Johannine Gospel. The three historical personages, John, Moses and Jesus Christ, who are introduced into what is predominantly a cosmic prologue, were examined in that order, to see whether the features and functions assigned to them are expanded and utilized in the rest of the Gospel.

The first figure, that of John, immediately raises literary and theological problems. Modern scholars have tended to see the verses about John in the prologue as insertions by the evangelist into an earlier hymnic structure. This view was refuted, and on the basis of C.K. Barrett's stylistic analysis the prologue was treated as a literary and theological unity. Further, it was argued that 1.15-18, and not 1.15 only, are to be taken as statements made by John. It was further argued that in the Gospel the final testimony of John is to be taken as stretching to 3.36.

Critical analysis of the Gospels has attempted to reconstruct from the traditions a unified historical picture of John; but, as W. Wink has emphasized, the figure of John in this gospel is a very different one from the Baptist figure of the synoptists.

An examination of the text showed that this John and his functions are almost entirely summed up in the concept of 'witness'. By this is to be understood an activity which asserts the true heavenly origins, status and qualities of what is being referred to. Hence John is the divinely appointed witness on earth to the Logos Creator as the cosmic source of life and light for humankind. This witness is the occasion of belief in human beings, of their consequent enlightenment, and of their capacity to become children of God. He is therefore the witness of the uniqueness, priority and pre-eminence of the Logos made flesh, and of participation in his fulness. This is then taken up in the opening chapters of the Gospel. He speaks of himself as a divinely appointed voice, which, whether to Jews or to disciples, proclaims the unique heavenly origin of the man Jesus as the Son of God, as the one who alone utters the words of God and gives the Spirit in fulness, is the owner of all things and the author of eternal life for believers (1.19-42; 3.22-36).

John's statements in the prologue are not limited to himself and his witness, but also serve to introduce the other two named historical persons who will figure in the drama, Moses and Jesus Christ. This is done by making some sort of link, which is also a contrast, between the law given (by God?) through Moses and the grace and truth that have come into being through Jesus Christ, who is here named for the first time. This is undoubtedly awkward in the context, and the text would run more smoothly with the omission of 1.17a, which is, however, forbidden in such a closely knit structure as the prologue. Nor is the force of the statement immediately clear. It is not that of the Pauline antithesis of law and grace. Nowhere is there an issue in this gospel of whether the Mosaic law is binding on Christians or not. 'Grace' and 'truth', which are associated in 1.14 with the Logos made flesh in his relation to the Father, have a wider meaning, which is more Hellenistic, with emphasis on the truth that Jesus is shown to be in the Gospel. Moses may be regarded as a figure with more than one face in the first century CE, and here, with the law, may be a symbol of the Jewish religion as a whole. As such there is a link between it and the divine grace and truth of Jesus Christ; for the God of the Christians is the same as the God of the Jews, and their Scriptures point to that truth.

Nevertheless there is also an antithesis, since in actual fact the Jewish religion in the person of its representatives is found consistently in opposition to Jesus Christ and what he represents, and serves as a foil rather than a stepping stone to the truth, and is overthrown by it.

In the body of the Gospel the Jewish religion makes an immediate appearance as the background to John's first public witness (1.19-28). In reply to interrogation by the religious authorities in terms of Jewish religious expectations he asserts the supremacy of the as yet unknown Jesus. Then at his direction disciples pass over to Jesus, applying to him various titles of Jewish aspiration, including 'him of whom Moses and the prohets wrote', though these are replaced by his own reference to the Son of Man (1.51). From then until the close of the public ministry in ch. 12 a great deal of the speech and action takes place in the setting of unremitting conflict with 'the Jews' over matters of Jewish belief and practice—sabbath observance, scriptural interpretation, divine sustenance, circumcision, sonship of Abraham and freedom, and messiahship. Sometimes this is not without a certain awkwardness, as in 1.17a; for example in the obscure parallel to Moses lifting up the serpent (3.14), his relation to the manna (6.32-33), to the law and circumcision (7.19, 22). What emerges from these conflicts is that the divine truths contained in the Jewish religion, but unrecognized or misunderstood by its practitioners, are a present reality only in and through Jesus, who is from God and alongside him before Abraham; who works the works of God, is himself the heavenly sustenance, and as the Son of God is the bearer of truth and the author of freedom.

The prologue, and John's witness in it, reach a conclusion and climax in the highly compressed statement in 1.18. In a manner characteristic of him the Evangelist moves through a negative to a positive. Over against the sweeping assertion that no one has ever seen God, which applies not simply to Moses but universally, is set Jesus Christ, who is now called μονογενὴς θεός—'a unique one, God'. This reading, recommended by Hort and others, is to be accepted. It returns to the opening verses of the prologue, and identifies Jesus Christ with the Logos, who has been said to be God. It is this one who 'communicates divine things'; this is the specialist meaning to be given to the verb ἐξηγεῖσθαι when used without an object. How this concluding statement of the prologue is explicated in the body of the Gospel was then explored by reference to the three dominant christological expressions there.

The first was 'the Son of Man'. This is not the eschatological figure coming on the clouds of the synoptic tradition, but one who is pre-existent with God—he alone can make the ascent to God since he alone has made the descent from God (3.13)—who by entering his creation as a man has established in himself a permanent route of heavenly inter-communication between God and humankind (1.51). Participation in his humanity, his flesh and blood, is the sole means to the possession of eternal life (6.47-58). Connected with this Son of Man is his being 'lifted up', a cryptic reference to his death as his exaltation to the Father. Through it the Jews will be able to apprehend the divine origin of himself and of his actions and words (8.28-29), and Gentiles his divine being ('glory', 12.20-36; cf. 1.14).

It is to be noticed that the term 'Son of Man', as distinct from the 'Logos Son', appears to be deliberately introduced since it contains within itself the idea of manhood. Thus the term provided the author with a concept to be utilised with special regard to the actuality of Jesus' human death without diminution of the concept of divine status. The former concept, Jesus' human death, is nonsense for the Jews whose God never entered human flesh, and for the Gentiles whose gods, when they took on flesh, did so only in appearance—for such gods were provided, by divine intervention, with an escape from the earthly reality of death. As for the latter concept, the divine status, this is crucial to the capacity of Jesus the Son of Man as one who communicates divine things; that is, as the actual route for ceaseless communication between God and humankind; as the divine communicator and as that which is communicated for the possession of eternal life.

The second christological expression was ἐγώ εἰμι. It was already in Judaism a divine mode of speech, but it was more widespread in various types of Hellenistic religion, especially when combined with a predicate. The speaker in this way identified himself and his functions with this or that heavenly entity, and with what was to be expected from them—in terms of truth, light, life, shepherd and the like. This type of saying on the lips of Jesus, which is peculiar to this gospel, contributes considerably to Jesus' presentation of himself and his functions. It occurs both in disputes with the Jews (the true, that is, real or heavenly, bread, ch. 6; the door, and the good—or perfect—shepherd, ch. 10), and in the instruction of disciples (the resurrection, ch. 11; the way, the truth and the life, ch. 14; the true, that is, real or heavenly, vine, ch. 15). It may not be without significance for the origin of these religious symbols in the Gospel that, apart from 'door' and 'resurrection', which may be of

Christian or Jewish-Christian origin, they are all found in the Jewish-Hellenistic writings of Philo attached in one way or another to the figure of the Logos, as Philo envisaged him.

As previously, so here, the person of Jesus who alone utters the ἐγώ εἰμι teachings claims certain divine functions. He asserts, by means of cryptic symbolism, that he is the provider of the means of access to, and the continuity of, eternal life. The veracity of his teaching stems from the divine authority which the Logos figure of the prologue alone can claim.

The third expression was 'the Son (of God)'. This, which is found throughout the Gospel, expresses at one and the same time the origin and source of Jesus and his actions in another, who is God the Father, and also his closeness to that other; the Son who is in the bosom of the Father. On the one hand 'son of' denotes derivation, where Jesus is 'from' (ἐκ)—an important question for the evangelist. His presence on earth is the result of mission; he is the one sent, and God is the 'Father who sent me'. He initiates nothing, but reproduces faithfully what he sees the Father doing and speaks what he hears the Father saying. On the other hand he and the Father work together. Like the Father the Son has life in himself—the prerogative of divinity, though this is given him by the Father and they can be called a unity ('one thing', 10.30). This issue comes to a head in ch. 17, which the evangelist chooses to place at the end of the ministry and immediately before the 'passion', and which constitutes a kind of counterpart to the prologue. This is a monologue in the presence of disciples in the form of a prayer of the Son to the Father. But as prayer it is *sui generis*, since, while it contains petition and intercession for the disciples, these are grounded in an account which the Son renders to the Father of his mission. He prays as the one who has already perfected the task the Father had given him; the one who has given the disciples the Father's name and kept them in it, and the Father's word and kept them in it as the truth; and has given them the glory that the Father had given him, so that they may reproduce the unity that he and the Father have—into which glory, which he had had with the Father before creation, he is about to return. This prayer is one that can belong only on the lips of the Son who is the Logos-Son and Creator-Son of the prologue.

The Son (of God) was implied in the prologue. The summary above expresses the manner in which he effects the communication of divine things, which is being examined here. This gives authentication to the oneness of the Jewish God and the Son of the prologue. Monotheism is not jettisoned for polytheism—which is vital to the author's case in claiming the God of the Jews for the Christians. Yet the veracity of Jesus' teaching and works demanded that the divine seal of approval was always his and that he had indeed been given all authority upon earth. If anything more than that written in chs. 1–16 were needed to carry the case for Christianity then the intensity of the whole of ch. 17 certainly provides it. Here the future intimacy for believers is finally established as fact by means of the Son's communicating with the Father as can no ordinary human being. Thus what has been hinted at in the prologue is fully stated here, but stated in such a manner as to leave no doubt that all that 1.1-18 applied to the Logos-Son was vital for understanding the Son (of God). All that had been allocated to his ordained life and work on earth in the prologue is offered to God as completed in ch. 17. Perhaps by means of ch. 17 the evangelist has made the greatest possible claim for the inviolable truths of which he writes. All heavenly truths are communicated by Jesus and ordained by God.

Finally chs. 18–19 (20–21) were examined, first with regard to the language used of the death. The theological ideas and terms used in the Synoptic Gospels were absent. This evangelist employs unique expressions which demand knowledge of Jesus' divine origins, mission and teachings. Thus his death is said to be a return journey to God (πορεύεσθαι, ὑπάγειν), while the elevation or hoisting up (ὑψοῦν) is understood as a *sēmeion*. The unique entry into full humanity made apparent God's 'glory'. Similarly, the death is unique, both in its physical character and in its divine function. Even the word 'passion' is inappropriate. Here we have an abundance of those techniques found only in this evangelist's work. He enlarges the vocabulary by giving common verbs a theological significance, for they now acquire a heavenly meaning. He continues to establish his theological perspectives thereby, and appeals to Hellenistic ideas (for example the idea of journeying to the sphere of the gods) without compromising the God of the Jews.

Secondly, these chapters take on something of the structure of drama. The readers already know from the prologue the inevitable theological outcome, and now, with the frequent use of *double entendre*, a dramatic irony is created. Moreover, the forces of opposition, cryptically expressed in the prologue, are brought together. The Jews, who were in fierce opposition throughout, and have condemned Jesus without trial, are now, as it were, off stage. Pilate takes centre stage and in a totally artificial way provides Jesus with the correct cues for his final teachings to the world at large. An authority which is not rooted in this world is at the heart of the matter. Unlike the characters on stage, the Logos Jesus has true authority. He alone has an unbroken relationship to God whence his authority comes, carrying with it those privileges and attributes accorded solely to the God of the Jews. This Jesus is in unity with God, *qua* Logos; he never forfeits that intimacy in life, *qua* human being Jesus, and he does not do so in death. Indeed, the authority invested in him, among other things, guarantees that he will effect his own resurrection. The will of God is inviolable. The Gospel events are enmeshed in that death. They are ordered and formulated from ch. 2 onwards.

However, it is to be remembered that the evangelist, by beginning his work with a prologue, placed the entire work within the literary sphere of Greek religious drama. Consequently it was directed to a widespread readership. The prologue's carefully constructed cryptic unity prepared for the reordering of events, the re-presentation of beliefs and the necessary background and personages for the redevelopment of the theological doctrines which followed. There is no clause, no phrase, no noun, no verb which does not play its part in this preparation. The introduction of the Logos into a literary construction which follows the convention of certain ancient Greek prologues in that preparation is vital for a correct understanding of the Johannine gospel. From the prologue onwards the evangelist skilfully unveils the full identity—the metaphysical identity, one might say—of the protagonist of this cosmic drama, the Logos μονογενὴς θεός, Jesus Christ.

APPENDIX:
THE LOGOS

It has been argued in the text that the prologue determines to a considerable extent the shape and character of the Fourth Gospel, and also that the figure of the Logos, which is introduced abruptly in the prologue and then dropped, affects the presentation of Jesus in that Gospel. In his discussion of the variant reading in 1.18 Hort judged the three salient verses in the prologue to be vv. 1, 14 and 18, and reached the conclusion that 'these verses by themselves would suffice to express the absolute primary content of S. John's message'.[1] The questions therefore arise of what is to be understood by 'the Logos' here, and of its origins and background. Discussion of these questions has been long and detailed in this century without any consensus being reached.[2] This has been because these questions have proved very difficult to answer, both because the possible thought backgrounds are not necessarily adequately documented, and also because of difficulties involved in such concepts as 'personification' or 'hypostatization'.

From the turn of the century attempts were made, especially by classically trained scholars, to trace the Logos to Greek religion and philosophy, where it was at home. It had originated with Heraclitus (c. 500 BCE) for whom it was another name for the Fire-God, or primal Fire, and was a term used to denote rule or order, that which governs the world processes. It was also reason or intelligence. All things happened through the Logos, which was universal, an all-pervading principle of reason

1. *Two Dissertations*, p. 15. Contrast the view of A. von Harnack, *The History of Dogma* (London: Williams & Norgate, 1905), I, p. 97, where he judges that 'the prologue of the Gospel is not the key to its composition', and that 'even the Logos has little more in common with that of Philo than the name, and its mention at the beginning of the book is a mystery, not the solution of one'.

2. The bibliography is considerable. For the commentaries, see Hoskyns, *Fourth Gospel*, Detached Note I, pp. 154-63; Barrett, *St John*, pp. 152-55; Brown, *John*, Appendix II, I, pp. 519-24; L. Morris, *The Gospel according to John: The English Text with Introduction, Exposition and Notes* (London: Marshall, Morgan & Scott, 1971), Additional Note A, pp. 115-26; Schnackenburg, *St John*, I, Excursus I, pp. 481-93. See also J. Ashton, 'The Transformation of Wisdom: A Study of the Prologue of John's Gospel', *NTS* 32 (1986), pp. 161-86; Dodd, *Interpretation*, pp. 263-85; J.D.G. Dunn, *Christology in the Making* (London: SCM Press, 1980), pp. 215-50; Harris, *Origin of the Prologue*; *idem*, 'Athena, Sophia and Logos'; E.F. Scott, *The Fourth Gospel: Its Purpose and Theology* (Edinburgh: T. & T. Clark, 2nd edn, 1908), ch. V, 'The Doctrine of the Logos', pp. 145-75; R.G. Bury, *The Fourth Gospel and the Logos-Doctrine* (Cambridge: W. Heffer & Sons, 1940); V.H. Stanton, *The Gospels as Historical Documents* (Oxford: Oxford University Press, 1920), pp. 161-86.

determining the structure of thought and the unity of being. Although this concept of the Logos played no part in the theories of other pre-Socratic philosophers, nor in those of Plato or Aristotle (for whom reason was denoted by Nous), it re-emerged in Stoic philosophy. In this system, as well as each object having its own 'Logos' which governs the form of its life, the totality of objects was constituted a cosmos by virtue of a single Logos, a single unitary cosmic principle. In attempting to define the place of humankind in such a general ordering of reality the Stoics developed a corresponding moral attitude; this was called the ὀρθὸς λόγος. It is not possible that Stoicism was here a direct influence on the evangelist, for it was by nature pantheistic, and the Logos was a principle and force totally immanent within the cosmos, whereas for John the Logos was, like God himself, transcendent over the world, and though the world was his creation it was not totally in harmony with him, but frequently at odds with him.[1]

By contrast there have been a line of scholars, especially those concerned to establish a 'biblical theology', who have claimed that it is not necessary to go outside the Old Testament and the Jewish religious sphere to account for the Logos in John. The Old Testament already contains a theology of the Word of God. This Word operates in creation—thus Ps. 33.6, 'By the word of the Lord were the heavens made' is a poetic and semi-personified form of the statement of creation in Gen. 1.3, 'God said "Let there be light"', and so on. This same Word operates through the prophets for revelation or judgment (cf. for example Jer. 1.4; 2.1), and can itself be said to effect salvation (Ps. 107.20). And it could be identified with the law, thus effecting what the law effected. It is, however, doubtful whether this usage stands immediately behind John's use of the Logos. It does not appear without a genitive—'the Word of the Lord' (or 'his', 'thy' or 'my word')—and it falls a good deal short of the personification of a pre-existent being with God, who can become incarnate. The only New Testament instance of 'the Word of God' as personal, Rev. 19.13, belongs to the apocalyptic tradition, which is different from that of John. Moreover it does not appear that such a theology of the Word of God had a continuing history in Judaism. It is absent from Jewish writings until the later Targums, where it appears, if anything, in a less personified form, being a mere periphrasis for God in order to avoid naming him.[2]

There was, however, a theological tradition, the development of which may be traced in the Old Testament and Judaism, which could offer a closer background to the prologue of John. This is the Wisdom tradition. Originally perhaps a borrowing from Egyptian religion—hence its feminine character—Wisdom, or the Wisdom of God, is a term reflecting in multiple ways the interpenetration of Judaism and

---

1.   But see Knox, *Hellenistic Elements*, p. 38 n. 1, who observes that the Stoic systems were not uniform, and that in some a place was found for the transcendent. He concludes that Philo, while undoubtedly indebted to Stoicism, will have been dependent on a 'transcendental type; a pure immanentism could find no place in Judaism'.

2.   For the weakness of the derivation of the Johannine Logos from the Memra or Word of God in the Targums, see Knox, *Hellenistic Elements*, p. 43, who comments that, even if such speculations about the Word of God were more prevalent in first-century Judaism than is now documented, they were due to Hellenistic influence.

Hellenism which took place in the last three centuries BCE and the first century CE, and in many places, though especially Alexandria.[1] It was used to commend Judaism to the intelligent Gentile, and to reconcile the two types of thought by bringing the transcendent God and his activity into an immanent relationship with the world and its life (Wisdom finds a place even in the apocalyptic tradition in Judaism). The striking parallels between this Wisdom tradition and the Johannine prologue have been noted frequently, especially by J. Rendel Harris.[2] Thus in the various statements about Wisdom to be found in Proverbs 8, Ecclesiasticus 24 and Wisdom 7–9 (cf. also *1 En.* 42.2; *2 En.* 30.8) there is presented a figure who was created by God before the world and was with him as a master worker and beside him on his throne; who was his agent in creation and 'the artificer of all things'; whose paths are the paths of life, and who is an effulgence from everlasting light and a mirror of God; who reaches from one end of the world to the other in ordering all things well, and who visits and indwells human beings to make them friends of God.

There are here close similarities between the character and functions of the figure of Wisdom and those ascribed to the Logos, and also a greater degree of personification or hypostatization than in the case of 'the Word of God'. It does, however, as Dodd observes, still fall a good way short of the statement in the prologue that 'the Word was God', and the visits of Wisdom to human beings, successful or unsuccessful, and her presence with them, do not have the same force as the incarnation at a single moment as veritably human of a divine pre-existent 'person'. For those who would see this Wisdom figure as the immediate background to the Johannine Logos the problem has been why the evangelist did not operate with it, and begin his prologue with 'In the beginning was Wisdom'. The suggestion that he did not do so because Wisdom was a feminine noun, and that in the circumstances he needed a masculine noun, is not altogether convincing.[3] And even if this were to have been the case it would raise again the questions of why, where and whence there was in existence this masculine term 'the Logos', which could be introduced as already recognizable to readers, and who was already invested with characteristics and properties which belonged to Wisdom, and which could enable it to be substituted for Wisdom.

This leads naturally to a particular person engaged in this synthesis of Judaism and Hellenism, Philo, and to a particular place in which it was being made, Alexandria. We now have the opposite problem; for whereas in investigating possible theologies of the Word of God or of Wisdom that might have been current in the evangelist's time and milieu the problem is that the surviving evidence is elusive and fragmentary, here

1. For the extent of this interpenetration, see M. Hengel, *Judaism and Hellenism* (2 vols.; London: SCM Press, 1974), *passim*; and for the place of Wisdom in it, see W.L. Knox, *St Paul and the Church of the Gentiles* (Cambridge: Cambridge University Press, 1939), pp. 55-89.

2. In *Origin of the Prologue*, which similarities are tabulated by Dodd, *Interpretation*, pp. 274ff. So also Ashton, 'Transformation of Wisdom', though with the important modification that the Wisdom figure in the background had already been given a significantly different mythical character under Christian influence.

3. A suggestion made by Harris, *Origin of the Prologue*, p. 12, and repeated by others. Petersen, in *The Gospel of John*, leans heavily upon this hypothesis.

the problem is the very plethora of evidence in the voluminous writings of Philo. This is compounded by the fact that Philo was not an original thinker nor a systematic writer. He was highly eclectic in his use of current philosophies and unsystematic in his presentation of what is largely exegesis of the Old Testament text. Nor is it certain whether he was a typical representative of Alexandrian Judaism or was idiosyncratic. The ground has been gone over frequently and different conclusions have been drawn.[1] One thing would appear to be clear with reference to our previous discussion, which is that in Philo the Logos has displaced Wisdom. Knox, in considering the relative paucity of references to Wisdom in Philo, judges that such references as there are 'would seem to go back to Philo's predecessors, since Wisdom in Philo is merely a duplicate for the Logos, who is tending to oust the earlier cosmic figure'.[2]

Among the multifarious statements in Philo in which he uses the Logos—there are twelve hundred of them or more—there are some which afford striking parallels to John's prologue, which have convinced some scholars that John is dependent on Philo, even that he might have read him. Such statements are that alongside although distinct from the eternal God there is another being, who can be called God's eldest son, the Logos, who is himself eternal and divine (θεῖος), and can even be called a 'second god'. He is an essential part of God as the divine reason, and was the instrument of divine creation. His action may be compared with that of light, and he is God's prophet or interpreter, the agent of God's revelation to human beings, whose coming to human beings makes them receptive of the good.[3] Other scholars, however, have stressed the great difference between Philo's thought and John's, the absence in John of typical expressions which are found in Philo in connection with the Logos, and the lack of full personality and of an explicit pre-existence in Philo's Logos in comparison with John's. These have tended to deny acquaintance with, or dependence on, Philo on John's part.[4]

There is, however, a third possible conclusion which may be drawn. This is that Philo's writings are themselves evidence that 'the Logos' was a term, philosophical and religious, which was widely diffused and current in the Greco-Roman world at the time, more widely than we would otherwise have known; and that it lay to hand for religious thinkers of various kinds to use in their own ways to express the relation of God to the world, as they conceived it. This view is present in the judgments of a number of scholars. Thus W.R. Inge, in his article on the 'Logos' in the *Encyclopedia*

1. See most recently Dunn, *Christology in the Making*, pp. 215-50.
2. *Hellenistic Elements*, p. 52. Cf. also Bury, *Fourth Gospel*, p. 8: 'the term "Wisdom" seldom denotes the cosmological principle, being for the most part discarded by Philo in favour of the term "Logos", partly perhaps because the latter is a more flexible term and one which had already received the seal of philosophical approval'.
3. See the discussion in Scott, *The Fourth Gospel*, ch. V, and Bury, *Fourth Gospel*, pp. 5-9. Also Dodd, *Interpretation*, pp. 276-85.
4. So Bernard, *John*, I, pp. cxl-cxli; Bury, *Fourth Gospel*, p. 10, comments that 'the tendency on the part of most English expositors, at least, is to underrate the dependence of St. John on Philo, and through Philo on Greek thought, and to magnify the differences between their conceptions'. He continues, 'But the only essential difference is that necessitated by the Christian problem—the identification of Christ with the Logos'.

of Religion and Ethics, concludes: 'It is clear from the tone of the Gospel that Philo's concept of the Logos, or something like it, was already familiar to those to whom the Evangelist wrote'.[1] Similarly, Knox, who regards it as fantastic to suppose the writer of the Fourth Gospel to have read Philo's works, or to suppose that 'the freedom and spontaneity of the Gospel were derived from the laborious pedantry of Philo', nevertheless concludes that

> the resemblance between them is easy to understand if both are drawing on a common stock of midrashic tradition, intended in the first instance to prove that the imagery of the Old Testament, if properly understood, revealed beneath the cloak of allegory the truths at which the great thinkers of Greece had only guessed and so to convert the Greeks or to preserve the educated Jew from apostasy. The Fourth Gospel uses the same imagery to prove that Jesus is the Logos of Greek philosophy manifested on the stage of history.[2]

This view would be further strengthened if Bultmann's contentions were acceptable. He insisted that the absolute use of the Logos must be taken with complete serious-ness, and not derived from 'the Word of God', and he assembled a great deal of material from Hellenistic and gnostic (including Mandaean) sources to show that the term or some equivalent of it was widely used in religious discussion and writing.[3] The date and character of these sources are, however, still matters of dispute, as is the whole question of whether there was a pre-Christian gnosticism.

Scott affirms that the Philonic Logos is to be understood by a double descent from Old Testament and Hellenistic thought.[4] Furthermore, he affirms that Philo's elabo-ration of the Logos doctrine in one respect, namely in its cosmic interest, is closer to Greek than to Jewish thought forms.[5] Of the Fourth Gospel's doctrines of the Logos, Scott maintains that 'it is closely similar' to that of Philo; and that the Philonic doctrine had 'naturalized itself in Christian thought' before being taken up by the Evangelist.[6] He concludes, as do others, that the Logos doctrine born of philosophical theory is wholly inadequate to explain the historical Jesus.

The recent work of Dunn explores the Logos in pre-Christian thought.[7] Of the Philonic concepts he says that they 'manifest to an unsurpassed degree how extensive and how sophisticated could be the interaction between the Jewish faith and Hellenistic philosophy'. This, he maintains, 'demonstrates the intellectual milieu out of which the Johannine prologue seems to have emerged'.[8] Having maintained that Philo merges Platonic cosmology with Jewish beliefs, and uses the Stoic concept of Logos, the divine reason which is both unexpressed thought in the mind and uttered

1.   W.R. Inge, 'Logos', in *Hastings's Encyclopaedia of Religion and Ethics* (Edinburgh: T. & T. Clark, 1915), VIII, p. 136.

2.   *Hellenistic Elements*, p. 44.

3.   Bultmann, *John*, pp. 21-23.

4.   Scott, *The Fourth Gospel*, p. 150.

5.   Scott, *The Fourth Gospel*, p. 152.

6.   Scott, *The Fourth Gospel*, p. 154.

7.   *Christology in the Making*, pp. 215-30.

8.   *Christology in the Making*, p. 216.

thought,[1] Dunn draws attention to passages which substantiate the view that Philo's logos is 'what is knowable of God; the logos is God in so far as he may be apprehended and experienced'.[2] Significantly, he sees Philo's importance in the fact that his writings demonstrate (1) the sort of cosmological speculation widespread at the time of the evangelist, and (2) the fact that Jews could use such speculation without compromising their monotheism.[3]

1. *Christology in the Making*, pp. 222-23.
2. *Christology in the Making*, p. 226.
3. *Christology in the Making*, p. 229.

BIBLIOGRAPHY

Aalen, S., '"Truth", a Key Word in St John's Gospel', *Studia Evangelica* II (1964), pp. 3-23.

Ashton, J., 'The Transformation of Wisdom: A Study of the Prologue of John's Gospel', *NTS* 32 (1986), pp. 161-86.

—*Understanding the Fourth Gospel* (Oxford: Oxford University Press, 1991).

Barclay, J.M.G., 'Manipulating Moses: Exodus 2.10-15 in Egyptian Judaism and the New Testament', in R.P. Carroll (ed.), *Text as Pretext: Essays in Honour of Robert Davidson* (JSOTSup, 138; Sheffield: JSOT Press, 1992), pp. 34-37.

Barrett, C.K., *The Gospel of John and Judaism* (London: SPCK, 1975).

—'The Holy Spirit in the Fourth Gospel', *JTS* NS 1 (1950), pp. 1-15.

—'The Prologue of St John's Gospel' (London: Athlone Press, 1971; reprinted in the collection *New Testament Essays* [London: SPCK, 1972]).

—*The Gospel according to St John: An Introduction with Commentary and Notes on the Greek Text* (London: SPCK, 2nd rev. edn, 1978).

Batey, R.A., *Jesus and the Forgotten City* (Grand Rapids: Baker, 1991).

Bauer, W., *Das Johannesevangelium erklärt* (HNT, 6; Tübingen: Mohr [Paul Siebeck], 1935).

Bernard, J.H., *A Critical and Exegetical Commentary on the Gospel according to John* (2 vols.; Edinburgh: T. & T. Clark, 1928).

Boismard, M.-E., *Le Prologue de Saint Jean* (LD, 11; Paris: Cerf, 1953).

Borgen, P., 'God's Agent in the Fourth Gospel', in J. Neusner (ed.), *Religions in Antiquity: Essays in Memory of E.R. Goodenough* (Leiden: Brill, 1968), II, pp. 137-48. Reprinted in J. Ashton (ed.), *The Interpretation of John* (Issues in Religion and Theology, 9; London: SPCK; Philadelphia: Fortress Press, 1986), pp. 67-78.

Borsch, F.H., *The Son of Man in Myth and History* (London: SCM Press, 1967).

Bowen, C.R., 'The Fourth Gospel as Dramatic Material', *JBL* 49 (1930), pp. 292-305.

Brown, R.E., *The Gospel according to John* (AB, 29, 29a; 2 vols.; Garden City, NY: Doubleday, 1966).

Buchsel, F., 'ἐξηγεῖσθαι', *TDNT*, II, pp. 907-908.

Bultmann, R., *The Gospel of John: A Commentary* (Oxford: Basil Blackwell, 1971).

Bury, R.G., *The Fourth Gospel and the Logos-Doctrine* (Cambridge: W. Heffer & Sons, 1940).

Carpenter, J.E., *The Johannine Writings* (Constable, 1927).

Chadwick, H., *Early Christian Thought and Classical Tradition* (Oxford: Clarendon Press, 1966).

Colpe, C., 'New Testament and Gnostic Christology', in J. Neusner (ed.), *Religions in*

Antiquity: Essays in Memory of E.R. Goodenough (Leiden: Brill, 1968), pp. 227-43.

Colson, F.H., 'Quintillian, the Gospels and Christianity', *Classical Review* 39 (1925).

Colwell, E.C., 'A Definite Rule for the Use of the Article in the Greek New Testament', *JBL* 52 (1933), p. 20.

Culpepper, R.A., *Anatomy of the Fourth Gospel* (Philadelphia: Fortress Press, 1983).

—'The Pivot of John's Prologue', *NTS* 27 (1981), pp. 1-31.

Deissmann, A., *Light from the Ancient East* (London: Hodder & Stoughton, 1910).

Derrett, J.D.M., *Law in the New Testament* (London: Darton, Longman & Todd, 1970).

Dodd, C.H., *The Bible and the Greeks* (London: Hodder & Stoughton, 1935).

—*Historical Tradition in the Fourth Gospel* (Cambrige: Cambridge University Press, 1963).

—*The Interpretation of the Fourth Gospel* (Cambridge: Cambridge University Press, 1953).

Dunn, J.D.G., *Christology in the Making* (London: SCM Press, 1980).

—'Let John be John: A Gospel for its Time', in P. Stuhlmacher (ed.), *Das Evangelium und die Evangelien* (Tübingen: Mohr, 1983), pp. 309-40.

Evans, C.F., 'Christ at Prayer in St John's Gospel', *Lumen Vitae* 24.3 (1969), pp. 579-96.

—*Explorations in Theology 2* (London: SCM Press, 1977), pp. 37-38.

Forestell, J.T., *The Word of the Cross* (Rome: Biblical Institute Press, 1974).

Gärtner, B., 'The Pauline and Johannine Idea of "To Know God" against the Hellenistic Background', *NTS* 14 (1968), pp. 209-31.

Gaffney, J., 'Believing and Knowing in the Fourth Gospel', *Theological Studies* 26 (1965), pp. 215-41.

Gager, J.G., *Moses in Greco-Roman Paganism* (*JBL* Monograph Series, 16; Nashville: Abingdon Press, 1972).

Glasson, T.F., *Moses in the Fourth Gospel* (SBT, 40; London: SCM Press, 1983).

Goodenough, E.R., *An Introduction to Philo Judaeus* (Oxford: Basil Blackwell, 2nd rev. edn, 1962).

—*By Light, Light: The Mystic Gospel of Hellenistic Judaism* (Oxford: Oxford University Press, 1935).

Hagner, D.A., 'The Vision of God in Philo and John: A Comparative Study', *JETS* 14 (1971), pp. 81-93.

Haigh, A.E., *Tragic Drama of the Greeks* (Oxford: Oxford University Press, 1925).

Hanson, A.T., *A Study in the Doctrine of the Incarnation* (London: SPCK, 1978).

Harnack, A. von, 'Über das Verhältnis des Prologs des vierten Evangeliums zum ganzen Werke', *ZTK* 2 (1892), pp. 189-231.

—*The History of Dogma*, I (London: Williams & Norgate, 1905).

Harris, J.R., 'Athena, Sophia and Logos', *BJRL* 7.1 (1922), pp. 56-72.

—*The Origin of the Prologue to St John's Gospel* (Cambridge: Cambridge University Press, 1917).

Harvey, A.E., *Jesus on Trial: A Study in the Fourth Gospel* (London: SPCK, 1976).

Havelock, E.A., Introductions to the Prentice Hall Drama Series (Englewood Cliffs, NJ: Prentice Hall, 1970).

Hengel, M., *Judaism and Hellenism* (London: SCM Press, 1974).

—*The Son of God* (London: SCM Press, 1976).

Hooker, M.D., 'John the Baptist and the Johannine Prologue', *NTS* 16 (1970), pp. 354-58.

—'The Johannine Prologue and the Messianic Secret', *NTS* 21 (1974), pp. 40-58.

Hort, F.J.A., *Two Dissertations* (London: Macmillan, 1876).

Hoskyns, E.C., *The Fourth Gospel* (ed. F.N. Davey; London: Faber & Faber, 2nd rev. edn, 1947).

Houlden, J.L., *A Commentary on the Johannine Epistles* (London: A. & C. Black, 1973).

Inge, W.R., 'Logos', in *Hastings's Encyclopaedia of Religion and Ethics* (Edinburgh: T. & T. Clark, 1915), VIII.

Jeremias, J., *The Parables of Jesus* (London: SCM Press, 1963).

—'Μωϋσῆς', *TDNT*, IV, pp. 848-73.

Käsemann, E., 'The Structure and Purpose of the Prologue to John's Gospel', in *New Testament Questions of Today* (London: SCM Press, 1969), pp. 138-67.

—*The Testament of Jesus* (London: SCM Press, 1968).

Kamberbeek, J.C., *The Plays of Sophocles. V. The Electra* (Leiden: Brill, 1974).

Kee, H.E., 'Aretalogy', *IDBSup*, pp. 52-53.

Kirk, K.E., *The Vision of God* (London: Longmans, Green & Co., 1931).

Knox, W.L., 'The "Divine Hero" Christology in the New Testament', *HTR* 41 (1948), pp. 228-49.

—'The Divine Wisdom', *JTS* 38 (1937), pp. 230-37.

—*Some Hellenistic Elements in Primitive Christianity* (Oxford: Oxford University Press, 1944). Reprinted 1980 by Kraus-Thornson, Munich, by permission of the British Academy, London.

—*St Paul and the Church of the Gentiles* (Cambridge: Cambridge University Press, 1939).

Kruijf, T.C. de, 'The Glory of the Only Son (Jn 1.14)', in *Studies in John* (NovTSup, 24; Leiden: Brill, 1970), pp. 111-23.

Lagrange, M.-J., *Evangile selon Saint Jean* (Paris: Gabalda, 1924).

Lightfoot, R.H., *The Gospel Message of St Mark* (Oxford: Clarendon Press, 1950).

—*St John's Gospel: A Commentary* (ed. C.F. Evans; Oxford: Clarendon Press, 1956).

Lindars, B., *The Gospel of John* (London: Oliphants, 1972).

—*Jesus, Son of Man* (London: SPCK, 1983).

Loisy, A., *Le Quatrième Evangile* (Alphonse Picard et Fils, 1903).

Louw, J.P., 'Narrator of the Father', *Neot* 2 (1968), pp. 32-40.

Maillet, H., '"Au-dessus de", ou "sur"? (John 1.51)', *ETR* 59 (1974), pp. 207-13.

Marshall, I.H., 'The Synoptic Son of Man Sayings in Recent Discussions', *NTS* 12 (1966), pp. 327-51.

Martyn, L., *History and Theology in the Fourth Gospel* (Nashville: Abingdon Press, 2nd edn, 1979).

Mastin, B.A., 'A Neglected Feature of the Christology of the Fourth Gospel', *NTS* 22 (1975), pp. 31-51.

McReynolds, P.A., 'John 1.18 in Textual Variation and Translation', in E.J. Epp and C.D. Fee (eds.), *New Testament Textual Criticism: Its Significance for Exegesis* (Oxford: Clarendon Press, 1981), pp. 105-18.

Meeks, W.A., *The Prophet-King: Moses Traditions and Johannine Christology* (NovTSup, 14; Leiden: Brill, 1967), pp. 17-29.

—'Moses as God and King', in J. Neusner (ed.), *Religions in Antiquity: Essays in Memory of E.R. Goodenough* (Leiden: Brill, 1968), pp. 354-71.

Michaelis, W., 'ὁράω', *TDNT*, V, pp. 315-82.

Michaels, J.R., 'Origen and the Text of John 1.15', in E.J. Epp and C.D. Fee (eds.), *New Testament Textual Criticism: Its Significance for Exegesis* (Oxford: Clarendon Press, 1981), pp. 87-104.

Moloney, F.J., *The Johannine Son of Man* (Bibliotheca de Scienze Religiose, 14; Las Libreria Ateneo Salesiano, 1976).

—'The Fourth Gospel's Presentation of Jesus as the Christ', *Downside Review* 95.321 (Oct. 1977), pp. 239-53.

Morris, L., *The Gospel according to John: The English Text with Introduction, Exposition and Notes* (London: Marshall, Morgan & Scott, 1971).

Moulton, J.H., *A Grammar of New Testament Greek*, I (Edinburgh: T. & T. Clark, 1906).

Muilenberg, J., 'Literary Form in the Fourth Gospel', *JBL* 51, pp. 40-53.

Nock, A.D., *Conversion* (Oxford: Oxford University Press, 1961).

—Review of *Galen on Jews and Christians* by R. Walzer, *Gnomon* 23 (1951), pp. 48-52.

Norden, E., *Agnostos Theos* (Leipzig: Teubner, 1913).

Odeberg, H.T., *The Fourth Gospel Interpreted in its Relation to Contemporaneous Religious Currents in Palestine and the Hellenistic Oriental World* (Stockholm: Almqvist & Wiksells, 1929).

Pancaro, S., *The Law in the Fourth Gospel* (NovTSup, 42; Leiden: Brill, 1975).

Petersen, N.R., *The Gospel of John and the Sociology of Light* (Philadelphia: Trinity Press International, 1993).

Pollard, T.E., *Johannine Christology and the Early Church* (Cambridge: Cambridge University Press, 1970).

Potterie, I. de la, 'Structure du Prologue de Saint Jean', *NTS* 30 (1984), p. 354-81.

—'Je suis la Voie, la Vérité et la Vie', *NRT* 88 (1966), pp. 907-42.

—*La Vérité dans Saint Jean* (AnBib, 73; Rome: Biblical Institute Press, 1977).

Pratt, D.B., 'The Gospel of John from the Standpoint of Greek Tragedy', *The Biblical World* 30 (1907), pp. 448-59.

Rengstorf, K.H., 'ἀπόστολος', *TDNT*, I, pp. 407-41.

Ridderbos, H., 'The Structure and Scope of the Prologue to the Gospel of John', *NovT* 8 (1966).

Robinson, J.A.T., 'The Relation of the Prologue to the Gospel of St John', *NTS* 9 (1963), pp. 120-29.

Sabourin, L., '"Who . . . was begotten of God", Jn 1.13', *BTB* 6 (1976), pp. 86-89.

Sanders, J.N., and B.A. Mastin, *A Commentary on the Gospel according to St John* (London: A. & C. Black, 1968).

Sandmel, S., *Philo of Alexandria* (Oxford: Oxford University Press, 1979).

Schnackenburg, R., *The Gospel according to St John* (3 vols.; London: Burns & Oates, 1968, 1980, 1982).

Schweizer, E., *Ego Eimi: Die religionsgeschichtliche Herkunft und theologische Bedeutung der johanneischen Bildreden, zugleich ein Beitrag zur Quellenfrage des vierten Evangeliums* (FRLANT, 38; Göttingen: Vandenhoeck & Ruprecht, 2nd edn, 1965).

Scott, E.F., *The Fourth Gospel: Its Purpose and Theology* (Edinburgh: T. & T. Clark, 2nd edn, 1908).

Smith, D.M., 'Johannine Christianity: Some Reflections on its Character and Delineation', *NTS* 21 (1975), pp. 222-48.

Stanton, V.H., *The Gospels as Historical Documents*, III (Cambridge: Cambridge University Press, 1920).

Stibbe, M.W.G., *John as Storyteller* (SNTSMS, 73; Cambridge: Cambridge University Press, 1992).

—*John* (Readings; Sheffield: JSOT Press, 1993).

Stoessl, F., 'Prologos', in PW, XXIII.I, cols. 631-41.

Strathmann, H., 'μαρτυρεῖν', *TDNT*, IV, pp. 474-512.

Suggs, M.J. 'Gospel, Genre', in *IDBSup*, pp. 370-72.

Talbert, C.H., 'The Myth of the Descending-Ascending Redeemer in Mediterranean Antiquity', *NTS* 22 (1976), pp. 418-40.

—*What is a Gospel?* (Philadelphia: Fortress Press, 1977).

Tasker, R.V.G., *The Greek New Testament* (Oxford: Oxford University Press; Cambridge: Cambridge University Press, 1964).

Teeple, H.M., *The Mosaic Eschatological Prophet* (SBLMS, 10; Atlanta: Society of Biblical Literature, 1957).

Trebilco, P.R., *Jewish Communities in Asia Minor* (SNTSMS, 69; Cambridge: Cambridge University Press, 1991), pp. 159-62.

Trites, A.A., *The New Testament Concept of Witness* (SNTSMS, 31; Cambridge: Cambridge University Press, 1977).

Walzer, R., *Galen on Jews and Christians* (Oxford: Oxford University Press, 1949).

Westcott, B.F., *The Gospel according to St John* (2 vols.; London: John Murray, 1908).

Williamson, R., *Jews in the Hellenistic World, Philo* (Cambridge: Cambridge University Press, 1989).

—'Philo and New Testament Christology', *Studia Biblica* 3 (1978), pp. 439-45.

Wilson, R.McL. *The Gnostic Problem* (London: Mowbrays, 1964).

—'Philo and the Fourth Gospel', *ExpTim* 65 (1953–54), pp. 47-49.

Wink, W., *John the Baptist in the Gospel Tradition* (SNTSMS, 7; Cambridge: Cambridge University Press, 1968).

Winston, F.N.D., *Logos and Mystical Theology in Philo of Alexandria* (Cincinnati: Hebrew Union College Press, 1985).

Wolfson, H.A., *Philo: Foundations of Religious Philosophy in Judaism, Christianity and Islam* (2 vols.; Cambridge, MA: Harvard University Press, 1968).

INDEXES

INDEX OF REFERENCES

OLD TESTAMENT

Genesis		Psalms		53.1	113
2.1-3	79	2.7	157	53.7-11	56
17.1	138	10.34	76	54.12-13	145
28.10-17	119	12.34	76		
28.12	119	15.25	76	Jeremiah	
		23.1	148	1.4-5	157
Exodus		24.5	68	2.21	152
3.14	131, 134,	25.5	68	9.24	157
	135	80.9-16	152	31.33-34	145
4.22	157	107.20	197		
23.20	151			Hosea	
24.9-11	23	Proverbs		11.1	157
33–34	23, 94, 95	8	16, 198		
33.6	94			Amos	
33.13	96, 97	Isaiah		3.7	157
33.19	96	5.1	152		
34.6	66	5.7	152	Wisdom of Solomon	
		6.8	157	7	16
Numbers		40–45	43	7–9	198
20.17	151	40.3	27		
21.6-9	121	43.25	131	Ecclesiasticus	
21.8-9	79	44.6	137	7.33	66
		44.24	137	24	16, 198
Esther		45.5-6	139	40.17	66
2.9	66	45.8	139	42.15	110, 114
2.17	66	45.19	131	43.21	110
		51.12	137, 139	43.31	112

NEW TESTAMENT

Matthew		12.11	161	17.12	174
4.3-6	155	14.27	130	21.42	174
7.13	147	16.16	157	27.51-53	127
11.25-27	156	16.21	174	28.19	156

Mark
1.1-5   21
1.1-13   21, 23
1.3   54
1.11   155
5.7   155
6.50   130
8.31   174
9.7   155
13.6   130
13.32   156
14.61   157
14.62   130
15.39   156

Luke
1.35   155
3.4   54
4.3-9   155
9.22   174
10.21-22   156
13.15   161
13.24   147
14.5   161
17.25   174
19.30   93, 100
20.17   174
21.8   130
22.15   174
23.11   174
24.26   174
24.35   174
24.46   174

John
1   27
1.1-18   21, 87, 91, 153, 194
1.1-17   108, 169
1.1-16   89, 90
1.1-14   92
1.1-13   24
1.1-12   22
1.1-5   18, 19, 23, 60
1.1-4   23
1.1-2   18, 37, 169
1.1   18, 108, 115, 128, 135, 168, 187
1.2   18, 37, 169
1.3-5   129
1.3   126, 169
1.4-9   163
1.4-5   161
1.4   46, 126, 133, 162, 169
1.5-13   24
1.5-11   169
1.5   24, 28, 46, 51, 168, 175
1.6-8   18-20, 26, 27, 29, 34, 35, 37, 40, 49, 55, 159, 160, 169
1.6   169
1.7-8   39, 40
1.7   31, 37, 51, 163
1.8   31
1.9-14   60
1.9-13   27, 129, 170
1.9-11   24, 28
1.9-10   169
1.9   51, 67, 68, 169
1.10   51, 60
1.11-12   159
1.11   51, 60, 168-71, 182
1.12-13   161
1.12   18, 19, 24, 28, 51, 163, 182
1.13   18, 24, 37, 51, 107, 161
1.14-18   23, 24, 77, 94, 95, 97, 104
1.14   18, 21, 23, 34, 35, 50, 67, 68, 80, 100, 101, 103, 104, 107, 108, 118, 120, 122, 127, 128, 155, 158, 159, 167, 173, 175, 190, 192
1.15-18   34, 35, 39, 42, 49, 54, 59, 60, 62, 80, 90-92, 160, 163, 189
1.15-17   60, 92
1.15-16   49, 50, 52, 55-57, 59
1.15   18-20, 27-29, 31, 34-40, 42, 54, 55, 59, 163, 189
1.16-18   33, 35, 37, 38
1.16-17   31, 33
1.16   31, 33, 35, 36, 50, 52, 59, 61, 67
1.17-18   19, 35, 90, 97, 170
1.17   18, 19, 31, 34-37, 49, 50, 52, 53, 59, 67, 68, 70, 71, 76, 77, 79, 82, 83, 86, 87, 90-92, 94, 101, 107, 108, 137, 159, 176, 190, 191
1.18   18, 19, 23, 24, 34, 36, 38, 46, 49, 59-61, 85, 90-95, 97,

	98, 100-102, 104, 106, 108-15, 122, 127, 128, 153, 156, 158, 160, 169, 171, 191, 196
1.19-51	22
1.19-42	190
1.19-34	27, 37, 53, 62
1.19-28	36, 40, 53, 59, 91, 191
1.19-27	60
1.19-20	37
1.19	32, 34, 36, 37, 39, 42, 53
1.20-27	41
1.20-23	40
1.20	37, 42
1.21	168
1.22-23	171
1.22	54
1.23	55
1.24-25	171
1.24	53, 168, 169
1.25	54, 168
1.26	42, 54, 60
1.27-36	80
1.27	54
1.29-34	53, 55, 160
1.29	37, 47, 55, 59
1.30-31	59
1.30	37, 42
1.31	55
1.32-34	39, 56, 155
1.32	56
1.33-34	60
1.33	58, 59, 80
1.34-36	58
1.34	37, 57, 61
1.36	55
1.37-51	116
1.41	23
1.42	37
1.43	37
1.45	76, 78
1.49	23, 163
1.50	118
1.51	21, 67, 98, 117, 118, 120, 124, 128, 150, 160, 176, 191, 192
2.1–3.21	62
2.1-25	22
2.6	23
2.11	23, 141
2.12	106
2.13-22	176
2.13	37
2.18-20	44
2.19-22	61
2.20	37
2.23	99, 137
3	77, 88
3.1-21	59, 160
3.2	37
3.3-21	58
3.3-8	62, 69
3.3	161
3.7	68
3.10	44
3.11-18	162
3.11-12	61
3.11	42, 98, 120
3.12	120, 161
3.13	93, 117, 120, 122, 150, 192
3.14-15	44
3.14	78, 106, 117, 120, 174-76, 191
3.16-18	61
3.16-17	44
3.16	80, 103, 104, 106, 108
3.17	127
3.18	103, 104,
3.19-21	61, 124, 161
3.19	37
3.21	68
3.22-36	53, 57, 190
3.22-30	28
3.25-36	160
3.25-26	60
3.26	37, 39, 59
3.27-36	42, 49, 60
3.27-30	49, 59
3.28	28, 42, 57
3.29	57
3.30	58
3.31-36	49, 58, 59
3.31-32	59
3.32-33	39, 61
3.32-30	59
3.32	42, 98
3.33	58
3.35-36	61, 161
3.36	49, 59, 61, 62, 161, 189
4.1-31	22
4.9	103
4.12	93, 94, 100
4.20-24	124
4.26	130, 135, 136
4.29	37
4.31-38	135
4.31	37
4.34	44
4.39-54	22
4.42	37
4.45	98
4.47	37
5	77, 78, 81, 82, 88, 161
5.1-18	22
5.14	80
5.17-47	46
5.17-32	80
5.17-29	183
5.17-18	177
5.17	79
5.18	44

Reference	Pages	Reference	Pages	Reference	Pages	Reference	Pages
5.19-27	44	6.36-41	85	8.12-53	163		
5.20-27	177	6.38	125	8.12	121, 124,		
5.21	80	6.40	99, 176		133, 136,		
5.22	80, 93	6.41-52	145		146, 175,		
5.24	48, 126, 176	6.41	69, 85, 136		176		
5.25	126	6.42	37	8.13-28	133		
5.26	127	6.44-51	163	8.14	39		
5.27	117, 126,	6.44-45	99	8.16	163		
	127, 129,	6.44	123	8.17	76		
	184	6.45	85, 145, 176	8.18	39, 136, 163		
5.28-29	126	6.46	85, 98, 100,	8.20	132		
5.29	39		101	8.21	47, 134		
5.30-47	183	6.47-58	192	8.23	68		
5.30	93	6.47-51	85	8.24	56, 127,		
5.32	39	6.48	69, 136		130, 133,		
5.36	39, 46	6.50-51	125		134		
5.37	93, 98, 100,	6.50	69	8.26	42		
	101, 163	6.51	69, 136	8.28-29	192		
5.39-47	81	6.53	117, 124	8.28	117, 121,		
5.39	46, 77, 79,	6.57	86, 163		122, 130,		
	81	6.58	69		133, 134,		
5.44-47	177	6.60-71	22		175		
5.44	183	6.62-63	86	8.32-36	70		
5.45-47	77, 79, 82	6.62	99, 117, 124	8.32	70		
5.47	78	7	88	8.33	93, 100, 101		
6	77, 79, 88,	7.1	177	8.35	163		
	146	7.19-24	82	8.38	98, 163		
6.1-25	22	7.19	76, 78, 83,	8.39-59	44		
6.1	37		191	8.48-59	177		
6.2	98, 99	7.22	191	8.58	122, 130,		
6.5-14	143	7.23	76, 83		133-35		
6.14	37	7.25-30	177	8.59	132		
6.20	130-32	7.25	177	9	79		
6.24-26	143	7.26	37	9.3	124		
6.26	125	7.28	35, 69	9.4	80		
6.27	117, 124,	7.30	132	9.13-10.39	44		
	125	7.32-36	177	9.13-41	80		
6.28	144	7.32	53	9.13	144		
6.30-32	85	7.33	175	9.20	37		
6.32-34	77	7.37	35	9.22	41		
6.32-33	191	7.40-44	177	9.24	37		
6.32	77, 82, 83,	7.40	54	9.26	144		
	125, 136	7.45-52	177	9.27	144		
6.33	84, 125, 136	7.45	53	9.31	144		
6.35-40	162	7.45	53	9.32	144		
6.35	69, 85, 93,	7.49	76	9.34	53		
	100, 101,	7.50-51	186	9.35-41	56		
	136	7.51	76	9.35	117		

9.39	176	12.34	117, 121	16.7-11	44, 47
9.41	47, 127	12.35-36	124	16.8-9	47, 56
9.50	144	12.35	175	16.9	127
9.51-57	144	12.37-50	181	16.13-15	48
9.52-63	144	12.37	141	16.13	68
10	147	12.38	112	16.16-20	98, 99
10.1-6	140	12.44-50	163	16.22	99
10.3-4	165	12.44-45	99	16.23-33	99
10.7	147	12.45	100	16.25-30	166
10.9	147	12.46-47	176	16.27-30	169
10.11-18	140	12.46	175	16.28	158, 175
10.11	147	13–17	22	16.33	176
10.14	147	13.1-3	165, 168	17	153, 164, 167
10.17-18	132, 149	13.1-2	168		
10.25	39	13.1	165, 175, 182	17.1-26	183
10.29-30	177			17.3	11, 37, 63, 69, 87, 100
10.30	148, 193	13.2	182		
10.31-33	177	13.3	165, 175, 182	17.4-5	183
10.39	177			17.4	185
11.23-24	176	13.4-5	168	17.5	173
11.25-26	180	13.5	169	17.11	173
11.40	98	13.12-19	133	17.12	182
11.45-53	177	13.19	130, 133	17.17	69
11.47-53	44	13.20	165	18.5	130-32
11.47	37, 53	13.25-30	182	18.6	130-32
11.49-50	183	13.31	117	18.8-9	183
11.50-52	44	13.36	175	18.8	130-32
11.50	181	13.38	41	18.12-14	184
11.52	181	14.1–16.33	165	18.13	53
12	123	14.1-6	166	18.15-27	141
12.1-11	178	14.3	165	18.19-24	184
12.1-2	180	14.4	175	18.25	41
12.9-11	180	14.6	149, 170, 176	18.28-32	184
12.17-19	180			19.1-7	184
12.17	39	14.7-9	98	19.7	76
12.19	178	14.9	100	19.8-16	185
12.20-26	181	14.12	166, 175	19.19-22	185
12.20-36	192	14.19	99	19.23-24	185
12.23-24	41	14.26	47	19.30	133, 174
12.23	117, 121, 177	14.28	175	19.32-36	185
		15	166	19.35	39
12.27-33	181, 183	15.1	69, 152	19.37	185
12.31-32	176	15.5	152	20–21	186-88
12.31	44, 127	15.12	37	20.2	186
12.32-33	141, 175, 177, 184	15.24	47, 98	20.9	186
		15.26	39, 47	20.11-18	187
12.32	123, 127, 145	15.27	39	20.17	187
		16	166	20.18	98

20.19-23	187	20	167	*Colossians*		
20.23	187	21.19	109	1.15-16	107	
20.24-29	187			1.18	110	
20.25	98	*Romans*				
20.27	187	1.3-4	156	*1 Thessalonians*		
20.31	157	3.27	76	1.10	156	
21.1-23	186	7.23	76			
21.24	39, 186	7.25	76	*Hebrews*		
21.25	186	8.2	76	6.6	156	
22.16	137	8.3	156	4.14	156	
		8.29	156			
Acts				*1 John*		
7.56	117	*2 Corinthians*		1.1	187	
10.8	109	1.19	156	4.9	103, 104	
15.12	109			5.20-21	169	
15.14	109	*Galatians*				
16.19	123	44	156			

PHILO

Agr.		*Leg. All.*		*Poster C.*	
51-54	148	3.101	97	145	51
		3.102	97		
Conf. Ling		3.172-73	145	*Rer. Div. Her.*	
62-63	158	3.173	146	79-80	145
Congr.		*Migr. Abr.*		*Somn.*	
51	97	174	151	1.75	147
173-74	146			2.172-73	152
		Mut. Nom.			
Det. Pot. Ins.		11ff.	135	*Vit. Mos.*	
118	145			1.24-25	74
		Op. Mund.		1.24	74
Deus Imm.		29-37	146	1.29	74
14.2	151	30	151	2.104	74
		36	151	2.292	74
Fug.					
137	145				

OTHER ANCIENT AUTHORS

Aristotle		*Poetics*		*Corpus Hermeticum*	
Rhetoric		1425b, 19-20	14	1.2	138
3.1414b,					
19-20	14	Clement of Alexandria		Homer	
3.1415a, 9	14	*Strom.*		*Iliad*	
		1.17	33	1.199.24.170	95
		3.3.17	96		

John Chrysostom
Homily
XIV   31

Josephus
Ant.
18.116-19   29

Origen
Adv. Haer.
3.10.2   33

Pollux
Onomasticon
VIII 12   114

Quintillian
De Institutione Oratoria
3.7-21   72

Tacitus
Histories
5.2-10   73
5.4   73

INDEX OF AUTHORS

Aalen, S. 67
Abbot, E. 102, 105
Ashton, J. 196, 198
Ausejo, S. de 20

Barclay, J.M.G. 178, 179
Barrett, C.K. 20, 27, 28, 36, 43, 47, 49,
    53, 64, 66, 84, 94, 103, 114, 122,
    125, 146, 189, 196
Batey, R.A. 179
Bauer, W. 49
Bernard, J.H. 18, 20, 118, 137, 199
Boismard, M.-E. 94, 110
Borgen, P. 45
Borsch, F.H. 117
Bousset 102
Brooke, A.E. 32
Brown, R.E. 20, 35, 42, 59, 65, 66, 78,
    94, 105, 111, 118, 122, 137, 149,
    150, 196
Buchsel, F. 113
Bultmann, R. 9, 10, 18-20, 26, 35-37,
    43, 46, 47, 49, 50, 52, 53, 59, 64,
    65, 67-69, 71, 77, 80, 82-84, 86,
    92, 94, 104, 106, 111-14, 118,
    122, 134, 138, 139, 144, 147-49,
    152, 200
Bury, R.G. 196, 199

Chadwick, H. 74
Colson, F.H. 72
Colwell, E.C. 127
Culpepper, R. 115

Deissmann, A. 137
Derrett, J.D.M. 45

Dodd, C.H. 21, 27, 28, 30, 35, 43, 49,
    53-55, 59, 66-68, 70, 75-77, 79,
    99, 100, 106, 121, 122, 131, 137,
    151, 152, 156, 157, 164, 167,
    196-98
Dunn, J.D.G. 196, 199-201

Evans, C.F. 168, 174, 178

Gaechter, P. 20
Gaffney, J. 97
Gager, J.G. 71-73
Gärtner, B. 97
Glasson, T.F. 73, 86
Goodenough, E.R. 74, 114, 115, 143
Green, H.C. 20

Haenchen, E. 20
Hagner, D.A. 97
Haigh, A.E. 13, 14, 16, 38
Harnack, A. von 9, 16-18, 105, 196
Harris, J.R. 106, 110, 196, 198
Harvey, A.E. 40, 42
Havelock, E.A. 15
Hengel, M. 156, 157, 198
Holtzmann 17
Hooker, M.D. 22, 23, 27, 38, 94, 96
Hort, F.J.A. 101-103, 105, 196
Hoskyns, E.C. 47, 48, 103, 110, 125,
    196
Houlden, J.L. 94

Inge, W.R. 199, 200

Jeremias, J. 65, 73, 140

Kamerbeek, J.C. 38
Käsemann, E. 20, 24, 28, 88, 94, 153, 158, 167
Kee, H.C. 10
Kirk, K.E. 95
Kittel, G. 86
Knox, W.L. 95, 97, 119, 135, 138, 144, 145, 148, 151, 152, 197-200

Lagrange, M.J. 64, 102
Lidzbarski, M. 151
Lightfoot, R.H. 21-23, 103, 110, 111, 165, 181
Lindars, B. 18, 43, 94, 105, 111, 114, 117
Lloyd-Jones, H. 15
Loisy, A. 65
Louw, J.P. 111, 112, 114

Maillet, H. 119
Marshall, I.H. 117
Mastin, B.A. 101-103
McReynolds, P.A. 101, 102, 106
Meeks, W.A. 54, 73
Michaelis, W. 95, 96, 150
Moloney, F.J. 117-19, 125
Morris, L. 196
Moulton, J.H. 93, 100

Norden, E. 130, 137

Odeberg, H.T. 119

Pancaro, S. 86, 87
Petersen, N.R. 133, 198

Pollard, T.E. 158
Potterie, I. de la 112, 149, 150

Reitzenstein, R. 138
Rengstorf, K.H. 45
Ridderbos, H. 21
Robinson, J.A.T. 20

Sabourin, L. 107
Sanders, J.N. 103
Sandmel, S. 143
Schnackenburg, R. 20, 43, 54, 94, 103, 107, 111, 112, 122, 137, 149, 151, 156, 170, 196
Schweizer, E. 131, 137, 138-40
Scott, E.F. 196, 199, 200
Stoessl, F. 14, 15
Stanton, V.H. 196
Stauffer, E. 167
Stibbe, M.W.G. 182
Strathmann, H. 41
Suggs, M.J. 9, 10

Talbert, C.H. 10, 11
Tasker, R.V.G. 103
Teeple, H.M. 73
Trebilco, P.R. 178
Trites, A.A. 40, 43, 45

Weizsäcker 17
Westcott, B.F. 105, 110-12
Williamson, R. 115
Wink, W. 29-31, 40, 41, 190
Winston, F.N.D. 142, 143
Wolfson, H.A. 96, 143

JOURNAL FOR THE STUDY OF THE NEW TESTAMENT

Supplement Series

1 THE BARREN TEMPLE AND THE WITHERED TREE
William R. Telford

2 STUDIA BIBLICA 1978
II. PAPERS ON THE GOSPELS
Edited by E.A. Livingstone

3 STUDIA BIBLICA 1978
III. PAPERS ON PAUL AND OTHER NEW TESTAMENT AUTHORS
Edited by E.A. Livingstone

4 FOLLOWING JESUS:
DISCIPLESHIP IN THE GOSPEL OF MARK
Ernest Best

5 THE PEOPLE OF GOD
Markus Barth

6 PERSECUTION AND MARTYRDOM IN THE THEOLOGY OF PAUL
John S. Pobee

7 SYNOPTIC STUDIES:
THE AMPLEFORTH CONFERENCES OF
1982 AND 1983
Edited by C.M. Tuckett

8 JESUS ON THE MOUNTAIN:
A STUDY IN MATTHEAN THEOLOGY
Terence L. Donaldson

9 THE HYMNS OF LUKE'S INFANCY NARRATIVES:
THEIR ORIGIN, MEANING AND SIGNIFICANCE
Stephen Farris

10 CHRIST THE END OF THE LAW:
ROMANS 10.4 IN PAULINE PERSPECTIVE
Robert Badenas

11 THE LETTERS TO THE SEVEN CHURCHES OF ASIA IN THEIR LOCAL
SETTING
Colin J. Hemer

12 PROCLAMATION FROM PROPHECY AND PATTERN:
LUCAN OLD TESTAMENT CHRISTOLOGY
Darrell L. Bock

13 JESUS AND THE LAWS OF PURITY:
TRADITION HISTORY AND LEGAL HISTORY IN MARK 7
Roger P. Booth

14 THE PASSION ACCORDING TO LUKE:
THE SPECIAL MATERIAL OF LUKE 22
Marion L. Soards

15 HOSTILITY TO WEALTH IN THE SYNOPTIC GOSPELS
    Thomas E. Schmidt
16 MATTHEW'S COMMUNITY:
    THE EVIDENCE OF HIS SPECIAL SAYINGS MATERIAL
    Stephenson H. Brooks
17 THE PARADOX OF THE CROSS IN THE THOUGHT OF ST PAUL
    Anthony Tyrrell Hanson
18 HIDDEN WISDOM AND THE EASY YOKE:
    WISDOM, TORAH AND DISCIPLESHIP IN MATTHEW 11.25-30
    Celia Deutsch
19 JESUS AND GOD IN PAUL'S ESCHATOLOGY
    L. Joseph Kreitzer
20 LUKE
    A NEW PARADIGM (2 Volumes)
    Michael D. Goulder
21 THE DEPARTURE OF JESUS IN LUKE–ACTS:
    THE ASCENSION NARRATIVES IN CONTEXT
    Mikeal C. Parsons
22 THE DEFEAT OF DEATH:
    APOCALYPTIC ESCHATOLOGY IN 1 CORINTHIANS 15 AND ROMANS 5
    Martinus C. de Boer
23 PAUL THE LETTER-WRITER
    AND THE SECOND LETTER TO TIMOTHY
    Michael Prior
24 APOCALYPTIC AND THE NEW TESTAMENT:
    ESSAYS IN HONOR OF J. LOUIS MARTYN
    Edited by Joel Marcus & Marion L. Soards
25 THE UNDERSTANDING SCRIBE:
    MATTHEW AND THE APOCALYPTIC IDEAL
    David E. Orton
26 WATCHWORDS:
    MARK 13 IN MARKAN ESCHATOLOGY
    Timothy J. Geddert
27 THE DISCIPLES ACCORDING TO MARK:
    MARKAN REDACTION IN CURRENT DEBATE
    C. Clifton Black
28 THE NOBLE DEATH:
    GRAECO-ROMAN MARTYROLOGY
    AND PAUL'S CONCEPT OF SALVATION
    David Seeley
29 ABRAHAM IN GALATIANS:
    EPISTOLARY AND RHETORICAL CONTEXTS
    G. Walter Hansen
30 EARLY CHRISTIAN RHETORIC AND 2 THESSALONIANS
    Frank Witt Hughes

31   THE STRUCTURE OF MATTHEW'S GOSPEL:
     A STUDY IN LITERARY DESIGN
     David R. Bauer

32   PETER AND THE BELOVED DISCIPLE:
     FIGURES FOR A COMMUNITY IN CRISIS
     Kevin Quast

33   MARK'S AUDIENCE:
     THE LITERARY AND SOCIAL SETTING OF MARK 4.11-12
     Mary Ann Beavis

34   THE GOAL OF OUR INSTRUCTION:
     THE STRUCTURE OF THEOLOGY AND ETHICS
     IN THE PASTORAL EPISTLES
     Philip H. Towner

35   THE PROVERBS OF JESUS:
     ISSUES OF HISTORY AND RHETORIC
     Alan P. Winton

36   THE STORY OF CHRIST IN THE ETHICS OF PAUL:
     AN ANALYSIS OF THE FUNCTION OF THE HYMNIC MATERIAL
     IN THE PAULINE CORPUS
     Stephen E. Fowl

37   PAUL AND JESUS:
     COLLECTED ESSAYS
     Edited by A.J.M. Wedderburn

38   MATTHEW'S MISSIONARY DISCOURSE:
     A LITERARY CRITICAL ANALYSIS
     Dorothy Jean Weaver

39   FAITH AND OBEDIENCE IN ROMANS:
     A STUDY IN ROMANS 1–4
     Glenn N. Davies

40   IDENTIFYING PAUL'S OPPONENTS:
     THE QUESTION OF METHOD IN 2 CORINTHIANS
     Jerry L. Sumney

41   HUMAN AGENTS OF COSMIC POWER:
     IN HELLENISTIC JUDAISM AND THE SYNOPTIC TRADITION
     Mary E. Mills

42   MATTHEW'S INCLUSIVE STORY:
     A STUDY IN THE NARRATIVE RHETORIC OF THE FIRST GOSPEL
     David B. Howell

43   JESUS, PAUL AND TORAH:
     COLLECTED ESSAYS
     Heikki Räisänen

44   THE NEW COVENANT IN HEBREWS
     Susanne Lehne

45 THE RHETORIC OF ROMANS:
   ARGUMENTATIVE CONSTRAINT AND STRATEGY AND PAUL'S
   DIALOGUE WITH JUDAISM
   Neil Elliott

46 THE LAST SHALL BE FIRST:
   THE RHETORIC OF REVERSAL IN LUKE
   John O. York

47 JAMES AND THE Q SAYINGS OF JESUS
   Patrick J. Hartin

48 TEMPLUM AMICITIAE:
   ESSAYS ON THE SECOND TEMPLE PRESENTED TO ERNST BAMMEL
   Edited by William Horbury

49 PROLEPTIC PRIESTS
   PRIESTHOOD IN THE EPISTLE TO THE HEBREWS
   John M. Scholer

50 PERSUASIVE ARTISTRY:
   STUDIES IN NEW TESTAMENT RHETORIC
   IN HONOR OF GEORGE A. KENNEDY
   Edited by Duane F. Watson

51 THE AGENCY OF THE APOSTLE: A DRAMATISTIC ANALYSIS OF PAUL'S
      RESPONSES TO CONFLICT IN 2 CORINTHIANS
   Jeffrey A. Crafton

52 REFLECTIONS OF GLORY:
   PAUL'S POLEMICAL USE OF THE MOSES–DOXA TRADITION IN
   2 CORINTHIANS 3.12-18
   Linda L. Belleville

53 REVELATION AND REDEMPTION AT COLOSSAE
   Thomas J. Sappington

54 THE DEVELOPMENT OF EARLY CHRISTIAN PNEUMATOLOGY
   WITH SPECIAL REFERENCE TO LUKE–ACTS
   Robert P. Menzies

55 THE PURPOSE OF ROMANS:
   A COMPARATIVE LETTER STRUCTURE INVESTIGATION
   L. Ann Jervis

56 THE SON OF THE MAN IN THE GOSPEL OF JOHN
   Delbert Burkett

57 ESCHATOLOGY AND THE COVENANT:
   A COMPARISON OF 4 EZRA AND ROMANS 1–11
   Bruce W. Longenecker

58 NONE BUT THE SINNERS:
   RELIGIOUS CATEGORIES IN THE GOSPEL OF LUKE
   David A. Neale

59 CLOTHED WITH CHRIST:
   THE EXAMPLE AND TEACHING OF JESUS IN ROMANS 12.1–15.13
   Michael Thompson

60 THE LANGUAGE OF THE NEW TESTAMENT:
    CLASSIC ESSAYS
    Edited by Stanley E. Porter
61 FOOTWASHING IN JOHN 13 AND THE JOHANNINE COMMUNITY
    John Christopher Thomas
62 JOHN THE BAPTIZER AND PROPHET:
    A SOCIO-HISTORICAL STUDY
    Robert L. Webb
63 POWER AND POLITICS IN PALESTINE:
    THE JEWS AND THE GOVERNING OF THEIR LAND 100 BC–AD 70
    James S. McLaren
64 JESUS AND THE ORAL GOSPEL TRADITION
    Edited by Henry Wansbrough
65 THE RHETORIC OF RIGHTEOUSNESS IN ROMANS 3.21-26
    Douglas A. Campbell
66 PAUL, ANTIOCH AND JERUSALEM:
    A STUDY IN RELATIONSHIPS AND AUTHORITY IN EARLIEST CHRISTIANITY
    Nicholas Taylor
67 THE PORTRAIT OF PHILIP IN ACTS:
    A STUDY OF ROLES AND RELATIONS
    F. Scott Spencer
68 JEREMIAH IN MATTHEW'S GOSPEL:
    THE REJECTED-PROPHET MOTIF IN MATTHAEAN REDACTION
    Michael P. Knowles
69 RHETORIC AND REFERENCE IN THE FOURTH GOSPEL
    Margaret Davies
70 AFTER THE THOUSAND YEARS:
    RESURRECTION AND JUDGMENT IN REVELATION 20
    J. Webb Mealy
71 SOPHIA AND THE JOHANNINE JESUS
    Martin Scott
72 NARRATIVE ASIDES IN LUKE–ACTS
    Steven M. Sheeley
73 SACRED SPACE
    AN APPROACH TO THE THEOLOGY OF THE EPISTLE TO THE HEBREWS
    Marie E. Isaacs
74 TEACHING WITH AUTHORITY:
    MIRACLES AND CHRISTOLOGY IN THE GOSPEL OF MARK
    Edwin K. Broadhead
75 PATRONAGE AND POWER:
    A STUDY OF SOCIAL NETWORKS IN CORINTH
    John Kin-Man Chow
76 THE NEW TESTAMENT AS CANON:
    A READER IN CANONICAL CRITICISM
    Robert Wall and Eugene Lemcio

77   REDEMPTIVE ALMSGIVING IN EARLY CHRISTIANITY
Roman Garrison

78   THE FUNCTION OF SUFFERING IN PHILIPPIANS
L. Gregory Bloomquist

79   THE THEME OF RECOMPENSE IN MATTHEW'S GOSPEL
Blaine Charette

80   BIBLICAL GREEK LANGUAGE AND LINGUISTICS: OPEN QUESTIONS IN
CURRENT RESEARCH
Edited by Stanley E. Porter and D.A. Carson

81   THE LAW IN GALATIANS
In-Gyu Hong

82   ORAL TRADITION AND THE GOSPELS: THE PROBLEM OF MARK 4
Barry W. Henaut

83   PAUL AND THE SCRIPTURES OF ISRAEL
Edited by Craig A. Evans and James A. Sanders

84   FROM JESUS TO JOHN: ESSAYS ON JESUS AND NEW TESTAMENT
CHRISTOLOGY IN HONOUR OF MARINUS DE JONGE
Edited by Martinus C. De Boer

85   RETURNING HOME: NEW COVENANT AND SECOND EXODUS AS THE
CONTEXT FOR 2 CORINTHIANS 6.14–7.1
William J. Webb

86   ORIGINS OF METHOD: TOWARDS A NEW UNDERSTANDING OF JUDAISM AND
CHRISTIANITY—ESSAYS IN HONOUR OF JOHN C. HURD
Edited by Bradley H. McLean

87   WORSHIP, THEOLOGY AND MINISTRY IN THE EARLY CHURCH: ESSAYS IN
HONOUR OF RALPH P. MARTIN
Edited by Michael Wilkins and Terence Paige

88   THE BIRTH OF THE LUKAN NARRATIVE
Mark Coleridge

89   WORD AND GLORY: ON THE EXEGETICAL AND THEOLOGICAL
BACKGROUND OF JOHN'S PROLOGUE
Craig A. Evans

90   RHETORIC IN THE NEW TESTAMENT
ESSAYS FROM THE 1992 HEIDELBERG CONFERENCE
Edited by Stanley E. Porter and Thomas H. Olbricht

91   MATTHEW'S NARRATIVE WEB: OVER, AND OVER, AND OVER AGAIN
Janice Capel Anderson

92   LUKE: INTERPRETER OF PAUL, CRITIC OF MATTHEW
Eric Franklin

93   ISAIAH AND PROPHETIC TRADITIONS IN THE BOOK OF REVELATION:
VISIONARY ANTECEDENTS AND THEIR DEVELOPMENT
Jan Fekkes

94   JESUS' EXPOSITION OF THE OLD TESTAMENT IN LUKE'S GOSPEL
Charles A. Kimball

95 THE SYMBOLIC NARRATIVES OF THE FOURTH GOSPEL:
THE INTERPLAY OF FORM AND MEANING
Dorothy A. Lee

96 THE COLOSSIAN CONTROVERSY:
WISDOM IN DISPUTE AT COLOSSAE
Richard E. DeMaris

97 PROPHET, SON, MESSIAH
NARRATIVE FORM AND FUNCTION IN MARK 14–16
Edwin K. Broadhead

98 FILLING UP THE MEASURE:
POLEMICAL HYPERBOLE IN 1 THESSALONIANS 2.14-16
Carol J. Schlueter

100 TO TELL THE MYSTERY:
ESSAYS ON NEW TESTAMENT ESCHATOLOGY IN HONOR OF
ROBERT H. GUNDRY
Edited by E. Schmidt and Moisés Silva

101 NEGLECTED ENDINGS:
THE SIGNIFICANCE OF THE PAULINE LETTER CLOSINGS
Jeffrey A.D. Weima

102 OTHER FOLLOWERS OF JESUS:
MINOR CHARACTERS AS MAJOR FIGURES IN MARK'S GOSPEL
Joel F. Williams

103 HOUSEHOLDS AND DISCIPLESHIP:
A STUDY OF MATTHEW 19–20
Warren Carter

104 THE GOSPELS AND THE SCRIPTURES OF ISRAEL
Edited by Craig A. Evans and W. Richard Stegner

105 THE BIBLE, THE REFORMATION AND THE CHURCH:
ESSAYS IN HONOUR OF JAMES ATKINSON
Edited by W.P. Stephens

106 JEWISH RESPONSIBILITY FOR THE DEATH OF JESUS IN LUKE–ACTS
Jon A. Weatherly

107 PROLOGUE AND GOSPEL:
THE THEOLOGY OF THE FOURTH EVANGELIST
Elizabeth Harris